Carters
Book for Gardeners

Carters
Book for Gardeners

A. G. L. HELLYER

M.B.E., F.L.S., V.M.H., A.H.R.H.S.

Written in collaboration
with the technical staff of
CARTERS TESTED SEEDS LTD

Drawings by Mike Taylor

HEINEMANN : LONDON

William Heinemann Ltd

15 Queen St, Mayfair, London W1X 8BE

LONDON   MELBOURNE   TORONTO
JOHANNESBURG   AUCKLAND

Several of the drawings have been inspired by illustrations that previously appeared in *The Gardening Year* and *The Complete Library of the Garden*, both published by The Reader's Digest Association Ltd, to whom full credit is given.

Printed in Great Britain by
Jarrold & Sons Ltd, Norwich

Contents

Foreword

We commissioned Mr A. G. L. Hellyer, who was for many years editor of *Amateur Gardening* and has great experience in explaining the technicalities of gardening to a very wide public, to write a book for gardeners with the widest possible appeal. In particular we asked him to consider the special needs of:

1. People with small, medium, or large gardens and those with greenhouses;
2. Amateurs, knowledgeable gardeners, and experts;
3. Those who garden as a hobby and those who like to enjoy a beautiful garden with as little labour as possible;
4. People who have no gardens but enjoy growing and nursing house plants.

The result is *Carters Book for Gardeners* which we hope, both for its contents and its very economical price, will be considered unique in the vast field of horticultural literature and will help to solve the many problems all gardeners experience from time to time.

We dedicate this book to the millions of gardeners whom we have been proud to serve for many generations.

Raynes Park,   CARTERS TESTED SEEDS LTD
London S.W.20

1 A Plan for the Garden

Today many gardens are so small that it is difficult to plan them by the traditional concepts of garden design. Since they will be used more as outdoor rooms than as places in which to grow any great variety of plants it is the principles of indoor decoration that can be applied to them most usefully. A first consideration will be the purpose for which the space will be required – for parties, perhaps, or for pleasant open air seclusion in fine weather, or for children to play in, or maybe for the cultivation of some specially loved plants. Furnishings such as chairs and tables can assume considerable importance in the planning of such tiny gardens and so can ornaments such as statues, vases or decorative plant containers.

There will most likely be a considered colour scheme, which, of course, does not mean that everything will be of similar colour, but that colours will be chosen to blend or contrast according to the mood it is desired to create. Contrasting textures will be seen as having considerable importance, and all kinds of fascinating possibilities may be considered with stonework, woodwork, water, grass, and carefully selected plants.

There will possibly be no very elaborate plan in the sense in which that term is commonly applied to garden design, but everything will be placed with a due sense of balance and proportion as well as with an eye to the convenience of those who will use this outdoor space for living.

There is certainly nothing in this catalogue of considerations which could not be applied to any garden, but the larger it is the more likely is it that other matters must be taken into account. Will the garden be used for games of any kind and if so will they be games played by children? What kind of plants will be grown in it and what are their requirements? And even more basically what kind of garden are we trying to make, for there are many possibilities. At one extreme of style are gardens which are completely symmetrical and rely for their effect on the patterns they contain and the colours of which they are composed. At the other are the entirely irregular landscape gardens in which the intention is to create series of living pictures much as an artist might paint.

All manner of intermediate ways may be considered, one that is very popular today being to plan the area adjacent to the house formally, perhaps making there a paved terrace or a level lawn, but to use a greater freedom of design and a more flowing line in the more distant parts.

Most gardens are adjacent to houses and so will often be looked at from the house windows. Take this into account when planning and be sure that the garden will look attractive from each of the principal rooms, including the bedrooms. Do not leave the view from the kitchen window out of account for it is likely that a good deal of time will be spent there also.

When design is based largely on pattern it is likely that the whole of each pattern will have to be seen to be fully effective, but if there is sufficient space it may well

1

be possible to have several quite different patterns within the same garden, each more or less concealed from the other and only to be revealed by exploration. The device of dividing a garden into separate compartments or 'rooms' is very old and has been brilliantly exploited in such twentieth century gardens as Hidcote Manor, Chipping Campden, Gloucestershire and Sissinghurst Castle, near Goudhurst, Kent. Both belong to the National Trust, are frequently open to the public, and are rich in ideas for garden makers.

Similarly the picture garden may be planned to concentrate on one picture only or on several, but the transition from one to the other is likely to be more gradual than in a patterned garden. Curving paths can invite exploration since everyone is curious to see what lies around the corner. In such gardens the pictures may be entirely composed within the garden or some may be planned to include outside features such as a church spire, a well placed tree or a view. Both the closed vista and the open vista have their place in garden planning.

Levels are a matter of great importance. A garden on sloping ground can be a great asset to the designer but it may well increase the cost of garden making. It certainly will do so if much terracing is attempted, for moving large quantities of soil can be a costly business and retaining walls are not cheap either. But terracing with good masonry or brickwork and with well planned flights of steps to link one level with another can add greatly to the charm of a garden.

SOIL

One thing is very necessary when moving soil in the garden. It is the top 20–30 cm (8–12 in.) that is always most fertile and the sub-soil below it may be a most unsatisfactory medium in which to grow plants. So, if existing levels have to be tampered with to any considerable extent, it is essential to remove the top soil first, stacking it conveniently near, and then adjust the level of sub-soil, after which the top soil can be replaced and spread in an even depth all over.

The nature of the soil should also be taken into account when preparing a plan for any garden since it may determine what can and cannot be grown. Fortunately most plants are extremely tolerant in this respect and will thrive in a wide variety of soils, but there are some notable exceptions. Rhododendrons and azaleas are well known examples of showy and popular shrubs which will not thrive in soils containing much free lime or chalk, and there are numerous other examples of this kind. It is quite easy to get soils tested to see if they are suitable for these lime haters, or small kits can be purchased at garden shops to enable one to do the test at home. Soils with free chalk or lime are usually alkaline, which is the opposite to acid; both are measured on a scale, known as the pH scale, in which neutrality, the exact balance between alkalinity and acidity, is represented by the figure 7. Readings higher than 7 indicate increasing degrees of alkalinity whereas figures below it represent increasing degrees of acidity. Since a great many plants enjoy slightly acid conditions, soils of pH 6 to 6·5 are ideal for gardening.

However, few people are able to choose their place of residence to suit the plants they would like to grow and, though the character of soils can be changed, it usually becomes a difficult and costly matter if one tries to change them too much. Hydrated lime or finely ground chalk are used to make soils less acid and can be forked in or applied as top dressings at rates up to 225 grammes per square metre (8 oz/sq yd). It is much more difficult to make soils less alkaline, though something can be done by working in heavy dressings of acid peat or of farmyard manure. However, old mushroom compost will actually make most soils rather more alkaline (or less acid) than they already are, since it contains a lot of chalk, which is necessary for the cultivation of mushrooms.

Texture of soil is important because it has considerable bearing on fertility and the way in which plants grow. Soil that is so close that air cannot penetrate soon becomes infertile and most plants grow poorly in it or not at all. Soil that is too open textured will neither hold water nor the chemicals that plants need as food and so again growth will suffer. The ideal is a soil of medium texture, one which crumbles fairly easily when it is moist, does not readily cake or clog when it is very dry or wet, and yet will hold water reasonably well.

Animal manures, peat, rotted garden refuse (often referred to as garden compost), old mushroom compost, spent hops, and seaweed are all substances which improve the texture of all soils, making more open those that are too close, and yet making more retentive those that are too coarse in texture. All can be worked into the soil so freely that it is really the availability of supplies and their price which determines how much is used.

Situation must also be considered when making a plan for the garden. Plants can be chosen to grow in full sun or in full shade and a few will grow in either, but they are not very numerous. The greatest difficulties occur when shade is caused by overhanging trees, the roots of which may impoverish and dry the soil, while the branches exclude light in summer and shed their leaves in autumn to smother many plants, unless promptly removed. However, there are good plants that will grow right under trees; or the shady garden can rely for its effect on the pattern of its stonework or woodwork, the clever placing of ornaments, and other 'architectural' features.

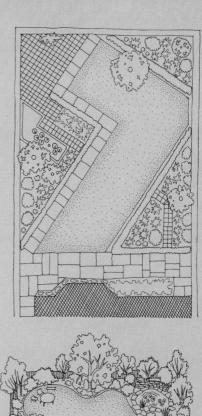

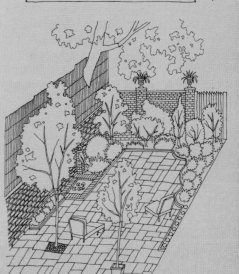

(above) **Plan for a small garden with L-shaped lawn set at an angle to increase the feeling of space to explore**
(centre) **A tiny 'glade' garden set in trees and shrubs**
(below) **Design for a little patio or outdoor room**

3

The best preparation for ground that is to receive plants or seeds is digging, but if this involves too much work a mechanical cultivator may be used to break it up. As a rule it is sufficient to cultivate soil to about 25 cm (10 in.) deep. Only if very special plants are to be grown or exceptional results are required will deeper cultivation be needed and then a process known as double digging must be used. To do this a trench must be opened at least 60 cm (2 ft) wide and 25–30 cm (10–12 in.) deep. Then the soil in the bottom of this trench is dug or forked where it lies. A further trench is then opened alongside the first, the soil from it being thrown into the first trench. In this way a further 60 cm (2 ft) of sub-soil is exposed and is dug or forked as before. So the work proceeds, trench by trench, until the whole area has been cultivated, when the soil removed from the first trench is used to fill in the last one.

But for ordinary purposes and on most soils it is sufficient simply to dig with a spade or fork, going to the full depth of the blade or tines and turning each lot of soil right over so that the grass or weeds which were on top are now down below, where most of them will rot. However, some weeds will come up through the soil even when buried upside down in this way. This is true of nettles, docks, dandelions, thistles, bindweed or wild convolvulus and couch grass. If any of these are seen when digging they should be picked out and later burned.

If any of the bulky soil dressings already mentioned, i.e. manure, peat, garden compost, etc., are available they can be worked into the soil as digging proceeds. The soil can also be lightly dusted with bone meal at about 100 grammes per square metre ($3\frac{1}{2}$ oz/sq yd). This is a good plant food that will last for a year or so.

AIDS TO PLANNING

When all the digging or mechanical cultivating has been completed the main features of the garden design can be marked out on the ground. It is often suggested that detailed plans should first be made on paper and this is excellent if one is competent to do it or if professional assistance is sought. But I think most people do no more than make a rough sketch of their ideas, and this works very well if one is doing all the work oneself since one can amend the plan and fill in the details as one goes along. It is much easier to visualize exactly what one is getting when one sees the beds, paths, etc., actually marked with pegs and string than from a plan on a sheet of paper. It is also wise at an early stage to make lawns, lay terraces and paths, erect any large structures, including sheds, greenhouses, summerhouses, pergolas, etc., and to plant trees and shrubs. The reason for this is that all these are both permanent and prominent features of the garden which will tend to dominate it and determine what kind of garden it is. As they are erected or planted the pattern and scale will become increasingly clear and alterations can be made if they seem necessary. Moreover these things immediately give the garden a 'made' appearance and that can be very satisfactory. Other items can be added later as they are required and as time and money are available, but in the meantime there will be some garden to be enjoyed.

Here are a few simple aids to accurate planning 'on the ground'. Mark the straight lines of paths, borders, lawns, etc., by driving in a peg at each end and stretching a garden line or string between them.

To make a right angle from such a straight line drive in a peg at the point where the angle is to be. From this measure 4 ft along the line already placed and

4

drive in another peg at this point. To it attach a piece of string exactly 5 ft long and attach another piece of string exactly 3 ft long to the first peg. Draw both strings taut and together until they just touch, at which point drive in a third peg. A line drawn taut between this peg and the first peg and extended to any desired length on either side will be at right angles to the first line. (Of course, equivalent metric lengths may be used providing the 4:5:3 ratio is preserved.)

Circles and arcs of circles are easily drawn by driving in a peg at the central point, and looping over this a piece of string exactly the radius (half the diameter) of the circle. Draw the line round the peg, keeping it taut, and using a pointed stick to trace on the soil the path followed by its extremity.

To mark an oval or segment of an oval is a little more difficult. First, two lines or pieces of string must be pegged out like a cross, bisecting one another at right angles, one exactly the greatest length of the oval and the other the greatest width. Then to one of the pegs marking the greatest width attach a piece of string half the greatest length of the oval and draw its tip round like a compass. It will touch the line marking the length of the oval at two points, one on each side of the cross. These are the focal points of the oval and must be marked with pegs. Now measure the length from one of these pegs to the furthest extremity of the oval. Make a loop of string exactly twice this length, throw it over the two pegs marking the focal points, and, using a pointed stick, stretch this loop taut, draw it around the focal points scratching the oval on the soil.

Irregular lines can be marked roughly with a series of small sticks after which a little hydrated lime can be trickled on the soil to mark the line more accurately, or it can be drawn in the soil with the corner of a hoe.

Levelling is done with a long straight plank, a spirit level, and a number of pegs. These are driven into the soil at distances apart that can be spanned by the plank which is laid on edge between them, first in one direction and then in another. The pegs are driven in or pulled upward until the spirit level laid on top of the plank indicates that they are exactly level. Soil, paving, etc., can then either be laid to the top of the pegs or, what is often more convenient, to a chosen distance below the top.

Even slopes can be made by nailing a short, straight-edged piece of wood against the side of the levelling plank and at exactly the angle to it that it is desired (this can be measured with a protractor). Then the spirit level is placed on this angled wood, but the plank is placed as before, on the pegs.

2 Lawns and Pavings

A well kept lawn can add greatly to the attractiveness of almost any garden, but when planning a very small garden it must be considered whether a lawn can be expected to stand the wear it is likely to receive. If not it will almost certainly be better to replace it with a paved area to provide the open space that is the necessary foil to well filled flower beds.

Paths can easily be overdone, and it is often possible to move about the garden just as conveniently on mown grass, but if there are areas of heavy traffic, as between house and greenhouse, arbour or shed, a path may be essential to avoid the wear which can quickly make a lawn unsightly, especially when the soil is wet. Even so it may be that stepping stones sunk flush with the surface of a lawn will provide all the protection necessary. They will certainly be cheaper and may quite likely be more sightly than a proper path.

Lawns can be made from seed, turf, by planting tufts of creeping grass, or by cultivating the natural turf on the site. Of these four, tufts have little to recommend them in the British climate, though they may provide a valuable means of making lawns in hotter and drier places. Turves have the merit that a usable lawn can be produced in a matter of weeks, but suffer from the drawbacks that they may contain unsuitable grasses, or even weeds, and that they are comparatively costly. Treatment of the natural turf of the site suffers similar drawbacks, for though it may appear the cheapest, in the long run it is quite likely to prove an expensive matter to rid it of weeds and unsuitable grasses.

Seed provides both the cheapest and, in the long run, the most effective method of making a lawn. There are numerous different kinds of lawn grass, each with its own characteristics and value, and, by making suitable selections of these, lawns can be produced to meet particular needs or suit special conditions.

Broadly the lawn grasses may be divided into two main groups, the slow growing kinds with small, narrow leaves which will produce the finest turf, and stronger growing kinds that will make coarser lawns capable of withstanding hard wear and growing in less favourable conditions. Into the first group come many of the fescues and bent grasses or agrostis species, into the second group the rye grasses and meadow grasses. There are others but they are less readily available and their use for lawns is not so significant.

It is very rarely that a lawn is made of one species of grass, more satisfactory results being obtained by mixing two or more, so giving a better coverage of the soil and reduced risk that the lawn will become patchy.

Seedsmen prepare mixtures to suit the main gardening requirements. Blends of tufted fescues with creeping fescues or bent grasses are for the finest quality lawns that will be mown closely and be well fed and watered. For hard wearing lawns needing less care and attention they may add perennial rye grass and for the coarsest lawns they offer cheap mixtures composed mainly of rye grass.

The meadow grasses, Poa trivialis and P. nemoralis, may be included in mixtures for shady places, and occasionally other grasses, such as the crested dog's tooth and timothy, may be used for special purposes. All that is necessary, therefore, is to buy a mixture prepared for the kind of lawn it is desired to make and the kind of soil or place in which it will have to grow. The finer the grasses the more the seed will cost, but the extra money spent will be well justified by the results, provided soil and situation are right and the turf is properly looked after.

Carters Chatsworth is a mixture of the very best grasses to produce the finest possible turf on soils of average quality; Sunshade will succeed in the drier shaded areas; Shaded Lawn will grow in damp, shady places, and Invicta is a mixture of dwarf grasses and perennial rye grass for a quick growing, hard wearing lawn.

Lawn sites must be thoroughly cleared of weeds before they are seeded. First they should be dug at least one spit deep, which means to the full depth of the blade of a spade or the tines of a fork, at least a month before lawn seed is sown. As soon as the surface begins to crumble readily it should be broken down with fork or rake and any final levelling done. Lawn seed can be sown at any time from March to October, but the two most favourable times are usually April and from about mid-August to mid-September. It is an advantage if the rough seed bed can be prepared about three weeks before sowing as this will give time for any weed seeds to germinate. The weeds can then be killed by watering them with paraquat (Weedol) or by light hoeing, and the grass seed will have a much better chance.

Immediately before sowing, dust the surface with a good compound fertilizer and then rake all over, so working the fertilizer in and leaving tiny furrows made by the teeth of the rake. Sowing can be done by hand or with a fertilizer distributor. The rate of sowing will depend in part on the kind of mixture used, since the fine grasses, which germinate and grow rather slowly, are best sown at 50 grammes per square metre (2 oz/sq yd), whereas the faster growing rye and meadow grasses will give a satisfactory coverage if sown at 25g/sq m (1 oz/sq yd). If the seed is sown by hand it will be wise to mark out the area in metre- or yard-wide strips, measure the correct quantity of seed for each and sow them separately.

After sowing rake the plot at right angles to the previous raking, thereby closing up the little furrows and covering most of the seed. Practically all lawn seed is pre-treated with bird repellent or else this is sold with the seed to be mixed with it prior to sowing. If this is done no further protection should be necessary.

Grass seed sown in mid-spring or early autumn usually germinates without any difficulty, but if seed is sown in summer it may require several waterings to bring it

Before sowing grass seed rake the surface quite level. Scatter the seed evenly either by hand, doing a one-metre wide strip at a time, or with a fertilizer distributor. Cover the seed by raking at right angles to the previous raking.

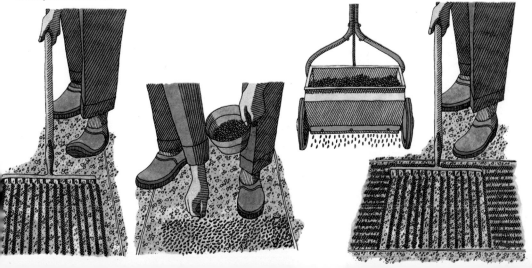

through. If so be very careful to water through a fine sprinkler so that the seed is not washed out of the soil, or the soil itself beaten down. Germination may take anything from one to six weeks according to weather and the kind of seed sown.

If many weed seedlings appear with the grass they can be destroyed by watering with ioxynil (Actrilawn) when the grass seedlings have made their second leaf, but if they are only annual weeds, such as groundsel and chickweed, there is no need to worry as they will quickly disappear with mowing. On no account must ordinary selective weedkillers such as 2,4-D and MCPA be used on seedling grass.

The first cutting should be given when the grass is 5–6 cm (2–2½ in.) high with a very sharp mower set to cut 2·5 cm (1 in.) above soil level. In subsequent mowings this level can be gradually decreased, but unless lawns are made of the finest grasses and are used for games requiring a very true playing surface, they should never be cut closer than 1 cm (½ in.).

Turves can be laid at any time of the year when the soil is not actually frozen, but it is difficult to get satisfactory establishment in summer unless very thorough watering is carried out, so in practice turfing is normally confined to spring and autumn. It is best to purchase turves specially grown from seed for lawnmaking as these are more likely to contain suitable grasses and fewer weeds than are those cut from meadows or building sites.

Preparation of the site is the same as for seeding except that it is not necessary to leave time for weed seeds to germinate since the turves will smother most of these. It is as necessary to feed the soil with a compound fertilizer as it is for seeding.

Turves are usually cut in 1 m by 30 cm (3 ft by 1 ft) strips, 4–5 cm (1½–2 in.) thick, but turves specially produced from seed in good nurseries are often much thinner, as little as 1 cm (½ in.). This is quite satisfactory provided the turves are laid at once and are well watered if the weather is dry.

Rake the surface quite level before commencing to lay the turves. Start along one edge of the lawn if it is straight, but if not start sufficiently far inside to be able to lay a straight line of turves. Take pains to see that each turf is level. If necessary remove or add soil beneath it to get it quite right. Then beat it down gently with the back of a spade, so that it is in the closest possible contact with the soil below.

Lay the next row alongside the first but start with a half turf so that the cross joins between the turves are not in line. Continue to stagger the cross joins in this way in each successive row so that the turves are bonded like the courses of brick in

Lay turves in straight lines with the turves in alternate rows staggered. Beat gently with the back of a spade to settle them firmly. Use a mixture of fine soil and peat to fill crevices. Trim away surplus turf with an edging tool.

a wall. If the edges of the lawn are curved or irregular fill these in after the straight rows have been laid. Finish the job by sprinkling a mixture of sifted soil and peat along the joins between the turves and brushing it in.

Turved lawns can be cut as soon as they commence to grow. Before cutting it will be wise to rake and sweep them well to remove any small stones or rubbish which might damage the mower.

Proper care of lawns has a great effect on their quality. Mowing should be done regularly from about mid-April until mid-October and just a few times during autumn and winter, as and when surface conditions permit. Set blades at 2 cm (1 in.) above soil level if the purpose of the

A good lawn from seed

lawn is simply to provide a good green carpet of grass, 1–1·5 cm ($\frac{1}{2}$–$\frac{3}{4}$ in.) for a neater effect in the more formal places, and at 0·5–1 cm ($\frac{1}{4}$–$\frac{1}{2}$ in.) for lawns used for putting, croquet, tennis, and other games requiring a smooth surface. All these heights can be varied a little according to the weather, since lawns can be cut more closely in summer than in winter but may be allowed a little extra coverage of grass to prevent scorching in very hot weather.

Where there is a sufficient area of grass, good effects can be obtained by mowing some closely and leaving others longer and rougher to give a contrast in textures.

Choice of mowing equipment is important. Rotary mowers are generally better than cylinder mowers for cutting long or wet grass but special models of cylinder mowers, usually with four blades only on the revolving cylinder or 'reel', are available for this purpose and are very satisfactory. If a rotary is to be used for close cutting it must be fitted with a grass box or bag, but for rough cutting this is not essential.

Cylinder mowers give the finest finish to a lawn provided they give sufficient cuts per metre (yard) of forward movement. Rough cut machines may give no more than 25 cuts per metre, the highest quality machine as many as 140 cuts per metre. Something like 40 to 50 is ideal for most hand propelled machines used for general garden purposes, and 70 to 80 for power operated machines whether electric or petrol engined. The more cuts per metre (yard) the more force is required to propel the machine.

Feed lawns each March with a good compound fertilizer, either one specially prepared for lawns, such as Carters Organic-based Lawn Fertilizer, or a general purpose fertilizer, using this at the rate per square metre (square yard) recommended by the manufacturer. Repeat at half this rate in late May and again in early July, but water these applications in well if the weather is dry. Never feed with an ordinary fertilizer after mid-August but use a special autumn lawn dressing, such as Carters Autumn/Winter Dressing, in September.

Only roll lawns occasionally unless they are used for games requiring a very true playing surface. Brush frequently to remove rubbish and rake with a spring toothed grass rake occasionally to drag out dead grass and moss. If the surface becomes hard through wear or too much rolling use a fork to spike it to a depth of 7–8 cm (3 in.) all over, or better still use a special spiking tool.

Water freely whenever the weather is warm and the soil becomes dry. Use a selective weedkiller in late April or early May and then spot treat with similar weedkiller any weeds that appear later.

PAVING

Paving of stone, slabs, bricks, or other suitable material may be used around the house or in any other place where there is likely to be considerable wear. All paving is more costly to buy than turf, but it costs little to maintain and, if well chosen and laid, can add greatly to the appearance and utility of a garden.

For good wear and comfort in use all paving materials are best laid in concrete made of 5 parts all-in ballast to 1 part of cement (or 3 parts gravel, 2 parts sand, and 1 part cement). But if plants are to be grown in the crevices it will be better to lay the paving on a good layer of coarse sand or sifted boiler ashes without any concrete. Either way there should be a minimum 10 cm (4 in.) foundation layer of stones or broken bricks beneath the paving to act as drainage and prevent freezing water heaving the surface up in winter.

Slabs can be purchased in various sizes, shapes, and colours and can be laid in many attractive patterns. Bricks can be laid flat or on edge in straight lines or in various patterns including the popular herringbone. Paving may be decorated with panels of other materials and carefully selected pebbles set in concrete are excellent for this purpose. A drawback to bricks is that they can become very slippery in wet weather.

Take great care to lay all paving materials level and true. Use a straight edged plank and spirit level to check frequently on the level and make the necessary adjustments immediately, before the concrete commences to dry. A neat finish can be made by pointing the crevices with a mixture of 3 parts sand to 1 of cement when the foundation concrete has hardened but before it has completely dried.

Paving slabs are the most satisfactory material for terraces, courtyards, and patios and are also excellent for paths, but for these last other cheaper materials may also be considered. These include gravel, concrete, and asphalt. There is the same necessity for a good foundation layer of rubble. The concrete should not be too wet since a better surface is obtained if only sufficient water is used to enable it to be spread properly. Long unbroken surfaces should be avoided since they are liable to crack with changing temperatures. Shuttering of greased planks can be used to divide the area into sections, the shuttering being removed when the concrete is quite dry. The surface can also be scored while soft with the point of a mason's trowel to give the appearance of paving slabs in any desired pattern.

Gravel for paths should have sufficient fine material and clay to bind well when watered and rolled. It should be at least 5 cm (2 in.) thick.

Asphalt is a good utility material but is not very attractive in appearance in the more ornamental parts of the garden, and plants do not take kindly to it. A minimum thickness of 2 cm (1 in.) is required over a good rubble base where there is likely to be heavy wear.

10

Paving to enhance a garden

It may be wise to lay 'mowing edges' of paving slabs between lawns and flanking flower beds. Plants can then flop or creep on to this strip without killing the grass or getting in the way of the mowing machine. A 30 cm (12 in.) wide strip is the minimum that is serviceable and 60 cm (2 ft) is to be preferred. When laying such a strip leave a little gulley 5 cm (2 in.) wide and deep so that grass can be neatly clipped and not permitted to encroach on the paving. Also lay the mowing strip dead level with the lawn or even fractionally below it so that the mower can be run on to it without damage. Take this same precaution when setting stepping stones in the lawn.

11

3 Screens and Hedges

The idea of the completely open garden, so popular in America, progresses slowly in Britain partly, no doubt, for traditional reasons but also because there are practical advantages in protecting a garden with screens and hedges. Our climate is changeable and often windy. Screens and hedges provide plants with valuable protection, besides making the garden a more pleasant place in which to work or rest. Moreover the British practice of using gardens primarily for personal relaxation provides a powerful argument for screening at least some part of the garden sufficiently to give complete privacy.

Screens may be living or inanimate: belts of trees in large gardens; evergreen shrubs or erections of stone, brick, concrete or timber in smaller ones. The perforated screen blocks now available in a variety of patterns and finishes have proved justly popular for they are easily erected, look well, and make excellent supports for climbing plants, particularly clematis, honeysuckles, jasmine, and the less vigorous climbing roses. Open horizontal boarding in the Canadian style can be used in a similar way and is considerably cheaper. Both these methods are excellent for screening a terrace, patio, or other small areas to be used primarily as an open air room.

Openwork screens of this kind give better protection from high winds than a solid wall or fence, since they slow the wind without causing violent turbulence. On sloping ground solid walls or fences can check the downward flow of cold air and so produce frost pockets which can be particularly dangerous to plants in spring. Openwork screens allow the cold air to flow through and continue its downward course.

For all these reasons large screens or windbreaks of trees or shrubs should also be arranged so that they absorb the wind pressure and permit some passage of air. If room permits, individual plants may be widely spread in two or more staggered rows. Where this is impossible the trees or shrubs may be set closer but some space kept open at the bottom to allow a slow flow of air.

Fast growing evergreen trees and shrubs suitable for screening are the Scots, Austrian, and Corsican pines, the Norway spruce, and the Leyland cypress. Holm oak is slower growing but stands clipping well and is particularly successful near the coast and so is the Monterey pine (Pinus radiata), one of the fastest growing trees.

Deciduous trees which may be used for screening include the fast growing poplars (but they spread their roots for a great distance and take a lot out of the soil); larch; sycamore (but its self-sown seedlings can be a nuisance); the Norway maple, particularly beautiful in its crimson leaved form; beech and hornbeam, both of which may be clipped and will then retain their dead leaves in winter; false acacia (Robinia); birch, particularly good on acid soils; and whitebeam which thrives on those containing chalk or lime.

If there is insufficient space for trees of this size, protection can be provided with smaller ornamental trees such as the flowering crab apples and cherries, almonds and peaches, laburnum, mountain ash or rowan, Venetian sumach (Rhus), and thorns.

Evergreen shrubs suitable for screening include aucuba, often known as the spotted laurel, Berberis darwinii, B. stenophylla, cherry laurel, Portugal laurel, hollies in many different varieties, pyracantha, rhododendrons and particularly the mauve flowered Rhododendron ponticum and the numerous hardy hybrids, many cypresses, particularly the various forms of Lawson cypress, and the rather similar varieties of thuya.

Near the coast tamarisk makes an excellent shelter belt and so does the grey leaved Atriplex halimus, both of which will stand salt-laden winds. Escallonias and hebes (shrubby veronicas) also do well and so do the Japanese euonymus, Pittosporum tenuifolium, and Griselinia littoralis, all three with green-leaved and variegated varieties.

None of the foregoing need to be clipped, though some can be without harm to their health. When it comes to choosing shrubs for formal hedges or for making into topiary specimens, the question of suitability for clipping becomes of paramount importance. This, plus its hardiness, account for the popularity of privet, both green and golden leaved. Holly, box, and yew stand clipping well and there is one form of box, known as edging box or suffruticosa, which is naturally low growing and can be kept to a height of 30 cm (1 ft) or less. This is the box used for edgings to formal beds and to make the complicated patterns in old fashioned knot gardens. Ordinary box and yew in both green and golden leaved varieties are the best shrubs from which to form topiary specimens.

All the cypresses and thuyas can be clipped, but the Monterey cypress (Cupressus macrocarpa) is apt to go brown at the base and then die as it ages. This trouble does not occur with Lawson cypress or its varieties and these are also much hardier.

Lonicera nitida makes an excellent hedge up to about 1·5 metres (5 ft) but its branches are too thin to make a more substantial hedge. It has something of the appearance of box and is faster growing. Japanese euonymus, Pittosporum tenuifolium, Griselinia littoralis, and Atriplex halimus can be close clipped if desired.

Another possibility is to make screens and hedges of roses. The outer ones, that are mainly to break the wind or keep out intruders, can be of vigorous shrub roses and the inner ones, that are mainly to mark the divisions between one part of the garden and another, of compact floribunda roses. Neither should be clipped, but they should be pruned each winter or early spring and can be further trimmed

(above) Berberis darwinii
(centre) Thuya plicata
(below) Viburnum tinus

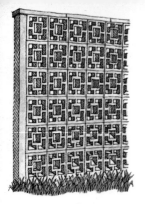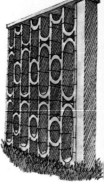

Open work walls are more decorative than solid walls and cause less air turbulence. They can be constructed with variously patterned walling blocks purchased ready for use or cast at home in special moulds. Alternatively open work brick walling may be used.

when the first flush of flowers is over in July.

There are also a number of varieties of the cherry plum or myrobalan (Prunus cerasifera) which make good deciduous hedges. One variety has green leaves and others have leaves in various shades of purple. These may be sold as P. pissardii and P. pissardii nigra or as Purple Flash and Blaze, in which case the green-leaved variety may be called Green Glow. They can be mixed together in various proportions and some nurserymen offer a mixture of one Green Glow to every two Purple Flash and sell it as Flamboyant. They will make good hedges up to 3 m (10 ft) high. Another allied plum, named P. cistena, is purple leaved and dwarf and will make a hedge 60–120 cm (2–4 ft) high.

Various other mixtures may be considered such as green leaved, copper, and purple beech; or silver and gold variegated hollies, possibly with green holly as well; green and golden yew or green and golden varieties of Lawson cypress.

Small hedges can also be made with lavender or rosemary and both can be allowed to flower and then be clipped when the flowers fade. Potentilla fruticosa will also make a very attractive hedge up to about 1 m (3 ft) high and if clipped in spring will flower most of the summer. In the milder parts of the South and West fine fuchsia hedges are to be seen, usually of the variety Riccartonii, but gracilis in both its green leaved and variegated forms can also be used.

The best time to plant screening and hedging shrubs of all kinds is between late October and the end of March; planting can continue in spring and even summer if plants are obtained in containers, are transplanted from these carefully with a minimum of root disturbance, and are kept well watered until they are established and growing freely.

It is an advantage if well rotted manure, garden compost, or peat can be dug or forked into the soil before planting. It is sufficient to cultivate a strip 1 metre (3 ft) wide for hedges, or individual circles 1·5 m (5 ft) in diameter for screen trees. The soil should be dusted with bone meal at 100 grammes per square metre ($3\frac{1}{2}$ oz/sq yd) prior to planting.

The best way to plant a hedge is to dig out a trench about 25 cm (10 in.) deep and 30 cm (1 ft) wide the whole length of the hedge, making certain with a garden line that it is quite straight, line out the plants in this at the correct spacing, and then return the soil a little at a time, breaking it up well and working it around the roots. Depth of planting should be such that the uppermost roots are covered by at least 5 cm (2 in.) of soil. When all the plants are in, tread the soil firmly around their

14

(left) Prunus cistena   (right) A hedge of green and purple leaved Prunus cerasifera

roots and then scatter a little more over the surface to leave it level, loose, and tidy.

To plant trees dig out a circle a little more than the diameter of the roots and 30 cm (1 ft) deep. Break up the bottom with a fork, drive a strong stake into the centre of the hole, place the tree against this and tie it to the stake if no one is available to hold it, and then return the soil and make it firm as just described for hedge plants.

Screening trees usually need to be 4·5–8 metres (15–25 ft) apart according to size; screening shrubs 1·5–3 m (5–10 ft) apart; hedge plants 30–60 cm (1–2 ft) apart. (*See* table at the end of the chapter for individual kinds.)

Most formal hedges need to be trimmed two or three times each year, first in early May when any hard cutting back of evergreens can be done, again in June, with a last trimming in August to leave everything tidy for the winter. More frequent trimming can be carried out if desired, and this may be necessary for topiary specimens, but deciduous hedges, e.g. beech, hornbeam, and tamarisk, should not be pruned too frequently in summer since it deprives them of foliage and may adversely affect their growth.

Pruning of large leaved shrubs, such as aucuba and cherry laurel, is best done with a pair of secateurs if time permits since shears leave ugly wounds on the sliced leaves. All other hedge shrubs should be pruned with sharp shears or a mechanical hedge trimmer. These latter are revolutionizing the outlook on both hedges and topiary specimens, since the work of trimming can be done in a fraction of the time required for hand trimming. The electrical models have the merit of complete reliability and quietness. They are available for operation by cable directly from the mains, or from a battery which may be the same as that used for the electric lawn mower, may be a small power pack slung from the shoulder, or a nickel-cadmium battery sufficiently small to be contained within the handle of the machine.

Simple topiary specimens, such as balls and cones, can be formed simply by clipping. More elaborate specimens such as bears, hens, and peacocks will almost certainly require some training as well as clipping. A frame may be constructed by lashing bamboo canes together or with stout wire bent to form the rough shape required. Young shoots are tied to this frame and the side growths are clipped to shape. If neatly made the frame can remain permanently concealed inside the specimen.

Hedges and topiary specimens need feeding. Well rotted manure or garden compost spread around them in spring is ideal, but failing this use peat with which

15

bone meal and hoof and horn meal have been mixed. Use 25 grammes of each meal per 0·5 kilogramme of peat (1 oz of each per lb) and spread this mixture at 2 kilogrammes per square metre (4 lb/sq yd).

Quick-reference Table of Hedging Plants

ABBREVIATIONS

Type	*E* evergreen; *D* deciduous.
Colours	*G* green; *Y* yellow (golden); *Yv* yellow variegated; *W* white; *Wv* white (silver) variegated; *Pl* purple; *Cp* copper; *M* mauve; *B* blue; *Bg* blue-grey; *O* orange; *R* red.
Other features	*Fl* flowers; *Ber* berries.

Name	Type	Foliage colour	Other features	Planting distance cm	in.	Useful hedge height m	ft
Aucuba	E	G Yv		45–60	*18–24*	1·5–2·5	*5–8*
Beech	D	G Cp Pl		30–45	*12–18*	2–4·5	*6–15*
Berberis darwinii	E	G	O Fl	45–60	*18–24*	2–3	*6–10*
„ stenophylla	E	G	Y Fl	45–60	*18–24*	2·5–3	*8–10*
„ verruculosa	E	G	O Fl	45	*18*	0·75–1	*2–3*
Box	E	G Y		40–45	*15–18*	0·5–1	*2–6*
Chamaecyparis lawsoniana (Lawson Cypress)	E	G Bg Y		60–80	*24–30*	2–3	*6–10*
Cherry Laurel	E	G		45–60	*18–24*	1·5–3	*5–10*
Cotoneaster simonsii	D	G	R Ber	30–45	*12–18*	1·5–2·5	*5–8*
Cupressocyparis leylandii (Leyland Cypress)	E	G		60–80	*24–30*	2–4·5	*6–15*
Escallonia Crimson Spire	E	G	R Fl	45	*18*	1·5–2·5	*5–8*
Euonymus japonicus	E	G Yv		40–45	*15–18*	1–2·5	*3–8*
Griselinia littoralis	E	G Yv		45–60	*18–24*	1·5–2	*5–7*
Holly	E	G Yv Wv	R Y Ber	45–60	*18–24*	1·5–3	*5–10*
Hornbeam	D	G		45–60	*18–24*	2–4·5	*6–15*
Laurustinus	E	G	W Fl	45–60	*18–24*	1·5–2·5	*5–8*
Lavender	E	grey	B Fl	30–40	*12–15*	0·5–1	*1½–3*
Lonicera nitida	E	G		30–40	*12–15*	1–1·5	*3–5*
Pittosporum tenuifolium	E	G Wv		45	*18*	1–2·5	*3–8*
Portugal Laurel	E	G		45–60	*18–24*	2–3·5	*6–12*
Privet (oval leaved)	E	G Yv		30–45	*12–18*	1–2	*3–6*
Prunus cerasifera	D	G Pl	W Fl	60	*24*	2–3	*6–10*
„ cistena	D	Pl	W Fl	45	*18*	0·75–1	*2–3*
Pyracantha	E	G	R Y Ber	45	*18*	1·5–2	*5–7*
Quickthorn	D	G	W Fl	15–20	*6–8*	1·5–2·5	*5–8*
Rhododendron ponticum	E	G	M Fl	60–80	*24–30*	2–2·5	*6–8*
Thuya plicata	E	G Yv		60–80	*24–30*	1·5–4·5	*5–15*
Yew	E	G Y		45–60	*18–24*	1–3	*3–10*

4 Annuals and Bedding Plants

Annuals are plants that grow, flower, and seed within a year and then die. For garden use they are divided into two groups: *hardy annuals* which can be sown and grown outdoors without protection from cold, and *half-hardy annuals* which are liable to be killed by frost and so are either sown in a greenhouse or frame and planted outdoors later, or are sown outdoors quite late in the spring when danger of frost is past.

These are the best plants with which to make a quick display in the garden since most can be had in flower within four months from sowing. Seed is readily produced and cheap to buy. Alternatively seedlings of many of the most popular kinds are produced on a vast scale commercially and offered for sale in boxes or other containers when it is time to plant them out. Most annuals continue to flower for two or three months, some longer, and the display of all can be increased if the faded flowers are picked off before the seed has a chance to develop and ripen.

By using annuals wisely it is possible to maintain colour in the garden from May to October and to fill quickly any gaps that may appear in the flower beds. Because of their relatively short life, they can be frequently renewed, so that changes can be made in the colour schemes, new varieties enjoyed, and all manner of interesting decorative possibilities exploited. Moreover, since the ground is periodically cleared of one lot of plants to make way for another, there is opportunity to cultivate the soil and clear it of weeds which does not occur so conveniently with other more permanent plants. For this reason annuals are particularly useful in new gardens, where it may take a year or so to get the soil into sufficiently good condition for planting perennials that will remain undisturbed for years.

BEDDING OUT

The process of renewing the garden display with plants raised from seed sown in a greenhouse, frame, or reserve garden, is known as bedding out. It may be a more or less continuous process from spring to autumn, and in public parks this is precisely what is done to maintain maximum display at all times. However there are two major periods for bedding out, one from early May to mid-June for summer flowering plants and the other in September and October for spring flowering plants, and this simple cycle satisfies the needs of most private gardeners.

Dwarf Annual Asters

Hardy annuals may be sown outdoors where they are to flower. Half hardy annuals are sown in well-drained pots or boxes filled with good seed compost made quite level. A little compost is sifted over the seeds and they are watered through a fine rose.

The term 'bedding-out plant' is used to describe all those plants specially grown for this kind of temporary display in the garden. It includes a great many half-hardy annuals which are raised in one place and then planted to flower in another and it is also used for numerous perennial plants, i.e. plants that will continue to live for many years, but which for one reason or another are seldom or never planted out permanently. Familiar examples are bedding geraniums (more correctly known as pelargoniums), marguerites, fuchsias, tuberous rooted begonias, dahlias, antirrhinums, penstemons, scarlet salvias, wallflowers, double daisies and polyanthus, and some useful grey and silver leaved plants such as Cineraria maritima, Centaurea ragusina, and Calocephalus brownii. Many of these plants can also be raised from seed in the same way as annuals, but some have to be propagated by cuttings, which may need to be overwintered in frost-proof greenhouses. Again this can be done quite easily at home if the necessary facilities are available, or young plants can be purchased when it is safe to plant them outdoors.

Some bulbs also enter into the bedding-out programme in a big way, especially for spring display, for which tulips, hyacinths, and daffodils are all extremely useful, but their separate requirements are dealt with in Chapter 5.

BIENNIALS

There is yet another class of plant that can be most useful in the bedding-out cycle and which can fill in the gap that sometimes occurs between the spring and summer flowering plants. These are the *biennials*, plants which grow, flower, seed, and then die in the manner of annuals, but spread this cycle over two years (or more accurately two growing seasons). Most biennials are sown in spring or early

18

summer, the seedlings are planted in a reserve bed to grow on and are removed to their flowering quarters in autumn. They then flower the following May or June and have ripened their seed by the end of the summer. Canterbury bells and forget-me-nots are true biennials and wallflowers, sweet williams, poly-anthus, and double daisies are plants which, though really perennial, are usually treated as biennial, since this is both convenient and produces the best results.

SOIL AND SITE

All annuals have a wide tolerance of soils and situations, though most prefer light situations that are open to the sky. However, there are useful kinds that can be grown in the shade, even under trees. All enjoy soils that have been well cultivated so that the soil is crumbly and easily penetrated by their roots. Such soil also makes the best seed beds and can be produced by working in plenty of peat. Annuals also like reasonably good soil, though not too rich as this may produce an excess of growth at the expense of flowers. Light dressings of well rotted manure or garden com-post, about a barrowload to 10 square metres (12 sq yd), can be forked in prior to sowing or planting and the soil can also be lightly dusted with a good general purpose fertilizer.

HARDY ANNUALS

Hardy annuals are sown outdoors from March to May and some kinds also in September for earlier flowering the following year (this almost makes them into biennials, but the growing season is shorter). The seed can be sprinkled evenly in patches and be covered by scattering a thin layer of fine soil over it, this process being known as broadcasting. Alternatively it can be sown in little furrows made with a pointed stick or the corner of a hoe and be covered by drawing back the displaced soil, this being known as sowing in drills. Broadcasting is quick and easy and is useful for filling small gaps and producing an informal effect in irregular drifts, but it is more difficult to care for the seedlings and to remove weeds from them.

In either case the covering of soil over the seeds should be quite light, certainly no more than 1 cm ($\frac{1}{2}$ in.). If the seeds are sown thinly only a little thinning out of the seedlings will be required and this should be done early while the seedlings are still only 2–3 cm

(above) Bartonia aurea
(centre) Candytuft Fairy Mixed
(below) Chrysanthemum carinatum tricolor

(1–1½ in.) high. If lifted carefully when the soil is moist many of the seedlings removed when thinning can be replanted elsewhere if there are spaces to be filled.

HALF-HARDY ANNUALS

Half-hardy annuals and summer flowering bedding plants that are to be raised from seed should be sown between January and May according to the facilities available and the time at which plants are required to start flowering. Most require a minimum night temperature of 13 °C (55 °F) for reliable germination and steady growth, and that means a fair amount of artificial heat in January and February. By March sun heat will maintain a sufficiently high temperature most days in a well constructed and properly placed greenhouse, but artificial heat will still be required most nights. By April it is possible to germinate most seeds in an unheated greenhouse or frame and by early May many half-hardy annuals will germinate in a sunny, sheltered place outdoors. Some kinds grow much more rapidly than others, and since the seedlings cannot be safely planted outdoors until May, or even early June in some cold districts, there is no point in sowing them very early. Other kinds grow more slowly and an early start is useful. These differences are noted with the descriptions of the various half-hardy annuals and bedding plants. But as a general rule most sowing can be done between the last week in February and the middle of March, provided the necessary minimum night temperature can be maintained. It is desirable that by day the temperature should rise 3–6 °C (5–10 °F) above the night temperature.

All seeds can be germinated in shallow seed boxes, trays, pans, or pots in either John Innes or peat seed compost. Do not quite fill these containers but leave a little space so that water is retained when applied. Sow thinly all over the surface and cover with a light sprinkling of the same seed compost. Water well from a can fitted with a fine rose, cover each container with a sheet of glass, and spread a sheet of newspaper on top to exclude light. Then place in the greenhouse or frame. Seedlings may appear in anything from five days to three weeks according to the variety. Examine containers daily and water if the compost appears to be dry. Directly the seedlings are seen pushing through the compost remove the paper covering and tilt the glass slightly to admit air. A day or so later remove it altogether and grow the seedlings with full light and free circulation of air. Use ventilation to control temperature which may average 16–18 °C (60–65 °F) by day and should be kept below 21 °C (70 °F) if possible.

When seedlings raised under glass make their first pair of true leaves, they must be very carefully transplanted, or pricked out, to other pots or boxes in which they can be spaced 4 cm apart. A notched stick is useful for lifting and holding these tiny plants.

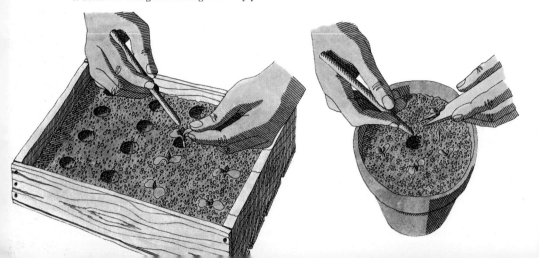

PRICKING OUT

The first leaves made by all seedlings are of a different character, and are usually simpler in shape, than those that follow. They are known as the seed leaves, or cotyledons, while those that follow are called the true or rough leaves. Seedlings should be transplanted to other containers as soon as they have produced their first true leaves. This process is known as pricking out and is necessary to give the seedlings more room to grow into sturdy plants. Similar compost can be used and also similar containers, boxes or trays 5 cm (2 in.) deep being ideal. Again they should not be quite filled with compost, so that there is room for water.

Water the seedlings well an hour or so before they are pricked out so that the soil is moist but surplus water has time to drain away. Then lift the seedlings carefully with a pointed stick or wooden plant label, separate them out without breaking their roots, and plant them 4 cm (1½ in.) apart each way in the new containers. The same wooden label may be used for this planting or a short, round ended stick about the size and shape of a fountain pen and known as a dibber. With this a hole can be made into which the roots are dropped and then the soil is gently pressed around them with dibber or finger. Professional gardeners often use their fingers for the whole operation, but unless a glove or finger stall is worn compost does accumulate under the nails and can become painful.

Water the seedlings in well through a fine rose to settle the compost still more around the roots and then stand them back in the greenhouse or frame under the same light airy conditions as before. Continue to water freely whenever the soil looks dry.

HARDENING OFF

From mid-April onward the plants should be gradually hardened off, which means that they must be accustomed to the lower temperatures they may have to face outdoors. This is done by discontinuing artificial heat unless it is exceptionally cold, for under no circumstances should the temperature be permitted to fall below 7 °C (45 °F), and by increasing ventilation. Plants in the greenhouse may be removed to a frame from which the

(above) Antirrhinum Intermediate Bedding Varieties
(centre) Salvia Blaze of Fire
(below) Polyanthus Pacific Hybrids

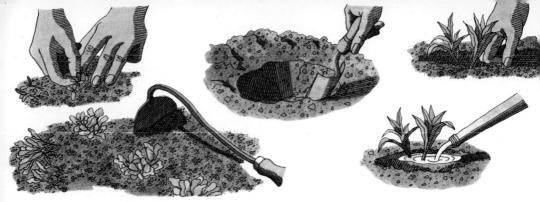

Seedlings raised out of doors must be thinned out either by hand or with a small hoe. Two fingers pressed on the soil each side of seedlings to be retained will prevent root disturbance. Plant out bedding plants with a trowel, firm well, and water in.

protective light can be completely removed on fine days. By May it may even be safe to stand them outdoors in a sheltered position, but be prepared to cover them at night with brown paper if there is a frost warning. Timing depends a great deal on locality since spring comes to the south and west of Britain two or three weeks earlier than to the north and east. Local knowledge is invaluable in these matters and can usually be provided by the local nurseryman, seedsman, or garden centre. Local horticultural societies are also useful in providing pools of expert local knowledge about such matters as these.

PLANTING OUT

Final planting out for most half-hardy annuals and summer bedding plants is between the third week in May and the second week in June, according to the variety and the locality. There is no need to be in too great a hurry as the late plants may catch up and even go ahead of the early plants if these are checked by cold nights.

Water the plants freely a few hours before planting. Remove them very carefully from their containers so that the roots are not unduly injured and the compost is retained around them. Plant with a trowel, put a handful of moist peat around each plant, and make it firm with the fingers or the handle of the trowel. Space the smaller kinds about 15 cm (6 in.) apart, the largest 45 cm (18 in.) apart, and others at intermediate distances according to their size and habit. Water in well after planting.

Very much the same treatment applies to purchased bedding plants except that those raised from cuttings, such as geraniums and fuchsias, are likely to be individually grown in pots. If each pot is turned upside down, two fingers are placed either side of the plant and the rim of the pot is sharply rapped with the handle of the trowel, the ball of compost and roots should slide out cleanly. Then it is only necessary to prepare a hole the correct size to receive it and work in a little moist peat, as with the box or tray grown seedlings. If bone meal is mixed with the peat in the proportion of a double handful to a 10 litre (2 gallon) bucket of peat, it will stimulate root growth and so get the plants quickly established.

All the subsequent care required is to keep beds clear of weeds, to remove faded flowers (this is not essential but it improves appearance and helps to keep plants flowering), and to stake tall plants such as larkspurs and cosmeas. This is most conveniently done by pushing some short brushy branches (such as the tops

22

of pea sticks) into the soil close to the plants at an early stage so that they grow up through the sticks, concealing them and finding their own support.

In seed catalogues some varieties are described as F_1 hybrids. F stands for filial, meaning offspring or generation, and 1 for first, so the sign F_1 means 'first generation hybrid'. These varieties have to be remade each year by the seed grower who produces them from two distinct parent stocks which are not distributed. This is a troublesome thing to do since usually a lot of hand work is involved, but it is justified by the improved vigour and uniformity of the resultant plants. However, it is no use saving seed from these plants in the hope of getting the same result again, since in the next generation there is likely to be considerable variation. In order to produce the required result the original parents, which are themselves maintained by in-breeding, must be recrossed and this is done year by year by the seed grower who introduced the variety and who is normally the only person capable of producing it.

FAVOURITE ANNUALS AND BEDDING PLANTS

Antirrhinum (Snapdragon). The popular name refers to the shape of the pouched flower, which, if pinched, opens like a mouth; but there are now varieties with double flowers and others with open funnel-shaped flowers which cannot be made to 'snap' in this way. All are perennials but are commonly grown as half-hardy annuals. It is an advantage to sow in January or February and to get strong plants which, if well hardened off, can be planted out in the latter half of May. Colours include almost everything except blue. Heights range from 15 to 90 cm (6–36 in.), the tallest varieties being excellent for cutting and the intermediate and dwarf varieties (such as Carters New Dwarf) being the best for garden display. Antirrhinums are sometimes attacked by rust, a disease which produces rust coloured spots on the leaves, which later wither and die. Rust resistant varieties are available and should be grown in districts in which this disease is troublesome.

Aster. The annual asters are more correctly known as *callistephus*. They belong

Gazania Longiscapa Hybrids   Mesembryanthemum criniflorum   Portulaca Double Mixed

to the daisy family and have showy flowers which may be single, semi-double, or double. The doubles may have long, thin, curled petals or quite short, straight petals or be intermediate in character like the medium length quilled petals of Apollo. Heights also vary from 30 to 75 cm (12–30 in.). Colours include lavender, blue, purple, crimson, rose, pink, and white. Sow in March and April under glass or sow the single varieties in April or May outdoors.

Begonia. There are a number of different kinds of begonia, some of which are purely greenhouse plants. However, the hybrid tuberous rooted begonias can either be grown in pots or be planted outdoors in summer and the many varieties of Begonia semperflorens are superlatively good bedding plants best treated as half-hardy annuals. This begonia grows from 15 to 30 cm (6–12 in.) high, has neat, slightly fleshy leaves which may be green or bronze according to variety, and clusters of small white, pink, carmine, or crimson flowers very freely produced all the summer.

The tuberous rooted begonias can be grown from seed in much the same way as the fibrous rooted Begonia semperflorens or from tubers obtained between January and April and started into growth in moist peat in a temperature of 15 °C (60 °F). Set the tubers shoulder to shoulder on the peat and barely cover them. Pot singly in John Innes No. 2 compost when leaves are 5–7 cm (2–3 in.) high. If desired large tubers can be carefully divided at this stage with a sharp knife, but take care that each piece has a growing shoot. This is the method used to increase the finest 'named' varieties, with immense double flowers in many shades of pink, red, crimson, yellow, and orange as well as pure white, since seedlings may vary from their parents but divisions do not.

Tuberous rooted begonias can be planted outdoors in late May or early June in good soil and sunny or semi-shady places, but they must be lifted and brought into a frost-proof place in late September or early October. Alternatively they can be grown as greenhouse pot plants in 12–15 cm (5–6 in.) pots. No artificial heat is required from May onwards, a temperature between 12 and 16 °C (55–65 °F) being ideal. Water fairly freely, shade from direct sunshine, and stake and tie the stems carefully to support the heavy flowers. Feed occasionally with weak liquid manure from June to August. Gradually reduce water from late September, allow plants to die down, and store the tubers in a frost-proof place until it is time to start them into growth again.

Seed of all begonias is very small and should be sown on the surface of fine compost and not covered.

Campanula. Many campanulas are hardy perennials or rock plants, but Campanula medium, the Canterbury Bell, is a hardy biennial; C. speculum, known as Venus' Looking Glass, is a hardy annual. Varieties of Canterbury Bell are also available which, if sown in a greenhouse in February, will flower outdoors that same summer and autumn. Canterbury Bells may have long, bell-shaped flowers, when they are known as single flowered varieties, or each bell may be backed by a ring of spreading petals, these being known as cup and saucer varieties. Heights vary from 45 to 75 cm ($1\frac{1}{2}$–$2\frac{1}{2}$ ft); colours include white, pink, rose, and various shades of blue.

Campanula speculum is 30–40 cm (12–15 in.) high with numerous widely opened violet flowers. It is also known as Specularia speculum-veneris.

Canna (Indian Shot). Perennial plants with broad green or purple leaves and stout 90–120 cm (3–4 ft) stems bearing showy scarlet, pink, yellow, or orange

flowers. They can be grown from seed in a temperature of 15–18 °C (60–65 °F), but seeds should be soaked in water for twelve hours before sowing. Alternatively roots can be purchased in spring and started into growth in moist peat in a temperature of 15–18 °C (60–65 °F). Cannas should not be planted outdoors before June, except in the mildest places. They enjoy sun and warmth, but also like to be well watered. Roots can be lifted in October and stored dry in a frost-proof place during the winter.

Carnation. The annual carnations resemble the greenhouse carnations in flower but are only 30–60 cm (12–24 in.) high. They are half-hardy annuals. Colours include white, pink, scarlet, crimson, salmon, and yellow. All appreciate lime or chalk in the soil.

Dahlia. These are among the most valuable of all summer bedding plants, because of their long season of flower from July to October, the great range of colours and flower shapes and also of heights from 45 cm to 1·5 m (18 in.– 5 ft). Varieties can be found to meet almost every need, from filling formal beds with gay flowers to planting with herbaceous perennials or shrubs to maintain continuity of colour. Many varieties are excellent for cutting. Pigmy is a particularly good dwarf variety 25–45 cm (12–18 in.) high with single flowers in all colours.

Dahlias are all half-hardy perennials, but they grow readily and rapidly from seed and if treated as half-hardy annuals will flower the same summer. This is a particularly good way to grow the dwarf varieties with either single or double flowers in mixed colours. The seedlings can be pricked out into boxes in the usual way but should be spaced 5 cm (2 in.) apart because of their rapid growth. It is even better to pot them singly in 7 cm (3 in.) pots in John Innes No. 1 or peat potting compost and plant them from these at the end of

(above) Foxglove Dwarf Foxy;
(below) Sweet William Mixed

25

May or early June, 25–45 cm (12–18 in.) apart. For culture of the taller varieties *see* Chapter 5.

Helichrysum (Strawflower). The popular name refers to the chaffy nature of the petals of this 'everlasting' flower, which is excellent for drying to use in winter decorations. It is a half-hardy annual, the flowers almost ball-like, in various shades of pink, crimson, yellow, and orange as well as white. Cut just before the flowers are fully developed, tie in small bunches, and hang upside down in a cool airy place to dry.

Impatiens. There are two different types of impatiens, one derived from Impatiens holstii and I. sultanii, popularly known as Busy Lizzie because the plants hardly ever stop flowering, the other derived from I. balsamina and known as garden balsam.

Busy Lizzies are really perennial, and if grown as pot plants in a frost-proof greenhouse or room will live for years. But they are readily raised from seed in a temperature of 21 °C (70 °F) without shading, and treated as half-hardy annuals for summer bedding. Heights range from 15 to 40 cm (6–16 in.) and colours from white and pale pink to scarlet and purple. The flowers are single. The balsams are half-hardy annuals and all the garden varieties have fully double flowers borne in spikes to 45 cm (18 in.) high. Colours are also from white to scarlet and they, too, make excellent pot plants, but for light greenhouses rather than for rooms.

Marigold. Several quite distinct plants are known as marigolds. The Pot Marigold or Calendula is a hardy annual with orange or yellow flowers, always fully double in the best garden varieties though liable to revert to single types if permitted to renew itself from self-sown seed, as it will so readily do. It is much better to grow from purchased seed each year, sowing outdoors from March to May where the plants are to flower.

The African and French Marigolds are varieties of Tagetes erecta and T. patula respectively. The former are 45–60 cm (18–24 in.) high with large, fully double yellow or orange flowers, the latter 15–40 cm (6–16 in.) high with single or double flowers which may be orange or yellow with chestnut red. However, the two races have been so much interbred that it is becoming increasingly difficult to draw any clear division between them. There are some excellent F_1 hybrids of both the French and African types, notable for their uniformity and free flowering. All are very showy half-hardy annuals, thriving in all soils but liking warm sunny places. They can also be sown outdoors in early May where the plants are to flower as they grow very fast.

Tagetes signata is also a marigold though it is seldom called one, but is referred to simply as 'Tagetes'. It is a low growing plant forming a mound of finely divided leaves starred all over with multitudinous small yellow or orange flowers. Cultivation is identical with that of French and African Marigolds. It is a first-rate edging plant.

Pelargonium (Bedding Geranium). There are two quite distinct types of bedding 'geranium', the zonal leaved pelargoniums which are bushy plants with stiff stems and roundish, slightly downy leaves, usually marked with a dark circle, and the ivy leaved pelargoniums with thinner, laxer, sprawling stems and smooth, angled leaves. Both produce their flowers more or less continuously for as long as the temperature permits the plants to go on growing. They are admirable bedding plants that can be grown from seed sown in a warm greenhouse in February or March or from cuttings taken in spring or late summer. From October to May plants must be kept in a cool or intermediate greenhouse (*see* Chapter 11). All enjoy sun and warmth.

Zonal leaved pelargoniums are available in white and shades of pink, salmon, scarlet, carmine, and crimson in single and double flowered forms. There are also varieties grown primarily for their foliage which may be golden or green, variegated with white, yellow, red, or black.

Ivy leaved pelargoniums are also available in single or double flowered forms, mainly in shades of pink, mauve, light purple, and red. They can be used as ground work, the sprawling shoots pegged down to cover the soil, or they can be trained up trellis work or canes or grown in hanging baskets, vases, window boxes, etc., and allowed to hang down.

Petunia. Showy half-hardy annuals with trumpet-shaped flowers in a great range of colours. Petunias will grow well in most soils, but enjoy good drainage and sun. There are a great many different varieties, the largest flowered (scarlet Gipsy Ballerina is a good example) being known as 'grandiflora' and those with smaller flowers as 'multiflora'. There are single and double flowered varieties in each type. All make mounded plants 30–45 cm (12–18 in.) high. In addition there are petunias of more trailing habit, known as 'cascade' petunias, or sometimes as 'balcony' varieties, which are specially useful for window boxes, vases, etc.

Polyanthus. Hardy perennials often grown as biennials and discarded after flowering, but if preferred the plants can be lifted when the flowers fade, split up into smaller pieces, and replanted in a reserve bed to grow on for use again another year. Polyanthus have primrose-like flowers, borne in clusters on sturdy 20–30 cm (8–12 in.) stems. They flower in spring and may be used for bedding or be planted more informally in borders, wild gardens, woodlands, etc. They enjoy rather rich soil and will grow well in sun or shade. Colours include white, shades of yellow, orange, pink, red, crimson, lavender, and blues.

Salvia. There are several kinds of salvia requiring quite different treatment. The scarlet salvia (S. splendens) is a half-hardy annual making a branching plant 30–40 cm (12–16 in.) high with spikes of scarlet flowers. There are now salmon, cerise, and purple varieties as well as dwarf varieties only

(above) **Annual Scabious Tall Double Mixed**
(centre) **Nigella Persian Jewels**
(below) **Giant Sweet Sultan Mixed**

15–20 cm (6–8 in.) high. It is desirable to grow the seedlings singly in 7 cm (3 in.) pots in John Innes No. 1 compost so that they can be transplanted without check.

Salvia patens is a perennial with tuberous roots like a dahlia and spikes of hooded gentian blue flowers. It can be grown from seed like a half-hardy annual or from the old roots stored for the winter in peat in a frost-proof place and restarted like dahlia tubers in the spring.

Salvia horminum is a hardy annual 45–60 cm (18–24 in.) high with slender spikes in which the purple, pink or white bracts (floral leaves) make the display. This is often known as clary but the name really belongs to Salvia sclarea, a 1 m (3 ft) hardy biennial with branched spikes of off-white and pink flowers. The best variety is called 'turkestanica'.

Stock. Half-hardy annuals derived from Matthiola incana. There are three distinct races: ten-week stocks, so called because they flower about ten weeks after sowing, and grown as half-hardy annuals; Brompton stocks which are biennials taking about nine months to flower; and East Lothian stocks which take about five months to flower and may be grown either as half-hardy annuals or as biennials. All have fragrant flowers in white and various shades of pink, red, lavender, and purple. It is the plants bearing fully double flowers that are most highly prized, but seed will not give all double flowered seedlings. However, in the 100 per cent stocks the seedlings that will produce double flowers can be recognized because they have lighter green leaves and the dark green seedlings can be discarded when pricking out. The colour distinction is most obvious when the seedlings are grown at temperatures below 10 °C (50 °F). Heights of these stocks vary from 30 to 60 cm (12–24 in.) according to variety.

In mild districts and on well-drained soils, especially near the coast, Brompton stocks can be planted in September where they are to flower the following spring and early summer, but in colder or damper places they should be overwintered in a frame and be planted outdoors in March.

East Lothian stocks are often sown in July to flower in pots in the greenhouse in winter.

(above) Wallflowers
(below) Sweet Pea Carlotta

Dwarf French Marigold Colour Magic

Sweet Pea. Hardy annuals, sweetly scented, in a wonderful range of colours, but not including full yellow. There are several distinct types differing in height, flower form, and the way in which the flowers are produced. Many fine varieties have been raised by Carters Tested Seeds Ltd.

The old fashioned sweet peas have relatively small flowers with unwaved petals, but some people regard them as the most fragrant. Spencer sweet peas have large flowers with elegantly waved petals. In this type there are both tall, climbing varieties and dwarf varieties ranging from 30 to 200 cm (12–80 in.) according to type. There are also types with more than the usual three to five flowers per stem and some bred specially for early flowering under glass.

For outdoor cultivation sweet peas can be sown in winter, spring, or autumn. January and February sowings are made in a greenhouse, minimum night temperature 7 °C (45 °F), the seedlings being hardened off for planting outdoors in April. March to May sowings are made outdoors where the plants are to flower. September to early October sowings are made in a frame or unheated greenhouse, the seedlings being hardened off and planted out in April. This is the best way to grow the tall varieties for the finest flowers for cutting.

Pinch out the tips of these early seedlings when they have made four pairs of leaves. Dig and manure ground for the seedlings liberally and plant out in April 25–30 cm (10–12 in.) apart, either in a single row or in a double row 30 cm (1 ft) wide, and if more than one row is required, leave at least 1·5 m (5 ft) alleyways. Place a 2·5 m (8 ft) bamboo cane to each plant and lash these canes to horizontal wires strained between posts. Reduce shoots to the one best per plant and tie this in regularly to its cane. Remove all side shoots, also tendrils, keeping each plant to a single stem. Water freely in dry weather and feed occasionally with a general purpose fertilizer from May onwards.

For ordinary decorative purposes sow seeds 2 cm (1 in.) deep and 5–7 cm (2–3 in.) apart in groups or rows where they are to flower: thrust long bushy pea sticks into the soil around them or erect netting between posts so that they can climb and find their own support. Let the plants branch naturally and do not remove the tendrils.

Short pea sticks, or the tops off pea sticks, will provide sufficient support for the dwarf varieties which can be grown in beds or be used as temporary flowering hedges.

Spray all sweet peas occasionally with a good greenfly killer.

29

Some varieties have hard black skins to their seeds and moisture does not readily penetrate to start germination. To overcome this chip the coat of each seed with the point of a penknife, but be careful to do this away from the 'germ' of the seed, visible as a small lump on the otherwise smooth round coat. The botanical name of the sweet pea is Lathyrus odoratus.

Sweet William. The ordinary varieties are hardy biennials, but there are also varieties which can be grown as hardy annuals. All carry their flowers in large flat-topped clusters, heights varying from 15 to 60 cm (6–24 in.) according to variety. Colours are white, pink, salmon, scarlet, and crimson and the auricula-eyed varieties have a coloured edge and white centre. Double and single flowered varieties are available. The botanical name of sweet william is Dianthus barbatus.

Viola. Under this name *Pansies* are included, since interbreeding between bedding violas and pansies is making the division between them ever more difficult to draw. All are low growing plants, the violas usually rather more tufted than the pansies which tend to sprawl further. Also the flowers of violas are often self-coloured, whereas those of pansies are usually blotched with one colour on another, but there are exceptions both ways. All may be treated as hardy biennials, seed being sown in pots or boxes in a frame, or direct outdoors in May or June, transplanted to a reserve bed, and moved again to flowering quarters in autumn or spring. Alternatively they may be treated as half-hardy annuals and sown in a greenhouse in January or February. All like rather rich soil and will grow in full sun or partial shade. All flower in spring and summer and the winter flowering varieties also whenever the weather is mild for a few days in winter.

Wallflower. Perennials usually grown as hardy biennials and among the most popular and useful of spring bedding plants. The flowers are richly fragrant. There are many varieties ranging in height from 30 to 45 cm (12–18 in.) and in colour lemon, yellow, apricot, orange, scarlet, blood red, purple, carmine-rose, and ruby violet. Good mixtures are available, such as Carters Art Shades. It is best to pinch out the tip of each seedling when 12–15 cm (5–6 in.) high to induce a more branching habit. If possible plant in flowering quarters in September so that plants have time to get established before the winter.

Zinnia. Half-hardy annuals with very showy flowers of pink, rose, salmon, apricot, orange, scarlet, purple, etc. There are several distinct types, Dahlia flowered having broad petalled ball-like flowers, Chrysanthemum flowered quilled or twisted petals, Lilliput small pompon flowers, and so on. Heights range from 15 to 90 cm (6 in.–3 ft). Though zinnias can be grown as half-hardy annuals even better results are obtained by sowing directly outdoors in May or early June where the plants are to flower, and hastening germination by covering with cloches if the district is a cold one. Zinnias do best in warm sunny places.

Verbena Sparkle   Nemophila insignis   Begonia semperflorens

Pampas Grass

ORNAMENTAL GRASSES

A number of grasses are grown for their coloured leaves or graceful flower heads and some can be dried and used in winter decorations. Some are hardy annuals to be grown from seed sown in spring where plants are to grow, a few are half-hardy annuals to be sown in spring in a frame or greenhouse and planted out when there is no longer danger of frost, and some are perennials which will grow for years and can be lifted and divided when overcrowded.

Quick-reference Table of Grasses

ABBREVIATIONS

HA hardy annual; *HHA* half-hardy annual; *HP* hardy perennial

Botanical name	Popular name	Type	Height cm	in.	Special beauty
Agrostis nebulosa	Cloud Grass	HA	45	*18*	Cloud-like flower sprays
Avena sterilis	Animated Oats	HA	100	*36*	Long twisting awns
Briza maxima	Quaking Grass	HA	45	*18*	Nodding flowers
,, minima	Small Quaking Grass	HA	40	*16*	Small nodding flowers
Coix lachryma-jobi	Job's Tears	HA	60	*24*	Pearly, bead-like seeds
Cortaderia argentea	Pampas Grass	HP	125–250	*50–100*	Plumes of silvery flowers
Festuca ovina glauca	Blue Sheep's Fescue	HP	30	*12*	Narrow blue-grey leaves
Hordeum jubatum	Squirrel-tail Grass	HA	30	*12*	Tassel-like flowers
Lagurus ovatus	Hare's-tail Grass	HA	30	*12*	Fluffy beige flower heads
Milium effusum aureum	Bowles' Golden Grass	HHA	30	*12*	Narrow golden leaves
Miscanthus sacchariflorus	Eulalia	HP	120	*48*	Grey-green leaves
,, zebrinus	Zebra Grass	HP	100	*36*	Leaves banded yellow and green
Molina coerulea variegata		HP	45	*18*	Blue and yellow leaves
Panicum violaceum		HA	100	*36*	Green and purple flower plumes
Pennisetum villosum		HA	100	*36*	Feathery flower plumes
Phalaris arundinacea	Ribbon Grass, Gardener's Garters	HP	100	*36*	Green and white leaves
Setaria italica	Foxtail Millet	HA	45	*18*	Arching brown flower plumes
Stipa pennata	Feather Grass	HP	75	*30*	Plumed flowers
Zea mays (varieties)	Maize	HHA	100	*36*	Variegated leaves or coloured seeds (cobs)

31

Quick-reference Table of Annuals and Bedding Plants

ABBREVIATIONS

Culture   *HA* Treat as a hardy annual, sowing seed outdoors in spring where the plants are to flower.
HA(S) Hardy annual which may also be sown outdoors in Aug–Sept.
HHA Treat as a half-hardy annual sowing under glass in Jan–Apr and planting out in May–June.
HHA(M) Treat as a half-hardy annual, but may also be sown outdoors in May or early June where the plants are to flower.
HHP Treat as a half-hardy perennial, keeping the plants in a frost-proof place from Oct to May and planting out in late May or early June.
HB Treat as a hardy biennial, sowing seed in May–June and planting in flowering beds in Sept–Oct.

Colour   *W* white; *Y* yellow; *O* orange; *P* pink; *R* red; *C* crimson; *Pl* purple; *B* blue; *M* mauve; *L* lavender; *G* green.

Flowering time   To cover the full times given it would be necessary to make several successional sowings of most annuals.

Botanical name	Popular name	Culture	Colour	Height cm	Height in.	Flowering time
Abutilon	Flowering Maple	HHA, HHP	W Y C	60–150	24–60	June–Oct
Acroclinium	Everlasting	HA	W P	38–46	15–18	June–July
Ageratum		HHA	B M Pl W	15–46	6–18	June–Aug
Agrostemma milas	Corn Cockle	HA(S)	M	90–120	36–48	July–Aug
Alonsoa	Mask Flower	HHA(M)	C	46	18	May–June
Alyssum maritimum	Sweet Alyssum	HA(S)	W Pl	10–15	4–6	May–Sept
Amaranthus caudatus	Love-lies-bleeding	HA	C G	75	30	July–Aug
,, hypocondriacus	Prince's Feather	HA	R C	60–120	24–48	July–Aug
,, tricolor	Joseph's Coat	HHA		60–90	24–30	Grown for its foliage
Anagallis	Pimpernel	HHA(M)	B R	15–20	6–8	June–Aug
Anchusa capensis		HA	B	40	16	May–June
Antirrhinum	Snapdragon	HHA	W Y O P R C	15–90	6–36	June–Sept
Arctotis	African Daisy	HHA	W Y O R Pl	30–60	12–24	June–Aug
Asperula azurea setosa	Oriental Woodruff	HA(S)	L	20	8	June–July
Aster: *see* Callistephus						
Bartonia		HA	Y	60	24	June–Aug
Begonia semperflorens	Fibrous rooted Begonia	HHA	W P R C	15–30	6–12	May–Oct
,, tuberhybrida	Tuberous rooted Begonia	HHP	W P R C Y O	20–40	8–16	May–Oct
Bellis monstrosa	Double Daisy	HB	W P R	15	6	Mar–May
Brachycome	Swan River Daisy	HHA(M)	B L W	15–20	6–8	July–Aug
Cacalia coccinea	Tassel Flower	HA	R	46	18	July–Aug
Calceolaria integrifolia	Bedding Calceolaria	HHP	Y C	50–60	20–24	June–Oct
Calendula	Pot Marigold	HA(S)	Y O	45–60	18–24	June–Sept
Californian Poppy: *see* Eschscholzia						
Calliopsis: *see* Coreopsis						
Callistephus	Annual Aster	HHA(M)	L B Pl C R P W	30–75	12–30	July–Sept

Botanical name	Popular name	Culture	Colour	Height cm	Height in.	Flowering time
Campanula medium	Canterbury Bell	HB	W B L P	45–60	*18–24*	June–July
,, speculum	Venus' Looking Glass	HA(S)	B	30–40	*12–16*	June–July
Candytuft: *see* Iberis						
Canna	Indian Shot	HHP	R P Y O	90–120	*36–48*	July–Sept
Canterbury Bell: *see* Campanula						
Carnation: *see* Dianthus						
Celosia plumosa		HHA	R Y	30–90	*12–30*	July–Aug
Centaurea cyanus	Cornflower	HA(S)	B L P R C W	30–90	*12–36*	July–Aug
,, moschata	Sweet Sultan	HA	W Y P L Pl	40–50	*16–20*	June–Aug
Cheiranthus allionii	Siberian Wallflower	HB	Y O	40	*16*	Mar–June
,, cheiri	Wallflower	HB	Y O R C Pl P	30–45	*12–18*	Mar–May
Chrysanthemum carinatum	Tricolor Chrysanthemum	HA	Y R O W	60–90	*24–36*	June–Aug
,, coronarium	Garland Chrysanthemum	HA	Y	40–90	*15–36*	June–Aug
,, multicaule		HA	Y	30–40	*12–16*	June–Aug
,, sagetum	Corn Marigold	HA	Y	30–45	*12–18*	June–Aug
Cladanthus arabicus		HHA	Y	40–50	*16–20*	June–Aug
Clarkia		HA(S)	W P R M Pl	45–60	*18–24*	June–Aug
Cleome spinosa	Spider Flower	HHA	P	90	*36*	July–Aug
Cobea scandens	Cathedral Bells	HHA	W Pl	climber		July–Sept
Collinsia bicolor	Innocence, Chinese Houses	HA(S)	L & W	30	*12*	June–Sept
Convolvulus tricolor	Dwarf Morning Glory	HA	B P	30–40	*12–15*	July–Aug
Coreopsis drummondii	Calliopsis	HA	Y C	45–60	*18–24*	July–Aug
Cornflower: *see* Centaurea						
Cosmidium		HA, HHA	C & Y	45–60	*18–24*	July–Aug
Cosmos bipinnatus	Cosmea	HHA(M)	C P W	45–60	*18–24*	July–Sept
,, diversifolius	Cosmea	HA	Y	60–90	*24–36*	July–Aug
,, sulphureus	Yellow Cosmea	HHA(M)	Y O	45–60	*18–24*	July–Sept
Crepis rubra	Hawkweed	HA	P	45–60	*18–24*	June–July
Cynoglossum amabile	Chinese Forget-me-not	HB	B	30	*12*	June–Aug
,, wallichii	,, ,,	HA	B	40–45	*16–18*	July–Aug
Dahlia		HHP	all	45–150	*18–60*	July–Oct
Delphinium ajacis	Larkspur	HA(S)	W P R Pl L	60–90	*24–36*	June–Aug
Dianthus barbatus	Sweet William	HB	W P R C	15–45	*6–18*	June–July
,, caryophyllus	Carnation	HA	W P R C L	45–75	*15–30*	July–Sept
,, sinensis	Indian Pink	HHA(M)	W P M R C	15–30	*6–12*	June–Aug
Diascea barbarea	Twinspur	HHA	P	20	*8*	June–Aug
Digitalis	Foxglove	HB, HA	R Pl P W	90–150	*36–60*	June–July
Dimorphotheca	Star of the Veld	HA	W Y O	15–40	*6–16*	June–Aug
Echeveria secunda		HHP	O	20	*8*	Grown for grey leaf rosettes
Echium		HA(S)	B L P W	30	*12*	June–Aug
Eschscholzia	Californian Poppy	HA(S)	O Y R C P W	30	*12*	June–Sept
Eucharidium	Fairy Fans	HA	P	30	*12*	July–Aug
Felicia bergeriana	Kingfisher Daisy	HHA(M)	B & Y	15	*6*	June–Aug
Foxglove: *see* Digitalis						
Gaillardia picta		HHA	Y R C	30–45	*12–18*	June–Aug
Gazania		HHP	Y P R O	10–30	*4–12*	June–Sept

Botanical name	Popular name	Culture	Colour	Height cm	in.	Flowering time
Geranium: *see* Pelargonium						
Gilia capitata		HA(S)	L	46	*18*	June–Sept
Godetia		HA(S)	P M R C W	20–60	*8–24*	June–Aug
Gypsophila elegans	Annual Gypsophila	HA(S)	W P	46	*18*	June–Aug
Helianthus annuus	Annual Sunflower	HA	Y C	60–250	*24–100*	July–Sept
Helichrysum	Strawflower	HHA(M)	Y O P C W	45–75	*18–30*	June–Sept
Heliophyla longifolia		HA	B & W	40–45	*16–18*	July–Aug
Heliotropium	Heliotrope, Cherry Pie	HHA, HHP	B Pl	45–60	*18–24*	June–Aug
Helipterum manglesii	Rhodanthe	HHA(M)	P W	30	*12*	July–Sept
Honesty: *see* Lunaria						
Iberis coronaria	Hyacinth-flowered Candytuft	HA(S)	W	40	*16*	June–Aug
„ umbellata	Annual Candytuft	HA(S)	W P Pl	20–40	*8–16*	June–Sept
Impatiens balsamina	Balsam	HHA	W P R	25–50	*10–20*	June–Aug
„ holstii and sultanii	Busy Lizzie	HHA, HHP	W P R Pl	15–40	*6–16*	May–Oct
„ roylei		HA	P Pl	150–175	*60–70*	July–Sept
Ionopsidium acaule	Violet Cress	HA	M	8	*3*	June–July
Ipomoea purpurea (Convolvulus major)	Morning Glory	HA	W P B Pl	climbing		July–Sept
„ rubro-coerulea	„ „	HHA	B	climbing		July–Sept
Jacobaea: *see* Senecio						
Kaulfussia amelloides		HA	B	10–15	*4–6*	June–Aug
Kochia	Burning Bush, Summer Cypress	HHA		60	*24*	Grown for foliage
Larkspur: *see* Delphinium						
Lathyrus odoratus	Sweet Pea	HA	W C R P Pl L M B	30–200	*12–80*	June–Aug
Lavatera trimestris	Annual Mallow	HA	P	90–120	*36–48*	June–Sept
Layia elegans	Tidy Tips	HA	Y & W	30–40	*12–16*	June–Aug
Leptosiphon: *see* Gilia						
Leptosyne stillmannii		HA	Y	40	*16*	June–Aug
Limnanthes douglasii		HA(S)	Y & W	20–30	*8–12*	May–July
Linaria maroccana	Annual Toadflax	HA(S)	all	20–30	*8–12*	June–Sept
Linum grandiflorum	Scarlet Flax	HA	R	30–40	*12–16*	June–Aug
Lobelia erinus	Bedding Lobelia	HHA	B Pl P C W	15–20	*6–8*	May–Sept
„ tenuior	Trailing Lobelia	HHA	B	trailing		May–Sept
Love-in-a-Mist: *see* Nigella						
Lunaria annua	Honesty	HB	Pl W	60	*24*	May–June
Lupinus hartwegii	Annual Lupin	HA	W L B P	45–60	*18–24*	June–Aug
Lychnis coeli-rosa (Viscaria oculata)	Rose of Heaven	HA	W P R	40	*16*	June–Aug
Malcomia maritima	Virginian Stock	HA(S)	R L W	20	*8*	June–Aug
Malope		HA	R Pl W	75–100	*30–40*	June–Sept
Marigold: *see* Calendula and Tagetes						
Matthiola bicornis	Night-scented Stock	HA	Pl	25–30	*10–12*	June–Aug
„ incana	Ten-week Stock	HA	W P R C Pl L	30–45	*12–18*	June–Sept
„ „	Brompton Stock	HA	W P R C L	45–60	*18–24*	Mar–May
„ „	East Lothian Stock	HHA, HB	W P R C Pl L	30–45	*12–18*	Apr–Sept

Botanical name	Popular name	Culture	Colour	Height cm	in.	Flowering time
Matricaria eximea (Chrysanthemum parthenium)	Feverfew	HP, HA	W Y	30–45	*12–18*	July–Sept
„ maritima (Chrysanthemum inodorum)	Scentless May-weed or Chamomile	HA	W	20–30	*8–12*	June–Sept
Mesembryanthemum criniflorum	Livingstone Daisy	HHA	P R O	trailing		June–Sept
Mignonette: *see* Reseda						
Molucella	Bells of Ireland	HHA	G	60	*24*	July–Sept
Morning Glory: *see* Ipomoea						
Myosotis	Forget-me-not	HB	B P	15–40	*6–16*	Mar–June
Nasturtium: *see* Tropaeolum						
Nemesia		HHA	all	20–30	*8–12*	June–Sept
Nemophila	Baby Blue Eyes	HA(S)	B	15	*6*	June–Aug
Nicandra	Apple of Peru, Shoo-fly Plant	HA	B	120	*48*	July–Aug
Nicotiana	Flowering Tobacco	HHA	R P W G	30–75	*12–30*	June–Sept
Nigella	Love-in-a-Mist	HA(S)	B P W	40–45	*16–18*	June–Sept
Nolana	Chilean Bell-Flower	HHA(M)	L	15	*6*	June–Sept
Pansy: *see* Viola						
Papaver nudicaule	Iceland Poppy	HB	Y O R P W	60–75	*24–30*	May–July
„ rhoeas	Shirley Poppy	HA(S)	W P R C	75	*30*	June–Sept
„ somniferum	Carnation or Peony Poppy	HA(S)	W P R Pl M	60–90	*24–36*	June–Sept

Carters Perfection Stocks

35

Botanical name	Popular name	Culture	Colour	Height cm	in.	Flowering time
Pelargonium peltatum	Ivy leaved Geranium	HHP	PRPlM	trailing		May–Oct
,, zonale	Zonal leaved Geranium	HHP	WPRC	45–60	18–24	May–Oct
Penstemon		HHP	WPRPlLM	25–60	10–24	June–Sept
➤Petunia		HHA	all	30–45	12–18	June–Sept
Phacelia campanularia		HA	B	20	8	June–Aug
Phlox drummondii	Annual Phlox	HHA	PRCPlW	15–45	6–18	June–Aug
Pink, Annual: see Dianthus						
Polyanthus: see Primula						
Polygonum capitatum		HHA	P	8–15	3–4	June–Aug
Poppy: see Papaver						
Portulaca		HHA(M)	PRCYW	15	6	July–Sept
Primula vulgaris	Primrose	HB or HP	all	15	6	Jan–May
,, ,, elatior	Polyanthus	HB or HP	all	30–40	12–16	Mar–June
Reseda odorata	Mignonette	HA	R & G	30	12	June–Aug
Rhodanthe: see Helipterum						
Ricinus communis	Castor Oil Plant	HHA		150	60	Grown for foliage
Rudbeckia hirta	Gloriosa Daisy	HHA(M)	YR	40–90	16–36	July–Sept
Salpiglossis		HHA	YPRCPlB	45–60	18–24	June–Aug
Salvia horminum		HA(S)	BPW	45–60	18–24	June–Aug
,, patens	Blue Sage	HHP, HHA	B	60	24	July–Sept
,, sclarea	Clary	HB	P	90	36	July–Aug
,, splendens	Scarlet Sage	HHA	RPPl	15–60	6–24	June–Sept
Saponaria vaccaria	Annual Soapwort	HA(S)	P	60	24	June–Aug
Scabiosa atropurpurea	Annual Scabious, Pincushion Flower	HHA(M)	PRCLBW	45–90	18–36	June–Aug
Senecio elegans	Jacobaea	HA	PRCPlW	40	16	June–Aug
Silene armeria	Annual Catchfly	HA(S)	PRW	15–60	6–24	June–Aug
Statice sinuata (Limonium)	Everlasting	HHA	WLBPRY	45	18	July–Sept
Stock: see Matthiola						
Sunflower: see Helianthus						
Sweet Pea: see Lathyrus						
Sweet Sultan: see Centaurea						
Sweet William: see Dianthus						
Tagetes erecta	African Marigold	HHA(M)	YO	20–60	8–24	July–Sept
,, patula	French Marigold	HHA(M)	YOC	15–30	6–12	July–Sept
,, signata		HHA(M)	YO	15–20	6–8	July–Aug
Tropaeolum canariensis	Canary Creeper	HA	Y	climbing		July–Aug
,, majus	Nasturtium	HA	YORCP	20–30 and climbing	8–12	July–Sept
Ursinia		HHA(M)	O	30–45	12–15	June–Sept
Venidium fastuosum	Monarch of the Veld	HHA(M)	O	60–90	24–36	June–Sept
Verbena hybrida	Bedding Verbena	HHA	PRCBM	15–30	6–12	July–Sept
Viola	Bedding Viola and Pansy	HB, HHA	WYOMLBPl	15–20	6–8	Mar–Oct
Wallflower: see Cheiranthus						
Zinnia		HHA(M)	PYORPl	15–90	6–36	July–Sept

5 Bulbs, Corms, and Tubers

Bulbs, corms, and tubers are all fleshy organs which enable plants to store food and water. In countries where they grow wild, many plants of this kind have to survive considerable periods of drought or other conditions unfavourable to growth and they rely on the reserves they have laid up to carry them over. That is why many such plants can be lifted and stored dry for weeks or months and many are sold in this dry, dormant condition and not as actively growing plants.

All the same, changes are often going on inside a bulb even when it appears outwardly to be most inactive. These changes prepare it for its next period of growth and they may be hastened or retarded by the conditions in which the bulb is stored. Some bulbs can be given carefully controlled temperature treatment while in store which will make them grow and flower much more rapidly when replanted. Such bulbs are described as 'prepared' and hyacinths that have been given this preparation are sold for potting and early flowering in greenhouses or rooms.

Another possibility is to hold bulbs or tubers in cool storage far beyond the normal season when they would start growth and use them to get flowers out of season. These are known as 'retarded' and lily-of-the-valley crowns (really fleshy roots) are kept back in this way and then forced for winter flowers.

However, generally plants with bulbs, corms or tubers should be permitted to follow their normal sequence of growth and many will do this quite naturally if simply left to grow without disturbance. Others benefit from being lifted periodically, dried off, and replanted.

Many of these plants are first rate to begin gardening with since they will give a very quick return and it is almost impossible to go wrong with them, at any rate during the first year. If good quality daffodils, tulips, hyacinths, crocuses or irises of the Spanish, Dutch, and English types are planted in the autumn it is as near certain as anything can be in gardening that they will all flower the following spring and early summer. Gladiolus corms planted in the spring will flower with the same

Erythronium White Beauty   **Leucojum Gravetye Giant**   **Dutch Iris**

degree of certainty from July to September, so with these bulbs alone it would be possible to ensure some colour in the garden for seven months of the year.

Apart from the fact that they all store food and water, plants with bulbs, corms, and tubers are of so many diverse kinds that it is impossible to generalize about their culture. Some are hardy and for outdoor culture throughout the year, some half-hardy and in need of winter protection except in the mildest parts of the country, some tender and for greenhouse cultivation only. There are bulbs suitable for sunny places and others for shady places. Most will grow in a great variety of soils but some have special requirements. All these matters are dealt with individually, but in this chapter only those kinds are included which can be lifted and sold dry. Plants with fleshy roots which should never be dried off will be found in Chapters 6 and 11.

Amaryllis belladonna (Belladonna Lily). Fine rose coloured, strongly fragrant, funnel-shaped flowers in clusters on stout 60–90 cm (2–3 ft) stems in September–October. Plant the large bulbs 30 cm (1 ft) apart, with tips just covered with soil, in a warm, sunny well-drained place, such as near the foot of a wall or fence facing south. Leave undisturbed for years. When overgrown lift in August, split up bulb clusters, and replant immediately. The greenhouse plants often known as amaryllis are really hippeastrum.

Anemone. By no means all anemones have tuberous roots but those that have include some very useful garden plants.

Anemone coronaria is known as the Poppy Anemone because of the shape of its flowers, which are in many shades of red, pink, lavender, blue, and purple, carried singly on 20–30 cm (8–12 in.) stems. De Caen or Giant French strain has single flowers in mixed colours, St. Brigid strain semi-double flowers in mixed colours. All like rich, well cultivated soil and warm sunny places. Plant the little tubers 5 cm (2 in.) deep and 10 cm (4 in.) apart, in April to flower in June–July; in June to flower in September; and in September–October to flower in February–May. Plants can also be grown from seed sown outdoors in spring to flower fifteen to eighteen months later.

Anemone apennina and A. blanda are low growing, spreading plants 10–15 cm (4–6 in.) high with blue, pink, rose or white flowers in spring. Plant in September–October 5 cm (2 in.) deep and 10 cm (4 in.) apart in sun or semi-shade and leave undisturbed.

Allium karataviense **Anemone St. Brigid**

Crocus. There are two quite distinct groups of crocus, one composed of the large flowered garden varieties, all of which flower in spring from February to April, and the wild species and their varieties some of which flower in autumn, some in winter, and some in spring. The garden varieties have a good colour range, including blue, purple, yellow, and white, and some have striped flowers. Most of the species have smaller, more fragile flowers. Among the best are Crocus speciosus, lavender or white, September–October; C. imperati, buff, mauve, and yellow, January–February; C. tomasinianus, lavender or purple, January–February; C. chrysanthus, white, cream, yellow, blue or purple, February; C. sieberi, lavender, February–March; and C. susianus, often called Cloth of Gold because of its golden yellow flowers, in February–March. All will grow in full sun or semi-shade and in all manner of soils. Plant the autumn and winter flowering kinds in August, spring flowering kinds in September–October 5 cm (2 in.) deep and 10–15 cm (4–6 in.) apart and leave undisturbed until overcrowded.

Cyclamen. There are both hardy and tender kinds, the latter very popular as winter and spring flowering pot plants for the greenhouse or home. All make bun-shaped tubers, but whereas dry tubers of the hardy kind are commonly offered for sale, the greenhouse cyclamen is almost invariably grown from seed or purchased as growing plants. (*See* Chapter 11.)

Start dry corms of hardy cyclamen in moist peat in an unheated greenhouse or frame. Bed the tubers into the peat but do not cover them. When growing pot them singly in J.I.P.1 or peat potting compost in small pots and grow in a frame until the pots are nicely filled with roots. Then plant out in a semi-shady place.

Hardy cyclamen succeed well under deciduous trees or on rock gardens in leafy or peaty soil, and should be disturbed as little as possible. Good kinds are Cyclamen orbiculatum, white to magenta, December–March; C. repandum, similar colours, March–May; C. europaeum, pink to carmine, July–September; and C. neapolitanum, white or pink, August–September.

Daffodil. *See* Narcissus.

(from top) **Anemone blanda; Chionodoxa gigantea; Crocus chrysanthus; Scilla tubergeniana**

39

Dahlia. The seed strains of short bedding dahlias (*see* Chapter 4) do not always make good tubers and are best renewed annually from seed. All other kinds which make good tubers can be stored dry in winter and small tubers are specially grown for sale 'dry' in the spring. Alternatively young plants can be grown from cuttings. These larger types can also be grown from seed like bedding dahlias, but seedlings may vary quite a lot in colour and shape.

Dahlias must not be planted outdoors until late May or early June. Dormant tubers can be planted in early May, covered with 7–10 cm (3–4 in.) of soil. Start stored tubers from February to April in soil or peat in a greenhouse or frame with minimum night temperature of 10 °C (50 °F). Sever young shoots as cuttings when 7–10 cm (3–4 in.) long. Insert in a mixture of equal parts coarse sand and sphagnum peat, and root in a still, moist atmosphere, which can be provided by slipping each pot or box of cuttings into a large polythene bag or by placing them in a propagator. Maintain a temperature of 16–18 °C (60–65 °F). When well rooted pot singly in small pots in J.I.P.1 or peat potting compost.

Alternatively, start tubers in the greenhouse or frame and divide them carefully when it can be seen where the new shoots are. Each division must have at least one shoot and one tuber. Pot these divisions and grow under glass until it is safe to plant outdoors.

Either way grow on in an average temperature of 15 °C (60 °F), but remove to an unheated frame at the end of April and harden off for planting outdoors at the end of May or early in June. Even a little frost may damage dahlias so do not plant out if the weather is cold. If it is unexpectedly cold after planting, cover the plants with inverted flower pots or brown paper at night.

Dahlias like fairly rich, well cultivated soil. Manure or garden compost can be dug in freely prior to planting and the soil dusted with a general purpose fertilizer.

Plant 0·5–1 metre (18–36 in.) apart according to the eventual height of the variety. Drive in at least one stout stake for each plant and tie all stems securely. Water freely in dry weather, feed every two or three weeks with a general purpose fertilizer, and remove all faded flowers regularly. If extra large flowers are required, remove the side flower buds and retain only one terminal bud on each stem.

When leaves have been blackened by frost in October, cut off all stems 10 cm (4 in.) above soil level, lift the plants carefully with a fork, and lay in a dry, frost-proof place for a few days. Then shake off all remaining soil and store in boxes filled with dry peat in a cupboard or similar frost-proof place.

There are a great many varieties of dahlia and for convenience of cataloguing and exhibiting they are classified according to the form and size of their flowers. Decorative dahlias have flowers composed of many broad petals. Cactus dahlias have narrower, more or less quilled petals. Ball dahlias have ball-like flowers and so have pompons, but normally under 5 cm (2 in.) in diameter. Collarette dahlias have single flowers with a circle of short petals, or petal-like segments, often in a contrasting colour. Singles have just one row of petals. There are yet other types, described in the catalogues of specialist growers.

Freesia. Delightfully fragrant winter or spring flowering plants, the funnel-shaped, white, cream, yellow, orange, red, lavender or blue flowers borne on slender 45–60 cm (18–24 in.) stems. Freesias can either be grown from seed or from corms. Pot corms successively from August to October, six or seven in each medium size pot in J.I.P.1 or peat potting compost. Water moderately and grow in a sunny greenhouse, minimum night temperature 7 °C (45 °F). Support stems with

Decorative Dahlias   **Pompon Dahlias**

small sticks and loops of string. From May gradually reduce the water supply and keep plants quite dry in July. Then shake out corms and repot.

Alternatively, purchase specially prepared corms in spring and plant from April to June 5 cm (2 in.) deep and 10 cm (4 in.) apart outdoors. Water freely to start corms into growth.

Sow seed from March to June in a greenhouse or frame, minimum night temperature 7 °C (45 °F). Sow thinly in medium size pots and do not transplant the seedlings. Grow in a frame or a sunny place outdoors in summer but bring back into the greenhouse at the end of September. After flowering treat as for freesias grown from corms.

Gladiolus. There are several distinct types of gladiolus and a great number of varieties, in a colour range that leaves little out except pure blue. All grow from corms, thrive in most reasonably good soils, and like open, sunny places.

The large flowered gladioli have spikes of closely placed flowers up to 1·25 metres (4 ft) high, produced from late July to mid-September. Butterfly varieties are similar but the flowers are smaller and often of two or more contrasted colours. Miniatures are 45–60 cm (18–24 in.) high with small flowers frequently with ruffled petals. Primulinus gladioli are 45–75 cm (18–30 in.) high with small, hooded flowers more widely spaced on a slender spike. Nanus, or Early Flowering gladioli, have small, rather star-shaped flowers in slender 45–60 cm (18–24 in.) spikes in May or June, or earlier under glass. Gladiolus byzantinus has slender 60 cm (24 in.) spikes of deep magenta flowers in May–June and is one of the few completely hardy kinds.

Plant the Large Flowered, Butterfly, Miniature, and Primulinus varieties from March to May, 10 cm (4 in.) deep and 20 cm (8 in.) apart, in ground well cultivated and enriched with a little well rotted manure or garden compost and give a light dusting of an all purpose fertilizer. Support the taller spikes individually with canes. Water freely in dry weather. Lift the corms six weeks after the flowers fade, cut off the top 2 cm (1 in.) above the corm, remove and discard the old withered corm from the base of the plant, and store the young corms in a cool, dry frost-proof place.

There may be a number of very small corms (known as cormels) clustering around the larger corms. If desired these can be kept separately and be 'sown' thinly, like seed, the following spring in drills 5 cm (2 in.) deep, but it may take a couple of years before they reach flowering size.

Plant Nanus or Early Flowering gladioli from September to November in pots, boxes or beds of good soil, in a greenhouse in which a minimum night temperature of 4·5 °C (40 °F) can be maintained. They can also be planted outdoors in warm sheltered places and well-drained soils. Lift after flowering in the same way as summer flowering gladioli.

Gloxinia. Greenhouse pot plants with velvety leaves and showy funnel-shaped flowers on short stems throughout the summer. Colours include pink, red, violet, and purple, often with a white throat or the colour veined or speckled on a white ground. The tubers are very similar to those of tuberous rooted begonias and cultivation is also similar. Gloxinias can be grown from seed sown in February–March in a temperature of 18 °C (65 °F). Transplant singly into small pots in J.I.P.1 or peat potting compost, grow on in a similar temperature, and move into 10 cm (4 in.) pots when the small ones are comfortably full of roots. Water fairly freely and from May onwards shade from direct sunshine. After flowering gradually reduce the water supply, allow plants to die down, and then lay the pots on their sides and keep quite dry until January–March, when the tubers can be shaken clean of soil and restarted into growth in moist peat. Tubers can also be purchased from January to March and a start made in this way.

Hippeastrum (Amaryllis). Popularly known as amaryllis, though botanically this name belongs to the belladonna lily. Hippeastrums have very large, widely trumpet-shaped flowers carried, two to four, on stout 45–60 cm (18–24 in.) stems from March to June. They are popular pot plants for warm greenhouses or light rooms.

Pot bulbs from February to April singly in 12 cm (5 in.) pots in J.I.P.2 or peat potting compost, leaving nearly half the bulb above soil level. Start into growth in a temperature of 15–18 °C (60–65 °F). Water moderately at first, freely later, and syringe daily with water except when in flower. Do not shade at any stage. Plants can stand outdoors from June to September. Feed occasionally all the summer. In October reduce the water and allow growth to die down. Store quite dry from November with pots on their sides in a minimum temperature of 10 °C (50 °F). Specially prepared bulbs can also be potted in September–October and grown in a similar manner to flower by Christmas.

Hyacinthus (Hyacinth). One of the most popular spring flowering bulbs for growing in pots or bowls and also excellent for spring bedding. There are numerous colours including white and shades of yellow, blue, pink, and red. Ordinary hyacinths carry their flowers in stout, well packed spikes 30–45 cm (12–18 in.) high, whereas Roman hyacinths have looser, more slender spikes and flower a little earlier. 'Prepared' bulbs are also available for forcing and will come into flower very quickly.

Outdoors plant hyacinths in October–November in fairly rich, well-drained soil and light position. Space bulbs 20 cm (8 in.) apart and cover with 10 cm (4 in.) of soil. Allow leaves to die down naturally after flowering, then lift bulbs and place them in a cool, dry place for a week or so. Then clean and store in a cool, dry shed until planting time.

For pots or bowls start in August–September and set bulbs almost shoulder to shoulder in J.I.P.1 or peat potting compost. If the bowls have no drainage holes use special bulb fibre consisting of peat with crushed shell and charcoal. Do not quite cover the tips of the bulbs. Water moderately and place in a cool, dark place for eight or ten weeks to allow roots to grow. Then bring into a light room or green-house and grow on in a temperature around 15 °C (60 °F). Keep well watered and feed occasionally with weak liquid manure. After flowering gradually reduce the water supply, let bulbs die down, and then shake out and store. They can be planted outdoors in the autumn but should not be forced a second time.

Iris. A number of irises grow from small bulbs which can be planted in the autumn. First to flower is Iris histrioides with bright blue flowers on 8 cm (3 in.) stems in January–February. Next comes I. reticulata with light blue, violet, or purple flowers on 15–20 cm (6–8 in.) stems in February–March, and I. danfordiae with yellow flowers on 10 cm (4 in.) stems in March. Cover bulbs of all these with 5 cm (2 in.) of soil and space 10 cm (4 in.) apart in well-drained soil and a sunny sheltered place. All are excellent for the rock garden.

The English, Spanish, and Dutch irises flower in May and June and are available in a number of different colours including white, yellow, bronze, blue, and purple, They grow 60–100 cm (2–3 ft) high and are excellent for garden display and cutting. Plant in good well cultivated soil 10 cm (4 in.) deep and 20 cm (8 in.) apart.

Leave all these irises undisturbed until overcrowded. Then lift when the leaves die down and store in a cool, dry place until September.

Lilium (Lily). There are hundreds of different kinds of lily, native to different countries in many parts of the world. It is not surprising that in gardens they prove to have different requirements and that some are difficult to grow. Yet they are nearly all beautiful plants and some are good tempered plants thriving in a wide variety of soils and situations. The number of these easy lilies has been greatly increased by the introduction of hybrid lilies, specially bred to meet garden

Tigridias

Large flowered Gladioli

Hyacinths Ostara, Pink Pearl, Myosotis, Princess Margaret

requirements. There are now so many of these that a grouping has been devised for them as it has for roses, dahlias, chrysanthemums, and other popular garden flowers. Among the best of these groups are the Asiatic Hybrids (including the popular Mid-Century Hybrids); the Martagon Hybrids, which do not mind chalk or lime; the American Hybrids, including the very good Bellingham Hybrids; the Trumpet Hybrids, including the Aurelian Hybrids; and the Oriental Hybrids.

In addition to these garden-bred lilies there are also a number of species, i.e. wild lilies, that are equally accommodating in the garden. Lilium regale, the regal lily, with fragrant trumpet-shaped white flowers flushed outside with maroon, will grow in any reasonably fertile soil in sun or partial shade and it does not mind lime or chalk. It is a first choice for every garden and can be readily raised from seed.

Lilium umbellatum (or hollandicum), with clusters of upward facing orange flowers, is another that all can grow. L. martagon, with hanging 'turk's cap' flowers and swept back petals in white and shades of purple, is easy to grow in semi-shady places and likes chalk soils.

Lilium tigrinum, a tall orange-red lily, also with the 'turk's cap' type of flower, grows readily but is often infected with virus disease without showing any symptoms, so it is best kept away from other lilies. L. henryi, which is similar but even taller, paler orange, does not suffer this drawback nor does L. willmottiae, a very graceful lily with reflexed orange-red flowers speckled with brown, carried on long arching stalks.

Lilium candidum, the white madonna lily, likes rather rich well manured soil. L. chalcedonicum, the scarlet martagon lily, likes chalk or lime in the soil. L. pardalinum, the panther lily, with orange-red, black spotted flowers, likes moist soils and can be planted near streams or pools. L. pyrenaicum, a yellow turk's cap lily, will grow almost anywhere but has a rather unpleasant smell. L. hansoni, rather similar in appearance, does not suffer from this drawback and is equally easy.

Lilium formosanum, with long white trumpet flowers, is very easily grown from seed, and seedlings will flower in their first year, but it is susceptible to virus disease and not very hardy. It is often grown as a pot plant in a cold or cool greenhouse. So is L. speciosum, with nodding white, or rose and white, flowers from July to September, but it does well outdoors in sheltered, semi-shady places.

Lilium auratum is one of the most handsome of all lilies, with immense bowl-shaped flowers either all white or white variously spotted and banded with gold or red. It is often known as the golden-rayed lily of Japan. It is very tall, dislikes lime or chalk, and succeeds best in semi-shade.

Lilium longiflorum is the Easter lily, with long white trumpet flowers. It is not hardy but is an excellent plant for cold or cool greenhouses, and can be readily forced into flower in March or April.

It will be seen from these descriptions that it is not easy to generalize about lilies. Nevertheless most kinds will grow in soil that is slightly acid (pH 6 to 6·5 is ideal) and that is well drained and not dry. Granulated peat can be worked in liberally to most soils with advantage and sharp sand also on soils that are apt to get wet and sticky.

Many lilies grow well among low growing shrubs or herbaceous plants which shade their roots but allow them to grow up into the light and air. All lilies should be planted as early as possible, Lilium candidum and L. testaceum in July or August, the bulbs barely covered with soil, most other kinds from September to November with about 10 cm (4 in.) of soil over the bulbs. Lilies can also be planted from February to April provided the bulbs have not been allowed to shrivel.

Lilies should not be disturbed unnecessarily. Allow them to grow on for years, but top dress every March with peat or leaf mould and also dust the soil with bone meal and hoof and horn meal 50 grammes of each per square metre (2 oz/sq yd). When they do get overcrowded, lift at the proper planting season, divide and replant at once.

Spray lilies frequently in spring and summer to keep down greenflies and other pests which spread virus disease. Water freely in dry weather. Lift and burn plants with leaves distorted or mottled with yellow or light green as these are probably virus infected.

For the greenhouse, pot lily bulbs singly in September–October, in 12–18 cm (5–7 in.) pots in J.I.P.1 or peat potting compost, without chalk or lime. Water sparingly in autumn and winter, freely in spring and summer.

(from top) Lilium Royal Gold; Lilium pardalinum giganteum; Lilium Destiny; Lilium regale

Shade from direct sunshine. Do not encourage temperatures above 18 °C (65 °F). Little artificial heat is required except in very cold weather. Repot bulbs every autumn.

Narcissus (Daffodil). There are a great many different varieties of daffodil, but they can be divided into several clearly recognizable types. The trumpet daffodils have a central cup, or corona, that is longer than the perianth segments that surround it. Daffodils with a corona shorter that the perianth are divided into large-cupped and small-cupped types, the former with the cup over one-third the length of the perianth segments, the latter with the cup one-third or less that length. Then there are narcissi with clusters of small flowers, others with double flowers, and many more types.

In addition to these garden varieties there are also wild narcissi some of which are very beautiful. The hoop petticoat narcissus, N. bulbocodium, is only a few inches high but its cup is comparatively large and shaped like a crinoline. Narcissus cyclamineus is also tiny, has a narrow tubular trumpet and narrow perianth segments turned right back. Both are delightful for the rock garden.

The poet's narcissus, N. poeticus, has a broad white perianth and very small orange-red cup which may have a green rim. There are numerous garden varieties with similar characteristics.

All daffodils and narcissi (they are really the same thing, though the popular name daffodil is often applied mainly to the trumpet varieties) are hardy and most are very easy to grow in almost any soil. They like soil that has been well cultivated and a dusting of bone meal improves growth. They will succeed in full sun or in shade.

Plant the bulbs from August to October, the earlier the better, 15–20 cm (6–8 in.) apart (the smaller kinds 10 cm or 4 in. apart) and cover with 7 cm (3 in.) of soil. Bulbs can be planted in grass provided their leaves are not cut off before about mid-June. A special tool can be obtained which will cut out a neat core of turf which can be replaced when the bulb has been planted.

Daffodils can be lifted every year when the foliage has died down and stored for a few weeks in a cool, dry place, but it is not necessary, and provided they continue to flower well, they can be left undisturbed for years to make clumps of ever increasing size. If left in this way feed each March with a good all purpose fertilizer.

Daffodils and narcissi can also be grown in pots in the greenhouse or in a light room. Plant the bulbs almost shoulder to shoulder in J.I.P.2 or peat potting compost. Place outdoors in a cool, shady place for eight to ten weeks to form roots, then bring into a frame or greenhouse, but not into a temperature above about 15·5 °C (60 °F). Water freely while in growth, but gradually withhold water as the foliage turns yellow and dies down. When it has completely withered, shake the bulbs out and store until planting time. These bulbs can be planted outdoors but should not be pot grown two years running.

If bulbs are grown in bowls or other containers without drainage holes special bulb fibre containing peat, charcoal, and crushed shell must be used instead of J.I.P. or peat potting compost. Another difference is that the bowls should not be placed where rain can fall on them or they may become filled with water, in which case the bulbs will be drowned.

Nerine (Guernsey lily). Bulbous plants with showy pink, rose, crimson or purplish funnel-shaped flowers borne in clusters on stout 30–45 cm (12–18 in.) stems in September–October. Nerine sarniensis and its numerous varieties are cool greenhouse plants, but N. bowdenii is fairly hardy and can be grown outdoors in sunny, sheltered places in well-drained soil. Plant the bulbs in August–September, only just covering them. Leave undisturbed for many years and only lift, divide, and replant when overcrowded. Give a light sprinkling of bone meal and hoof and horn meal each March.

Pot bulbs for greenhouse cultivation in August in J.I.P.1 compost. Leave the upper third of each bulb uncovered. Start to water when the flower spikes appear and from then on keep the soil moist until the leaves die down in May, after which plants should be kept quite dry and in as warm and sunny place as possible until September. Repot in August every third or fourth year. Do not shade at any time and only use artificial heat to maintain a minimum night temperature of 4·5 °C (40 °F).

Tulipa (Tulip). There are a great many different varieties of tulip, ranging from quite small plants suitable for the rock garden to splendid bedding and cutting varieties with stems up to 75 cm (30 in.) long. Like many other plants that have been highly developed in gardens, they are split into groups for convenience of cataloguing and description. The early flowering varieties flower in April, are mostly rather short stemmed and have single or double flowers. The Kauffmanniana varieties flower in March–April and are sometimes known as waterlily tulips because of the shape of their short stemmed flowers. They are very suitable for rock gardens. The Greigii Hybrids, often known as peacock tulips because of their gaily contrasted colours, are April flowering, have medium length stems, and the leaves are often striped with chocolate. The May-flowering, Darwin and Darwin Hybrid varieties are the tallest and have large flowers in May. Late doubles, or Peony-flowered tulips, have very large double flowers, also in May. Parrot tulips have fringed petals and are often flecked with green and other colours on a ground

(above) Narcissus
Mrs R. O. Backhouse

(centre) Narcissus Cragford

(below) Four Narcissi: Verger (top left);
Pomona (top right); Edward Buxton (bottom left);
and Chinese White (bottom right)

47

colour. There are other types, including some with several flowers to a stem instead of the usual solitary flower. The colour range is immense, covering almost every shade except pure blue. In some varieties two contrasted colours appear in elaborately veined or flaked patterns. These are known as 'broken' tulips and the Rembrandt varieties have this characteristic.

Tulips thrive in sunny places and fairly rich, well cultivated and well drained soils. They are not always so permanent as daffodils, but some varieties will go on increasing for years.

Plant the bulbs in September–October, 15–20 cm (6–8 in.) apart and cover with 7 cm (3 in.) of soil. Spray the foliage in spring with thiram to prevent tulip fire, a damaging disease. Lift the bulbs in July when the leaves have withered, cut off the tops, and store in a cool, dry place until October.

Tulips can also be grown in pots, four or five bulbs in a 12 cm (5 in.) pot in J.I.P.1 or peat potting compost. Pot in September and keep in a cool dark place for eight to ten weeks to allow the bulbs to make roots, then bring into a light greenhouse. Water moderately throughout. Artificial heat is not necessary, but a temperature of around 15 °C (60 °F) will produce earlier flowers. After flowering, stand pots outside in a sunny place and keep watered until the foliage commences to yellow, when water should be withheld and the bulbs allowed to dry off. They can be replanted outdoors in the autumn, but should not be pot grown two years running.

If bulbs are grown in bowls or other containers without drainage holes special bulb fibre must be used and other precautions taken as described for daffodils on page 46.

(opposite) A fine garden display of Double and Single Tulips and, in the foreground, the Multiflora Tulip Scarlet Spray

Freesias

Gloriosa Rothschildiana

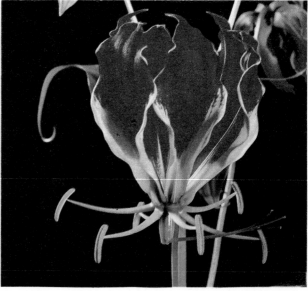

Hippeastrum

Quick-reference Table of Bulbs, Corms, and Tubers

ABBREVIATIONS

Colour W white; Y yellow; O orange; P pink; R red; C crimson; Pl purple; B blue; M mauve; G green; Bl black.

Place Sn sunny place outdoors; Sh shady place outdoors; Cd cold greenhouse; Cl cool greenhouse; In intermediate greenhouse. *See* Chapter 11 for further details of greenhouse temperatures.

Rest WR winter rest. Keep quite dry in winter. If outdoors lift in autumn and store in a cool, dry, frost-proof place until planting time.
PWR partial winter rest. Keep fairly dry in winter.
SR summer rest. Keep quite dry from about midsummer until August.
PSR partial summer rest. Keep fairly dry in summer.
NR no rest. Will take normal rainfall outdoors. Under glass water freely Apr–Sept, moderately Oct–Mar.

Plant Best planting months shown in figures.

Depth Amount of soil over top of bulb. E top of bulb exposed.

Lift A lift and replant, or repot, annually; O lift and replant, or repot, only when overcrowded. Months for lifting in figures.

Name	Colour	Season	Height cm	in.	Place	Rest	Plant	Depth cm	in.	Lift
Acidanthera	W & Pl	Aug–Sept	90	*36*	Sn Cd	WR	4–5	8	*3*	A:11
Allium coeruleum	B	June–July	60	*24*	Sn	N	9–10	5	*2*	O:8
„ giganteum	M	June–July	90–120	*36–48*	Sn	N	9–10	5	*2*	O:8
„ karataviense	W	May–June	15	*6*	Sn	N	9–10	5	*2*	O:8
„ moly	Y	June–July	20	*8*	Sn Sh	N	9–10	5	*2*	O:8
„ ostrowskianum	P	June–July	60	*24*	Sn	N	9–10	5	*2*	O:8
„ neapolitanum	W	Mar–May	30	*12*	Sn	N	9–10	5	*2*	O:8
„ rosenbachianum	Pl	June–July	45	*18*	Sn	N	9–10	5	*2*	O:8
„ sphaerocephalum	Pl	July–Aug	45	*18*	Sn	N	9–10	5	*2*	O:8
Amaryllis belladonna	P W	Sept–Oct	60	*24*	Sn	WR	8	2	*1*	O:8

50

Name	Colour	Season	Height cm	in.	Place	Rest	Plant	Depth cm	in.	Lift
Anemone apennina	B P W	Mar–Apr	15	*6*	Sh	N	9–10	5	*2*	O:8
,, blanda	B P R W	March	10	*4*	Sn Sh	N	9–10	5	*2*	O:8
,, coronaria	R Pl P B	Feb–Oct	20–30	*8–12*	Sn Cd	N	4–10	5	*2*	after flowering
Babiana	B Pl C Y	May–June	15–30	*6–12*	Sn Cl	SR	9–10	2	*1*	O:8
Brodiaea (Ipheion, Triteleia)	B	Apr–May	20	*8*	Sn	N	9–10	5	*2*	O:8
Calochortus	all	May–July	15–90	*6–36*	Sn Cl	WR	3–4	5	*2*	A:11
Camassia	B	May–June	60	*24*	Sn	N	9–10	5	*2*	O:9
Canna	R C Y	July–Sept	90	*36*	Sn Cl	WR	3–4	8	*3*	A:10
Chionodoxa	B & W	Mar–Apr	15	*6*	Sn	N	9	5	*2*	O:9
Colchicum	P M W	Sept–Oct	10–15	*4–6*	Sn Sh	N	7–8	2	*1*	O:7
Crinum	P W	July–Aug	90	*36*	Sn Cl	N	4–5	2	*1*	O:4
Crocosmia	O	July	60	*24*	Sn	N	3–4	7	*2*	O:3
Crocus	W Y B M Pl	Oct–Apr	7–10	*3–4*	Sn Sh	N	8–10	5	*2*	O:8
Cyclamen europaeum	P C	July–Sept	7	*3*	Sh	N	10	E		O:7
,, neapolitanum	W P	Aug–Sept	10	*4*	Sh	N	10	E		O:7
,, orbiculatum (including C. coum)	W P C	Dec–Mar	7	*3*	Sh	N	8–9	E		O:8
,, repandum	W P C	Mar–May	7	*3*	Sh	N	8–9	E		O:8
,, greenhouse varieties: *see* Chapter 11										
Daffodil: *see* Narcissus										
Dahlia	all	July–Oct	60–150	*24–60*	Sh	WR	5–6	7	*3*	A:10
Eranthis	Y	Feb–Mar	5–7	*2–3*	Sh	N	8–9	5	*2*	O:8
Eremurus	W Y O P	June–July	100–200	*36–72*	Sh	N	9–10	7	*3*	O:9
Erythrina	C	July–Sept	120	*48*	Sn Cl	PWR	4–5	5	*2*	O:4
Erythronium	P Y W	Mar–Apr	10–30	*4–12*	Sh	N	9–10	5	*2*	O:9
Freesia	all	Dec–July	45–60	*18–24*	Sn Cl	SR	8–10	5	*2*	A:8

Large cupped Narcissus Aranjuez

Name	Colour	Season	Height		Place	Rest	Plant	Depth		Lift
			cm	in.				cm	in.	
Fritillaria imperialis	Y O	May	100	36	Sn	N	9–10	7	3	O:9
,, meleagris	W Pl & G	April	30–45	12–18	Sn Sh	N	9–10	5	2	O:9
Galanthus (snowdrop)	W & G	Jan–Mar	15–20	6–8	Sn Sh	N	8–9,3	7	3	O:3
Galtonia	W	July–Aug	100	36	Sn	N	9–10	7	3	O:9
Gesneria	R	July–Aug	45	18	Cl In	WR	3–4	1	½	A:10
Gladiolus byzantinus	Pl	May–June	60	24	Sn	N	8–10	10	4	O:8
,, garden varieties	all	July–Sept	45–120	18–48	Sn	WR	3–5	10	4	A:10
,, nanus	P W	May–June	45–60	18–24	Sn Cl	SR	9–11	5	2	A:8
Gloriosa	C & Y	July–Sept	climbing		In	WR	2–5	5	2	A:2
Gloxinia: see Chapter 11										
Haemanthus	W R	July–Sept	30–60	12–24	Cl	WR	3–4	1	½	A:3
Hesperantha	P R Y	May–June	30–40	12–16	Sn Cl	SR	10–11	5	2	O:9
Hippeastrum	R C P W	Mar–June	45–60	18–24	Cl In	WR	2–4	E		A:2
(greenhouse varieties)										
Hippeastrum pratense	C	May–June	30	12	Cl Sn	PWR	3–4	2	1	O:2
Hyacinthus (hyacinth)	all	Dec–May	30–45	12–18	Sn Cd	SR	8–11	10	4	A:7
Hymenocallis (Ismene)	W	June–July	45	18	Sn Cl	WR	3–5	5	2	A:10
Iris danfordiae	Y	March	10	4	Sn	N	9–10	5	2	O:7
,, histrioides	B	Jan–Feb	8	3	Sn	N	9–10	5	2	O:7
,, reticulata	B Pl	Feb–Mar	15–20	6–8	Sn	N	9–10	5	2	O:7
,, tuberosa	G & B	Apr–May	20–30	8–12	Sn	N	9–10	5	2	O:7
(Hermodactylus)										
,, xiphium (Spanish,	B Pl Y W	May–June	60–90	24–36	Sn	N	9–10	5	2	O:7
Dutch, and English)										
Ixia	R C O Y W	May–June	60	24	Sn Cl	SR	10–11	5	2	A:7
Ixiolirion montanum	M	May–June	30–45	12–18	Sn Cl	SR	10–11	5	2	A:7
Lachenalia	Y O	Jan–May	20–30	8–12	Cl	SR	9–10	5	2	A:7
Leucojum aestivum	W & G	Apr–May	45	18	Sn Sh	N	9–10	5	2	O:6
,, autumnale	W & P	Sept	20	8	Sn Sh	N	7–8	5	2	O:9
,, vernum	W & G	Feb–Mar	20	8	Sn Sh	N	9–10	5	2	O:4
Lilium (lily)	W Y O R C P	Mar–Oct	60–200	24–72	Sn Sh	N	10–11, 3–4	10	4	O:7–10
Montbretia	O R	July–Sept	60	24	Sn	N	3–4	5	2	O:3
Muscari (grape hyacinth)	B W	Apr–May	10–15	4–6	Sn	N	9–10	5	2	O:8
Narcissus (daffodil)	W Y O R P	Feb–May	10–60	4–24	Sn Sh	PSR	8–10	7	3	O:7
Naegelia: see Smithiantha										
Nerine bowdenii	P	Sept–Oct	30	12	Sn	PSR	8–9	1	½	O:8
,, sarniensis	P R C Pl	Sept–Oct	30–45	12–18	Cd Cl	SR	8	E		O:8
(greenhouse varieties)										
Ornithogalum thyrsoides	W	July–Aug	45	18	Sn Cl	WR	4	2	1	A:10
,, umbellatum	W	Apr–May	30	12	Sn Sh	N	9–10	5	2	O:9
Polianthes (Tuberose)	W	June–Sept	60–90	24–30	Cl In	WR	2–5	2	1	A:10
Puschkinia	B	March	15	6	Sn	N	9–10	5	2	O:8
Ranunculus asiaticus	Y O R C P	May–June	20	8	Sn	WR	2–4	5	2	A:7–8
Scilla bifolia	B Pl W	March	8–10	3–4	Sn	N	9–10	5	2	O:8
,, hispanicus	B P M W	May	30–40	12–16	Sn Sh	N	9–10	10	4	O:8
,, nonscriptus (bluebell)	B W	May	30	12	Sn Sh	N	9–10	10	4	O:8
,, siberica	B	April	15	6	Sn	N	9–10	5	2	O:8
,, tubergeniana	B	April	10–15	4–6	Sn	N	9–10	5	2	O:8
Smithiantha	Y O R P	July–Sept	40	16	Sl In	WR	3	1	½	A:2
Sparaxis	R C Pl Y O	Apr–May	30–40	12–16	Sn Cl	SR	10–11	5	2	A:7
Sprekelia	C	May–July	20	8	Sn Cl	SR	8	2	1	A:8
Tigridia	Y O R P	July–Sept	45–60	18–24	Sn Cd	WR	4–5	5	2	A:10
Tritonia	Y O P W	May–June	20–30	8–12	Sn Cl	SR	10–11	5	2	A:7
Tulipa (Tulip)	all	Dec–May	15–75	6–30	Sn Cl	N	9–10	7	3	A:7
Zephyranthes	W P Y	Aug–Sept	10–30	4–12	Sn Cd	N	3–5	2	1	O:3

6 Hardy Plants

The full description of the plants included in this chapter is *hardy herbaceous perennials*. This means that they are sufficiently hardy to be grown outdoors, winter and summer, in most parts of the British Isles, that they have growth that is renewed annually, and will continue to live for years. In all these respects they differ in degree, some being hardier than others, some dying right to ground level each autumn, others having evergreen leaves or growing from a crown or root-stock, and some having great longevity while others may need renewal from divisions, cuttings or seeds every few years.

Some of the most popular plants belong to this great group. It includes delphiniums, lupins, phlox, peonies, and bearded irises, all of which have numerous garden varieties, as well as many other plants which have not been quite so highly developed.

Traditionally these plants are grown in herbaceous borders, i.e. borders devoted solely or primarily to them, but this is by no means essential since almost all kinds are good mixers. In small gardens it is usually more convenient to associate hardy plants with shrubs, bulbs, annuals, and bedding plants. Some kinds look best when planted in small groups of a variety, but many are effective as single plants.

Very few are fussy about soil. They will grow well in a variety of soils provided they have been well cultivated and are reasonably fertile. Lupins are not happy in soils containing a lot of lime or chalk, but there are not many examples of this kind.

Ground should be prepared by thorough digging or forking, during which well rotted manure, decayed garden compost or old mushroom compost can be worked in freely, but do not use mushroom compost where lupins are to be planted since

Paeonia sinensis

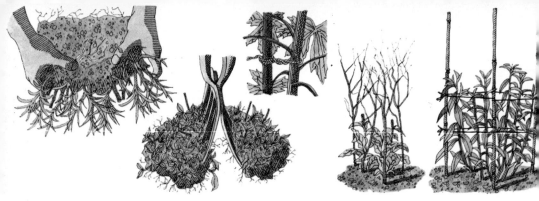

Many hardy plants need to be divided occasionally. Two forks may be used to break up tough clumps. Two methods of supporting plants are shown. If stems must be tied individually make a double twist between stake and stem so that there is room for expansion.

it contains a lot of chalk. Granulated peat can also be used to improve the texture of the soil and is particularly useful forked or raked into the top soil. Bone meal can be scattered over the surface at 100 grammes per square metre ($3\frac{1}{2}$ oz/sq yd) prior to planting.

All hardy plants can be lifted and replanted in spring, March and April being usually the two most favourable months. A few, notably bearded irises and pyrethrums, can be planted in June or July as soon as they have finished flowering, and some can be planted in September–October. All can be planted from containers at any time of the year when the soil is in reasonably good working condition.

Many hardy plants can be raised from seed sown outdoors or in a frame or unheated greenhouse between April and June. A few, if sown in February–March in a warm greenhouse, will flower the first year, but generally it is wise to take a longer view, grow the seedlings in a nursery bed the first summer, and transfer them in the autumn or the following spring to the beds in which they are to flower. The seeds do not always germinate rapidly, like those of annuals, and so it is wise to start with a clean, weed-free seed bed. Alternatively seeds may be sown in pots filled with John Innes or peat seed compost. This is usually the most convenient way of handling small quantities of seed and pots should not be discarded for at least six months, even longer with some slow germinating kinds.

Alternatively a great many hardy plants can be increased by division. Strong roots are lifted and split into a number of pieces, each of which must have some roots and at least one shoot or growth bud. Many plants can be pulled apart by

Dicentra spectabilis

Aquilegia Spring Song

A well-planted herbaceous border

hand, but for tough roots use two hand forks, or border forks, thrust back to back through the middle and then levered apart. Occasionally a sharp knife must be used to cut through thick crowns or rootstocks, e.g. peonies, hellebores, delphiniums, and Caucasian scabious, but great care is needed not to sever roots from shoots.

Some hardy plants can also be increased by cuttings prepared from firm young shoots, usually in March–April.

Some hardy plants spread quite rapidly and are best lifted, divided, and replanted every second or third year. A few do not like disturbance and are best left alone for years.

Delphiniums are not usually long lived, for old plants tend to rot in winter, so it is desirable to raise some plants annually from seed or cuttings. Seed sown in February or March in an unheated greenhouse or frame and transplanted in May or June will often give some flower by August or September, but the main flowering season is in June–July and second or third year plants usually give the best display. The best germination is obtained by sowing seed as soon as it is ripe in August–September and overwintering the seedlings in a frame or greenhouse. Both seedlings and mature plants may be severely damaged by slugs, particularly from February to April. They should be protected by metaldehyde or methiocarb slug bait. Some varieties are also subject to powdery mildew in summer. This may also affect some varieties of phlox and michaelmas daisies, so all should be sprayed occasionally from June to August with thiram or colloidal sulphur.

Many hardy plants are self supporting, but some of the taller kinds need staking or can be allowed to grow up through branching sticks thrust firmly into the soil or through special plant supports that can be purchased for this purpose.

Faded flowers should be removed both for the sake of tidiness and to prevent seed production which is a strain on the plants and may result in hundreds of self sown seedlings that can be a nuisance. Each autumn all dead and dying growth should be cleared away and the surface soil broken up with a fork, but only to a depth of about 5 cm (2 in.). Each spring rotted manure or garden refuse or old mushroom compost can be spread around the plants. Alternatively use peat plus a good compound fertilizer at the rate recommended by the manufacturers.

The only other routine work is to remove weeds by hand weeding, hoeing, or the careful use of paraquat applied directly to the weed leaves and kept off all garden plants and lawn grass.

FERNS

There are a number of beautiful hardy ferns which can be grown in shady places. They like soil containing plenty of peat or leaf mould and can be increased by division in the spring, which is also the best planting season. Ferns are best left undisturbed for years. Among the finest kinds are the Hard Fern (Blechnum spicant), the Hart's Tongue Fern (Phyllitis scolopendrium), the Lady Fern (Athyrium felix femina), the Male Fern (Dryopteris felix mas), the Ostrich Fern (Pteretis struthiopteris), the Common Polypody (Polypodium vulgare), the Shield Fern (Polystichum aculeatum), and the Royal Fern (Osmunda regalis).

Meconopsis baileyi

Delphinium Carters New Giant

Quick-reference Table of Hardy Plants

ABBREVIATIONS

Colour   *W* white; *Y* yellow; *O* orange; *R* red; *C* crimson; *Pl* purple; *P* pink; *B* blue; *M* mauve; *G* green.
Duration *S* short, lift and divide or otherwise renew every two or three years; *L* long, leave undisturbed until overcrowded.
Place   *Sn* likes a sunny or light place; *Sh* likes a shady or semi-shady place.
Increase *D* by division; *C* by cuttings; *Rc* by root cuttings; *S* by seed.

Botanical name	Popular name	Colour	Season	Height cm	ft	Dura-tion	Place	In-crease
Acanthus	Bear's Breech	Pl & W	July–Aug	125	*4*	L	Sn Sh	D S
Achillea filipendulina	Yarrow	Y	July–Aug	125	*4*	S	Sn	D
,, millefolium	Milfoil	P	June	60	*2*	S	Sn	D
,, ptarmica	Sneezewort	W	June–Sept	60	*2*	S	Sn	D
Aconitum	Monkshood	B Pl Y	July–Sept	100	*3*	L	Sn Sh	D S
Agrostemma (Lychnis) coronaria	Rose Campion	C	June–July	60	*2*	S	Sn	S
Alstroemeria	Peruvian Lily	O P	July	100	*3*	L	Sn	S D
Althaea rosea	Hollyhock	W P M R C Y	July–Aug	150–250	*5–8*	S	Sn	S
Anchusa angustifolia		B	May–July	30	*1*	S	Sn	S Rc
,, italica	Alkanet	B	May–June	125	*4*	S	Sn	S Rc
,, myositidiflora		B	April	30	*1*	L	Sn Sh	D
Anemone japonica	Japanese Anemone	P W	Aug–Oct	100	*3*	L	Sn Sh	D
,, pulsatilla	Pasque flower	M Pl	Apr–May	20	*⅔*	L	Sn	S D
Anthemis tinctoria	Golden Marguerite	Y	June–Sept	60	*2*	L	Sn S	C
Aquilegia	Columbine	all	May–June	40–100	*1½–3*	S	Sn Sh	S D
Armeria	Thrift	P R	May–July	15–60	*½–2*	L	Sn	S D
Aster amellus	Michaelmas Daisy	B M P	Aug–Sept	60–100	*2–3*	S	Sn	D S
,, noviae-angliae	,, ,,	P R Pl	Sept–Oct	150–200	*5–6*	S	Sn Sh	D S
,, novi-belgii	,, ,,	W M B R Pl	Sept–Oct	30–200	*1–6*	S	Sn Sh	D S
Astilbe	Spirea	W P R C	June–July	30–100	*1–3*	L	Sh	D
Auricula	Dusty Miller	B C Pl Y G	Mar–May	15	*½*	S	Sn	S D
Bergenia	Large-leaved Saxifrage	P C W	Mar–May	30	*1*	L	Sn Sh	D
Campanula carpatica	Tussock Bellflower	B W	July–Aug	20	*⅔*	S	Sn Sh	D S
,, glomerata	Clustered Bellflower	Pl	June–July	30	*1*	S	Sn Sh	D S
,, lactiflora	Milky Bellflower	B M	July–Aug	30–200	*1–6*	S	Sh	D S
,, persici-folia	Peach-leaved Bellflower	B W	June–July	100	*3*	S	Sn Sh	D S
Carnation, Border: *see* Dianthus								
Catananche	Cupid's Dart	B	June–Sept	60	*2*	S	Sn	S D
Centaurea dealbata	Perennial Corn-flower	P	June–Aug	60	*2*	S	Sn	S D
,, macro-cephala	,, ,,	Y	June–Aug	100	*3*	S	Sn	D S
,, montana	Mountain Corn-flower	B	May–June	45	*1½*	S	Sn	D S
Centranthus	Valerian	P R W	June–July	60	*2*	L	Sn	D S
Cerastium	Snow in Summer	W	May–June	20	*⅔*	S	Sn	D
Chelone		R P	July–Sept	100	*3*	L	Sn	S C
Chrysanthemum maximum	Shasta Daisy	W	June–Aug	100	*3*	S	Sn	D S
Convallaria	Lily of the Valley	W	May–June	30	*8*	L	Sh	D

Botanical name	Popular name	Colour	Season	Height cm	ft	Dura-tion	Place	In-crease
Coreopsis auriculata	Tickseed	Y & C	July–Sept	60	2	S	Sn	S D
,, verticillata	,,	Y	June–Aug	45	1½	S	Sn	D
Delphinium bella-donna	Perennial Larkspur	B Pl P W	June–July	100	3	S	Sn	S C D
,, elatum		B Pl M P W	June–July	100–200	3–6	S	Sn	S C D
Dianthus allwoodii	Perpetual Pink	W P R C	May–Aug	30–45	1–1½	S	Sn	C S
,, caryophyllus	Border Carnation	W P R C Pl M Y	June–July	60	2	S	Sn	C S
,, plumarius	Pink	W P R C	May–June	30	1	S	Sn	C D S
Dicentra eximea	Keys of Heaven	P	May–June	30	1	S	Sn Sh	D
,, spectabilis	Bleeding Heart	P & W	May–June	60	2	S	Sn Sh	D
Dictamnus	Burning Bush	W Pl	June–July	100	3	S	Sn Sh	S
Doronicum	Leopard's Bane	Y	Apr–May	30–60	1–2	S	Sn Sh	D
Echinacea	Purple Coneflower	Pl	Aug–Sept	100	3	S	Sn	D
Echinops	Globe Thistle	B W	July–Aug	100–150	3–5	L	Sn	S
Erigeron	Fleabane	B P C	June–Aug	45–60	1½–2	S	Sn	D S
Eryngium	Sea Holly	B W	July–Aug	60–100	2–3	L	Sn	S Rc
Euphorbia	Spurge	Y G O	Apr–May	30–60	1–2	S	Sn	D
Gaillardia	Blanket Flower	Y R C	June–Oct	30–75	1–2½	S	Sn	S Rc D
Galega	Goat's Rue	B M W	July–Aug	125	4	S	Sn Sh	D
Geranium armenum	Crane's Bill	C	July–Aug	100	3	S	Sn	D S
,, endressii	,, ,,	P	June–Sept	50	1½	S	Sn	D S
,, ibericum	,, ,,	B	June–July	30	1	S	Sn	D S
Geum	Avens	Y O R	June–Sept	30–45	1–1½	S	Sn	SD
Gypsophila paniculata	Chalk Plant	W P	July–Aug	60–100	2–3	L	Sn	S C
Helenium	Sneezewort	Y C	July–Aug	60–150	2–5	S	Sn	D S
Heliopsis		Y	July–Sept	100	3	S	Sn	D S
Helleborus niger	Christmas Rose	W	Dec–Mar	20–30	⅔–1	L	Sh	D S
,, orientalis	Lenten Rose	W P Pl	Mar–Apr	30–45	⅔–1	L	Sh	D S
Hemerocallis	Day Lily	Y O P R C	July–Aug	100	3	L	Sn Sh	D S
Hesperis matronalis	Sweet Rocket, Dame's Violet	W Pl	May–June	100	3	S	Sn Sh	S
Heuchera	Alum Root	P R	July–Aug	45–60	1½–2	S	Sn	D S
Hollyhock: see Althaea								
Hosta	Plantain Lily	W M	July–Sept	45–100	1½–3	L	Sn Sh	D
Incarvillea	Trumpet Flower	P R	May–June	45–60	1½–2	L	Sn	S
Iris germanica	German Iris, Bearded Iris	all	May–June	20–100	⅔–3½	S	Sn Sh	D
,, sibirica	Siberian Iris	W B Pl	June–July	100	3	S	Sn Sh	D
,, unguicularis	Algerian Iris	B	Nov–Mar	30	1	L	Sn	D
Kniphofia	Red Hot Poker, Torch Lily	Y O R	June–Oct	60–125	2–4	L	Sn	D S
Liatris	Blazing Star, Gay Feather	Pl	July–Aug	45–100	1½–3	L	Sn Sh	D S
Ligularia	Giant Groundsel	Y O	July–Aug	125	4	S	Sn Sh	D
Limonium latifolium	Sea Lavender	B	Aug–Sept	60	2	L	Sn	S Rc
Lobelia cardinalis	Scarlet Lobelia	R	July–Oct	60	2	S	Sn	D S
,, vedrariensis		B	July–Sept	100	3	S	Sn	D S
Lupinus polyphyllus	Lupin	all	May–June	60–125	2–4	S	Sn	S C
Lychnis chalcedonica	Maltese Cross, Jerusalem Cross	R	Aug–Sept	100	3	S	Sn	S
Lysimachia num-mularia	Creeping Jenny	Y	June–Aug	creeping		S	Sn Sh	D
,, punctata	Yellow Loosestrife	Y	June–Aug	100	3	S	Sn Sh	D S
Lythrum	Purple Loosestrife	Pl P	July–Aug	100	3	S	Sn Sh	D

Botanical name	Popular name	Colour	Season	Height cm	ft	Duration	Place	Increase
Meconopsis baileyi	Thibetan Blue Poppy	B	May–July	100	*3*	S	Sh	S
,, cambrica	Welsh Poppy	Y	Apr–Oct	45	*1½*	S	Sn Sh	S
Monarda	Bergamot	P R Pl	July–Aug	100	*3*	S	Sn Sh	D S
Nepeta	Catmint	B	May–Sept	30	*1*	S	Sn	D S
Oenothera fruticosa	Evening Primrose	Y	June–Aug	45	*1½*	S	Sn	D S
,, missouriensis	Creeping Evening Primrose	Y	July–Sept	30	*1*	S	Sn	D S
Paeonia albiflora	Chinese Peony	W P R C	May–June	100	*3*	L	Sn Sh	D
,, mlokosewitschii	Yellow Peony	Y	May	60	*2*	L	Sn Sh	D S
,, officinalis	European Peony	P R C	May–June	100	*3*	L	Sn Sh	D S
Papaver orientale	Oriental Poppy	R C P W	May–June	75	*2½*	S	Sn	S Rc
Phlox decussata	Herbaceous Phlox	W P R B M	July–Sept	30–100	*1–3*	S	Sn Sh	D Rc S
Physalis	Winter Cherry, Chinese Lantern	orange pods	July–Oct	45	*1½*	S	Sn	D S
Physostegia	Obedient Plant	P W	Aug–Oct	45–100	*1½–3*	S	Sn Sh	D
Pink: *see* Dianthus								
Platycodon	Balloon Flower	B	July–Aug	40	*1¼*	L	Sn	S D
Polemonium	Jacob's Ladder	B W	May–June	45	*1½*	L	Sn Sh	S D
Polygonatum	Solomon's Seal	W & G	May–June	100	*3*	L	Sh	D S
Polygonum bistorta	Bistort	P R	July–Oct	60	*2*	S	Sn Sh	D
Potentilla	Cinquefoil	Y O R C	June–Aug	15–45	*½–1½*	S	Sn	D S
Pulmonaria	Lungwort	B Pl R	Mar–Apr	15–20	*½–⅔*	L	Sh	D
Pulsatilla: *see* Anemone								
Pyrethrum		W P R C	May–June	60	*2*	S	Sn	D
Rudbeckia	Coneflower	Y	Aug–Sept	100–125	*3–8*	S	Sn	D
Salvia superba		B Pl	July–Aug	45–100	*1½–3*	S	Sn	D
Scabiosa caucasica	Caucasian Scabious	B W	July–Oct	60–100	*2–3*	S	Sn	D S
Schizostylis	Kaffir Lily	P R	Sept–Nov	45	*1½*	L	Sn	D
Sedum spectabile	Stonecrop	P R	Aug–Sept	30	*1*	S	Sn	D
Sidalcea		P R	July–Aug	60–125	*2–4*	S	Sn Sh	S D
Solidago	Golden Rod	Y	July–Sept	60–150	*2–5*	S	Sn Sh	D S
Spiraea aruncus	Goat's Beard	W	June–July	150	*5*	L	Sn Sh	D S
Statice lanata	Lamb's Ears	P	June–Aug	30	*1*	S	Sn	D
Thalictrum aquilegifolium	Meadow Rue	Pl	June	100	*3*	S	Sn Sh	D S
,, dipterocarpum	,, ,,	M W	July–Aug	150	*5*	S	Sn	D
Tritonia: *see* Kniphofia								
Trollius	Globe Flower	Y O	May–July	60–100	*2–3*	S	Sh	D S
Verbascum	Mullein	W Y P Pl	June–July	100–200	*3–6*	S	Sn	S Rc
Verbena bonariensis	Vervain	Pl	July–Sept	150	*5*	S	Sn	S
,, venosa	,,	Pl	July–Sept	45	*1½*	S	Sn	S
Veronica gentianoides		B	May–June	45	*1½*	S	Sn	D S
,, spicata		B P	June–Aug	30–60	*1–2*	S	Sn	D S

Kniphofia   **Scabiosa caucasica**   **Russell Lupins**

7 Roses

Roses can be used in many different ways in the garden. Beds can be filled entirely with them to make a concentrated display over as long a period as possible, so that they virtually serve the purpose of permanent summer bedding plants. For this hybrid tea and floribunda varieties are best since they make plants of moderate size and flower recurrently from June to October or even later, with major displays in late June and early July and again in September. Roses grown in this way need thorough annual pruning to keep them shapely and producing the succession of young growth on which the best flowers are produced. Hybrid tea varieties have the finest flowers, but floribunda varieties produce large clusters of bloom and make a more solid mass of colour.

Roses can also be grown like shrubs, either as isolated bushes or in association with other kinds of shrub. For this purpose shrub roses, old fashioned roses, and species (wild roses) are very suitable though some of the most vigorous floribunda roses can also be used. These roses will only require light pruning and some varieties will only flower for four or five weeks each year between late May and early July. Some kinds also have attractive foliage or showy fruits (hips) in the autumn and at least one, Rosa omiensis pteracantha, has ornamental thorns which run together like crimson wings along the branches.

Yet another possibility is to group roses with hardy plants so that they extend or vary the display. For this purpose floribunda roses are usually the best.

Shrub roses and bushy floribunda roses can also be planted as hedges, provided these are allowed to grow fairly informally and are not regularly clipped, which would prevent them flowering.

Climbing roses can be used to cover walls and can also be trained over arches, pergolas and screens, or up pillars or tripods which can be used as dominant features in the design or as a background to borders. Climbing roses do not climb naturally, but have long whippy stems which sprawl about if left to their own

Prepare planting holes for roses with a spade, making each hole large enough to accommodate all roots spread out. Sprinkle a little bone meal in the hole. Plant so that the point where stems join stock is slightly below soil level as indicated by stick.

devices. They must be tied up to suitable supports and they need annual pruning to keep them in good condition. Some can be allowed to sprawl and be used to cover banks, the pink variety Max Graf being particularly suitable for this. Most modern climbing roses are repeat flowering from about June to October, like hybrid teas and floribundas, but some of the older varieties and most ramblers (which are very vigorous climbers) flower once only each summer for from four to six weeks, usually in July and August.

Standard and half standard roses can be used like miniature trees in the garden or may be planted among bush roses to make high banks of bloom.

All roses succeed best in light open places, preferably with some direct sunshine, but some will grow in shade. All like rather rich, well cultivated soil. Ground should be well dug or forked and well rotted manure, decayed garden refuse or some other manure substitute such as prepared town refuse or treated sewage, worked in freely. The surface can also be dusted with bone meal at about 100 grammes per square metre (3–4 oz/sq yd) before it is finally broken down and levelled for planting.

There are two ways of buying roses: lifted from the open ground with bare roots or growing in containers. The former is the only practical way if plants have to be dispatched any distance, but the roots must be protected in transit so that they do not dry out. Bare-root roses pre-packed in polythene are sold in many shops. It is important that the package is well sealed so that roots remain moist. The planting season for bare-root roses is from mid-October to late March.

Container grown roses can be planted at any time of the year provided the plants have been growing in the containers sufficiently long to fill the soil with their roots, so binding it together and making it possible to remove the container with little or no disturbance of the soil. Then the whole ball of soil and roots is planted, just as it is, in a hole large enough to contain it and allow the top of the soil ball to be covered with a further 1–2 cm ($\frac{1}{2}$–1 in.) of soil. Container plants weigh a lot and so this system is only practicable if the plants can be collected. Garden centres stock such plants for their cash-and-carry trade.

If bare-root roses seem at all dry stand them in a bucket of water for a few minutes before planting. Also cut off any broken pieces of root and shorten long thin roots. Plant in holes sufficiently large to

(above) Floribunda Rose Dearest
(centre) Hybrid Tea Rose Buccaneer
(below) Climbing Rose Delbard

61

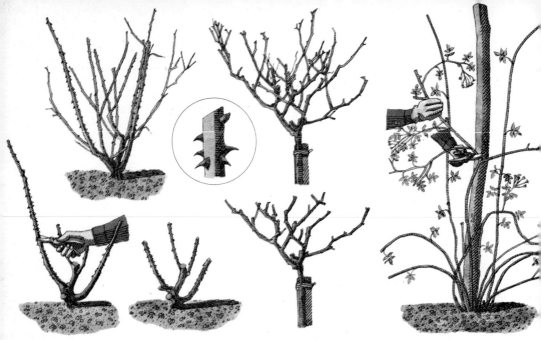

Prune roses by first removing damaged, diseased or old stems and then shortening young stems. Keep centres of bushes (left) and standards (centre) open. Make a cut just above a growth bud (inset) or to a branch stem as in the climbing rose on the right.

contain all the roots comfortably when spread out in a natural manner and to permit the uppermost to be covered with 5 cm (2 in.) of soil. Mix some moist peat and bone meal 50 g (2 oz) of the latter to each 10 litre (2 gallon) bucket of peat and put two or three handfuls of this around the roots. Then return the soil, breaking up well and making it firm by treading. Complete the work by scattering some loose soil over the foot marks.

Plant bush roses 45–60 cm (18–24 in.) apart; standard and half standard roses 1·25–1·5 m (4–6 ft) apart; climbing roses at least 2 m (6 ft) apart; and shrub roses 1–1·5 m (3–5 ft) apart according to their vigour.

Container planted roses purchased between April and September need not be pruned after planting. Bare-root roses and container grown roses planted in autumn or winter should be pruned the following March unless already pruned by the nurseryman. Each bush plant will probably have two or three good stems each of which should be shortened to within 15 cm (6 in.) of soil level. If there are some weaker stems cut them down to 5–8 cm (2–3 in.). Make each cut immediately above a growth bud, visible as a little lump on the stem. It is from these buds that new shoots will grow in the spring.

Standard and half standard roses will have heads of several branches on a bare stem anything from 60 cm to 1·5 m (2–5 ft) high. Each sturdy branch must be shortened to 12–15 cm (5–6 in.) and weaker ones to 5–8 cm (2–3 in.). There should be no growths on the main stem or 'trunk', but if there are they must be cut right out.

Prune newly planted climbers like bush roses except those known as climbing sports. These always have the word 'Climbing' before their names, e.g. Climbing Allgold, Climbing Ena Harkness, etc., so it is easy to recognize them. Only shorten strong stems of these by about one-third and weaker stems by two-thirds. Hard pruning of these roses may cause them to revert to the bush habit of the varieties whose name they bear and from which they were obtained as natural sports or mutants.

In subsequent years pruning can be spread over a much longer period and done as convenient, any time between November and March, though in cold districts it is best to leave it until March. The object is to get rid of diseased, damaged, and old wood and to shorten the healthy young stems sufficiently to obtain the kind of plant and the quality of flower required. The more severely stems are cut back the smaller the plants will be and the fewer the flowers, but individually they are likely to be larger. Most exhibitors therefore prune their roses rather hard, whereas if grown solely for garden display they may be pruned more lightly.

Start by cutting out all stems with splits, cankers, or black or purple patches indicating disease. Also cut out as much as possible of the old wood, recognizable by its darker more gnarled bark. This is practically all the pruning that many shrub roses, old fashioned rose, and all species require.

With hybrid tea and floribunda roses the remaining young stems must also be pruned, strong ones by one-third to one-half their length, weaker ones by about two-thirds, if fairly large bushes are required. But if the object is to have smaller bushes or the largest possible flowers or flower clusters, pruning can be harder, strong stems being shortened by one-half to two-thirds their length and weaker ones cut back to 5–8 cm (2–3 in.). Again, it is important to make each cut just above a growth bud, if possible one pointing outwards from the centre of the plant as this will encourage outward growing shoots and a well balanced, shapely plant. Towards the end of April look over the plants, and if some of the stems have made growth which is not from the uppermost bud, but from one lower down, cut back to this. Pieces of stem without growth will die and decay may spread.

(above) Rambler Rose Albertine; (centre) Shrub Rose Nevada; (below left) Moss Roses; (below right) Climbing Rose Message

Climbing roses are pruned on the same lines. Vigorous ramblers often make much of their new growth near the base and with these all the old stems can be cut right out as soon as the flowers have faded, the young ones being tied in at full length or shortened as necessary to fill available space. But most repeat flowering climbers make a lot of new growth from higher up on old stems, so it is impossible to cut out all the old growth every year. Some is removed each year, but the best young growth is retained and shortened a little – a very little in the case of climbing sports.

Standards and half standards are pruned just like bushes except that a little more attention should be paid to the shape and balance of the heads of branches since these are so conspicuous.

As the flowers of hybrid tea, floribunda, and repeat flowering climbers fade in summer, cut them off with a short length of stem, again making each cut immediately above a growth bud (there will be one where each leaf stalk joins its stem) or a good new shoot. This will encourage further strong new growth, and more flowers.

Because roses flower on young growth, it is essential to maintain a constant succession of this. Correct pruning will help to this end, but regular and substantial feeding is also essential. Spread well rotted manure, decayed garden refuse, spent mushroom compost or a manure substitute around the roses each February or March. In April sprinkle a good compound fertilizer (preferably one specially prepared for roses) for at least 30 cm (1 ft) around each plant at the rate recommended by the manufacturer. Repeat at half rate in early June and again about mid-July. Water freely in dry weather, especially after applying fertilizer to dissolve it and make it available to the plants. If leaves tend to become yellow apply iron and magnesium sequestrols in spring or early summer as advised by the manufacturer.

Roses must be kept free of the competition of weeds. This can be done by pricking over the surface of the beds lightly with a fork immediately before applying manure in late winter or early spring and by occasional hoeing from April until October. Never disturb the soil near roses to a greater depth than 5 cm (2 in.) since many roots are near the surface. Alternatively weeds can be killed by watering them with paraquat and further weed growth prevented by watering the soil with simazine. Both these weedkillers must be used strictly according to manufacturer's instructions. They are best applied from a special plastic applicator with an 8 cm (3 in.) sprinkle bar, so that the weedkiller can be applied directly to the weed leaves (or to the soil with simazine) and kept off the leaves of roses, other garden plants and lawn grass. Special formulations of simazine for rose beds must be used.

Roses are commonly attacked by greenflies in late spring and summer, the green 'lice' clustering around the young shoots and flower buds and sucking sap from them. Monthly spraying from May till September with a systemic insecticide

(left) Rosa hugonis; (right) Miniature Rose Perle de Montserrat

OUTSTANDING HYBRID TEA ROSES (in rows from top)

Ena Harkness	Super Star	
Anne Letts	My Choice	Peace
Rose Gaujard	Montezuma	Stella
Silver Lining	Perfecta	

such as menazon, dimethoate (Rogor) or formothion will eliminate these pests. Special formulations of one or other of these chemicals with other insecticides such as trichlorphon or BHC can be purchased and if these are used there are unlikely to be any caterpillars, slugworms, thrips, capsid bugs, or other pests on the rose bushes.

Black spot and mildew are the commonest diseases. Black spot is rarely seriously troublesome in town gardens and mildew is most likely to occur in closed-in places where there is little circulation of air. Fungicides containing chemicals such as captan, phaltan, maneb, thiram, and dinocap can be used to control these and other

diseases, but need to be applied fortnightly from mid-April until late September to be fully effective. Whether such regular spraying is considered necessary or not will depend greatly upon experience of disease in former years or, if one is new to the district, on what neighbouring rose growers report. Some varieties are more susceptible to disease than others.

There are hundreds of rose varieties and many new ones are added every year. Selection from these is very much a matter of personal taste and is best done by seeing roses growing in nurseries, in the special display gardens maintained by many nurserymen, in public parks, the trial gardens of the Royal National Rose Society, the Royal Horticultural Society, the Northern Horticultural Society and other bodies, and in the private gardens of other rose enthusiasts.

(above) Rose Waltz Time
(centre) Hybrid Tea Rose Margaret

(below left) Hybrid Tea Rose Pink Favourite
(below right) Hybrid Tea Rose Brilliant

8 Shrubs and Climbers

Shrubs, together with trees, provide the permanent plant framework of the garden. They will remain for many years and most cannot be readily moved once established, so they should be sited with care. Moreover many shrubs and climbers increase in size for a good many years and though some can be checked by pruning, in general it is necessary to allow for this expansion when planting them. If they are planted at the full spacing necessary for eventual development there will almost certainly be considerable bare ground for a few years and this may be occupied by hardy plants, bulbs, annuals, or bedding plants. Alternatively shrubs may be planted deliberately too thick at the outset with the intention of removing some later on. Most shrubs are about as wide as they are tall so height gives some indication of eventual spacing.

Shrubs and climbers may be *deciduous* or *evergreen*. The former lose all their leaves in the autumn and produce a new lot in the spring. In winter stems are therefore bare, but often present an attractive tracery of twigs and branches and some kinds have attractively coloured bark. There is also usually a change in colour of leaves from spring to autumn and some kinds have leaves that colour brilliantly before they fall.

Evergreen shrubs retain their leaves throughout the year and, though some do fall, their place is taken by others. They help to keep the garden sheltered in winter and give it a well furnished appearance then, when their solid shapes stand out in sharp contrast to surrounding bareness. However, too many evergreens can give a garden a heavy and rather depressing appearance.

Shrubs may also be either *broad leaved* or *coniferous*. There are evergreen and deciduous kinds in both these groups, but whereas broad leaved shrubs may be grown for foliage, flowers or fruit, conifers are grown mainly for their foliage.

Most shrubs will grow in a wide variety of soils, but some dislike soils containing lime or chalk. Principal among these are azaleas, camellias, some heathers (calluna and some ericas), magnolias, and rhododendrons. However, it is possible to grow all these shrubs even where there is chalk or lime if special beds of lime free soil are built up for them above the existing soil level or if they are fed several times a year with iron and magnesium sequestrols.

Tamarix pentandra **Choisya ternata** **Cotoneaster horizontalis**

(above) Mahonia aquifolium

(above) Camellia Alba Plena
(below) Deutzia scabra

Sites for shrubs and climbers should be prepared by thorough digging or forking. Manure or manure substitutes, plus bone meal, should be used as for roses (*see* page 61). Also like roses, shrubs and climbers may be lifted from the open ground, in which case the planting season is from mid-October to April, or may be grown in containers from which they can be planted at any time of the year provided the ball of soil and roots can be kept intact. Unlike roses, some shrubs do not like having the soil shaken from their roots, however carefully these may be kept moist. Even from the open ground they must be lifted with a good ball of soil and with the more difficult kinds, such as conifers and hollies, good nurserymen ensure that the soil does not fall off in transit by wrapping it tightly in sacking or polythene. Such plants may cost more to buy and transport, but losses will be far less.

Lifted evergreens transplant best rather early or late in the planting season, i.e. in October or April rather than in mid-winter.

Only plant when the soil is in good working condition, not when it is frozen or very wet. Plant in holes sufficiently large to accommodate all the roots and allow the uppermost to be covered with 5–7 cm (2–3 in.) of soil. Stake and tie large shrubs, especially kinds such as brooms and genistas which have rather small roots and so are easily blown over until established. Water in shrubs well if the soil is dry and keep them well watered during warm weather for the first few months until their roots have had time to penetrate deeply.

If possible plant wall climbers a foot or so away from the wall as the soil close to walls is often very dry. For the same reason it is particularly important to keep wall climbers well watered until established and growing freely.

Most shrubs and climbers will grow with a minimum of attention, but they do benefit from annual feeding with a good compound fertilizer, applied in spring as directed on the label, or with bone meal and hoof and horn meal each at 100 grammes per square metre ($3\frac{1}{2}$ oz/sq yd) applied to the soil under the full branch spread of the shrub or for 1 metre (3 ft) around the base of a climber.

68

(opposite)
(left) Weigela; (right) Viburnum carlesii

Weeds must be suppressed and the same methods can be used as for roses (*see* page 64) except that simazine may damage some surface rooting kinds. Shrubs can be grown as isolated specimens in grass, but if so a circle of clean soil almost as wide as the branch spread should be maintained around each, either by surface cultivation or the use of paraquat, for the first five or six years.

Pruning may be done for one or both of two reasons: to keep shrubs and climbers smaller or neater than they would otherwise be, or to improve the quality of their flowers, leaves, stems or fruits. Most shrubs that flower in late summer, e.g. buddleia and Hydrangea paniculata, can be pruned fairly hard in March–April, since they flower on the new shoots made after that date. Many shrubs that flower before mid-summer, e.g. forsythia, brooms, weigela, deutzia, and philadelphus, can be pruned immediately after flowering by cutting out the old flowering stems but preserving all new shoots or non-flowering stems. With brooms it is unsafe to cut back into hard, old wood from which new shoots are unlikely to grow. Most shrubs can be moderately thinned by removing some of the older branches in February–March, if it is merely a question of reducing the size of plants. Special cases are dealt with in the notes on particular shrubs which follow.

SOME FAVOURITE SHRUBS AND CLIMBERS

Azalea. These are closely related to rhododendron and are regarded by botanists as part of the genus rhododendron. There are both evergreen

(from top) Varieties of Hydrangea macrophylla;
Hypericum Hidcote; Hardy Hybrid Rhododendron

and deciduous kinds, the former with small leaves and small to medium size flowers in white, lilac, and shades from pink to carmine and scarlet; the deciduous kinds are mainly larger flowered, in many shades of yellow, apricot, orange, salmon, flame red, and pink. The common yellow azalea has specially fragrant flowers and some other deciduous kinds are fragrant, though few as richly as this.

All azaleas like lime free soil and partially shaded places though they will grow in full sun. The evergreen kinds are from 0·60 to 1·25 m (2–4 ft) high, usually considerably broader. Deciduous azaleas are 1·25–2·5 m (4–8 ft) high and through. All transplant well even when quite large. The evergreen kinds are usually increased by summer cuttings, deciduous kinds by cuttings or seed.

Camellia. Beautiful evergreen shrubs with shining, dark green leathery leaves and showy single or double flowers produced in winter and early spring. There are a great many varieties of Camellia japonica ranging in colour from white and pale pink to crimson, and in height from about 2 to 3 m (6–10 ft), flowering March to May. There are fewer varieties of C. williamsii, all in whites or shades of pink, flowering March–April. C. reticulata has the largest flowers, rose-pink, and makes a very large, wide spreading shrub, but needs a warm, sheltered place. So do the varieties of C. sasanqua, white or in shades of pink, flowering from November to March.

All camellias like lime free soil. They grow most rapidly in semi-shade but usually flower more freely in sunnier places. Varieties of Camellia japonica and C. williamsii are fairly hardy, but their flowers can be spoiled by frost, so it is best to give all camellias as sheltered a position as possible. They can be trained on walls, especially those facing west, and also grow well in tubs or large pots if well watered. They need no pruning and are increased by cuttings in summer.

Ceanothus. There are both evergreen and deciduous kinds, all bearing small flowers in clusters, the evergreen kinds all blue, the deciduous ones blue or pink. The evergreen kinds are all rather tender and are often trained against sunny walls like climbers, as they are more likely to survive in such sheltered places. However, near the sea and in mild districts some can be grown as bushes in the open. Two of the hardiest are Ceanothus impressus, deep blue flowers in May, 1·5–2·5 m (5–8 ft) high and considerably more through and C. thyrsiflorus, powder blue flowers in May, 3–3·5 m (10–12 ft) high. C. burkwoodii has deep blue flowers from July to October and is 1·5–2·5 m (5–8 ft) high. All the evergreen kinds can be pruned immediately after flowering, and this is necessary when ceanothus are trained on walls in order to shorten stems growing forward. The deciduous kinds all flower from July to September and can be pruned quite severely each April if desired. They grow 1·5–2·5 m (5–8 ft) high. All kinds are increased by cuttings in summer.

Chaenomeles (Japanese Quince). These early flowering deciduous shrubs were formerly known as Cydonia and this name is still frequently used. To many gardeners, they are just 'japonicas'. All make freely branched, rather tangled shrubs if left to their own devices, but are usually trained against walls or fences as climbers. When so grown they should be pruned each June, when forward pointing stems can be shortened and growth generally thinned and tied in to wires or trellis. As a bush chaenomeles only grows 1·25–1·5 m (4–5 ft) high but may be twice as much through. Trained on a wall it can reach a height of 2·5–3·0 m (8–10 ft). There are numerous varieties with white, pink, scarlet or crimson flowers, all produced from March to May, even earlier in a warm place. All can be increased by suckers dug up in autumn with roots attached.

A well-planted heather garden

Clematis. Slender climbers which can be trained on walls and screens, over arches and pergolas, up poles or allowed to scramble up into small trees. There are many varieties, differing greatly in vigour, size, and colour of flower, and time of flowering. Clematis montana, with small white or pale pink flowers very freely produced in May, will climb to 6 m (20 ft) but can easily be trained along a fence or pergola. C. macropetala will only reach a few feet and has very beautiful, nodding, lavender-blue or soft pink flowers in May. C. armandii is vigorous, evergreen, has white flowers in March–April and needs a sunny, sheltered wall as it is less hardy than most. C. jackmanii has large violet-purple flowers in July and August and will reach 3–3·5 m (10–12 ft). C. orientalis and C. tangutica have small yellow flowers from July to August, and will reach 3–3·5 m (10–12 ft). There are many other varieties, some with very large flowers, some with double flowers, in white and many shades of lavender, purple, violet, and carmine.

All these clematis enjoy rather rich, well cultivated soil, preferably with lime or chalk. They do not transplant well so should be purchased in containers and moved from these with the soil ball unbroken. The early flowering kinds, such as C. armandii, C. macropetala, and C. montana, can be pruned after flowering, when some of the older stems can be cut out and overgrown stems cut back. The large flowered garden varieties, flowering from June onwards, benefit from regular pruning each February–March, when previous year's growth can be shortened considerably to strong growth buds or new shoots.

Large flowered clematis sometimes wilt and die. This is due to a disease which can be checked by spraying with a copper fungicide. Cut out and burn wilting shoots and paint wounds with Arbrex or Medo. Clematis can be raised from seed, but the large flowered garden varieties are produced by grafting on to seedlings of the wild clematis vitalba or from cuttings.

Fuchsia. Many fuchsias are best grown as greenhouse pot plants, but some are sufficiently hardy to be grown outdoors. Near the sea and in other mild localities

71

they may make permanent bushes, but in colder places are killed to ground level each winter and shoot up again in spring. They are not fussy about soil and will grow in full sun or partial shade. They enjoy plenty of moisture in summer. Among the hardiest kinds are Fuchsia magellanica, available in several forms, one named gracilis with slender pale pink to carmine-purple flowers; another named riccartonii, with small scarlet and purple flowers; and garden varieties such as Margaret, Brutus, and Mrs. Popple, all scarlet and purple; Lena, flesh pink and purple; Alice Hoffmann and Madame Cornelissen, pink and carmine with white; and Tom Thumb, carmine and violet, dwarf and compact. All are readily raised from spring or summer cuttings. All can be pruned in the spring.

Heather. There are many different kinds of heather or heath, some derived from the Scottish heather or ling, Calluna vulgaris, others from various species of erica. The Irish heath or heather is Daboecia polifolia. Most dislike lime or chalk, but varieties of Erica carnea, E. darleyensis, E. mediterranea, and E. stricta will succeed in moderately chalky or limy soils, particularly if these are well dressed with peat.

Heathers vary from completely prostrate, spreading plants to erect bushes, up to 2·5 m (8 ft) high. There are white varieties and many shades of pink, purple, and carmine. Some have double flowers and some yellow or coppery coloured foliage. Varieties can be chosen to be in flower every month of the year. Among the most useful kinds are Calluna vulgaris, 0·60–1·0 m (2–3 ft), white, pink to crimson, autumn flowering; Daboecia polifolia, 60 cm (2 ft), deep purple or white, June to October; Erica arborea, 2–2·5 m (6–8 ft), white, March to May; E. carnea, 30 cm (12 in.), white, pink to red, December to March; E. cinerea, 30–45 cm (12–18 in.) white, rose-pink to purple, June to August; E. darleyensis, 45 cm (18 in.), purplish pink, November to April; E. mediterranea, 1·25–1·5 m (4–5 ft), white or rosy red, March to May; E. stricta (also known as E. terminalis), 0·60–1 m (2–3 ft), rose-pink, June to September; E. vagans, 30–45 cm (12–18 in.), white, rose-pink to carmine, August to November; and E. veitchii, 1·5–2·0 m (5–6 ft), white, March to May.

All heathers prefer open, sunny places. Some peat placed around them when planting helps to get them started. They can be lightly clipped over after flowering. Propagation is by layers or summer cuttings.

(above) Chaenomeles
(centre) Jasminum nudiflorum
(below) Pyracantha

72

Hydrangea. Deciduous shrubs, and one climber, all with large clusters of bloom in summer. Hydrangea arborescens, 1–1·25 m (3–4 ft) and H. paniculata 1–2 m (3–6 ft) are the hardiest, both white flowered. There are many garden varieties of H. macrophylla, varying in hardiness, in height from 1·0 to 2·0 m (3–6 ft) and in colour from white, pink, and pale blue to crimson and purple. The colour of coloured varieties changes according to the character of the soil, tending to pinks and reds in alkaline soils (those containing chalk or lime) and to blues and purples in acid soils. In some varieties the whole of each flower head is composed of flowers with large petals, and in others, known as 'lace-caps', only an outer ring of flowers is of this type and all the inner ones are small and bead-like. The Climbing Hydrangea, H. petiolaris, has white flowers of the lace-cap type and climbs by aerial roots like an ivy.

All hydrangeas like good, rich, well-drained soils. They will grow in sun or partial shade. Hydrangea paniculata can be pruned almost to ground level each spring. Other varieties should only have faded flower heads and dead stems removed in spring, and may be thinned a little then if overgrown. All are readily raised from summer cuttings.

Pyracantha (Firethorn). Evergreen shrubs with clusters of small white flowers in June, followed by heavy crops of crimson, orange-red or yellow berries. They are frequently trained as climbers against walls or fences, but can equally well be grown as bushes 2–2·5 m (6–8 ft) high. If used as climbers badly placed or overgrown stems should be shortened after flowering when it is seen which are going to bear berries. Pyracantha will grow well in most soils in sun or shade and can be increased by cuttings.

Rhododendron. Flowering evergreens covering a great range of species and varieties ranging from prostrate plants to trees 6 m (20 ft) high. All dislike lime or chalk and many succeed best in semi-shade, but the hardy hybrids will grow equally well in sun or shade. These are the most useful for general garden planting. They are all shrubs, eventually 2·5 m (8 ft) or more high but taking many years to reach these dimensions and capable of being transplanted even when quite large. Their flowers are borne freely in large trusses in late May and June and cover a wide colour range from white,

(above) Wistaria
(centre) Passiflora coerulea
(below) Ceanothus dentatus

73

lavender, and pale pink to scarlet, crimson, and purple. There are also yellow and apricot flowered hybrids, but these prefer semi-shade to full sun.

All rhododendrons grow well in thin woodland, especially woodland composed of oak and pine, which do not rob the soil too much or cast too heavy a shade. They like peat or leafmould and it is desirable to mix some with the soil when planting and to spread some more round the plants each spring. They also appreciate moisture in summer and may be well watered in dry weather.

The species, or wild rhododendrons, and also first generation hybrids from them, show great variations in flower form, some having hanging, bell-shaped or tubular flowers, some open flowers like those of azaleas, to which they are closely related, botanists uniting them both under the name 'rhododendron'. In general these species and pedigree hybrids are a little more exacting than the hardy hybrids and some are distinctly tender. Some have very fragrant flowers and flowering is spread from February to July. Most prefer half shade and are more successful in country than in town gardens.

The only regular pruning required is removal of the faded flowers, but overgrown bushes can be cut back in April, with the loss of one year's bloom. All rhododendrons can be raised from seed, but the hybrids may show considerable variation from seed and so are increased by layers, cuttings or grafting on to plants of the common purple Rhododendron ponticum.

Viburnum. There are many different kinds of viburnum, varying greatly in character. Viburnum fragrans and V. bodnantense are deciduous, winter flowering shrubs 2·0–2·5 m (6–8 ft) high, one white and pink, the other all pink, both scented. V. carlesii, V. burkwoodii, and V. juddii are more richly fragrant, white, April–May flowering, deciduous, and 1·25–1·5 m (4–5 ft) high. V. carlcephalum is similar but has larger flower clusters.

Viburnum opulus is the British guelder rose, deciduous 2·5–3 m (8–10 ft) high, with clusters of white flowers in June followed by shining scarlet berries. There is a dwarf 1·5 m (5 ft) variety named compactum. Another variety, sterile, the snowball tree, has large ball-like flower clusters but no berries.

Viburnum tomentosum mariesii is 2–2·5 m (6–8 ft) high, deciduous, with horizontal branches bearing flat clusters of white flowers in May. Its variety plicatum has ball-like flower clusters, smaller than those of the snowball tree.

Viburnum tinus is the laurustinus, a fine evergreen, eventually 2·5–3 m (8–10 ft)

Some shrubs give best results when cut hard back each spring (left). Others may be pruned immediately the flowers fade when old flowering stems are removed (centre), but young growth is retained. Others benefit from a thinning out of old stems in winter or early spring (right).

Large flowered Clematis

high with clusters of pink and white flowers from November to April. It can be used as a hedge or screen, trimmed to shape after the flowers fade.

There are other useful kinds all quite easily grown in most soils and in sun or semi-shade. All can be increased by cuttings or layers and some sucker.

SHRUBBY CONIFERS

All the following are evergreens.

Cypress. Mostly trees, but there are some very slow growing or bushy kinds. Among the most useful to be planted on lawns or other places where their distinctive shape and colour can be displayed are Chamaecyparis pisifera plumosa, feathery leaved, and available both in grey and golden forms and C. pisifera filifera aurea with hanging whip-like golden branchlets. All grow slowly to about 2·5 m (8 ft).

Juniper. There are several useful spreading kinds. Juniperus horizontalis is completely prostrate, green, blue-grey, or cream variegated according to variety. J. sabina tamariscifolia is grey-green, eventually 60 cm (2 ft) high and 2·0–2·5 m (6–8 ft) in diameter. J. chinensis pfitzeriana makes a broad green shuttlecock eventually 1·5 m (5 ft) high and 2–2·5 m (6–8 ft) in diameter.

Spruce. Only a few are small enough to be called shrubs, but Picea albertiana conica make a neat cone of light green leaves slowly reaching to a height of 1·5 m (5 ft).

Thuya. The best shrubby variety is Thuya occidentalis Rheingold to 1·25 m (4 ft) high, gold in summer, turning bronze in autumn.

BAMBOOS

There are numerous kinds, all evergreen and spreading into large clumps by underground shoots. They will grow in most soils and places, look specially well by the waterside, but are often scorched by wind and so are best given some shelter. The popular kinds are all quite hardy and can be increased by division in spring, which is also the best planting season.

75

Among the best kinds are Arundinaria nitida, Phyllostachys henonis, and Pseudosasa japonica also known as Arundinaria japonica and Bambusa metake. All grow 3 m (10 ft) or more high. Sasa veitchii is 1 m (3 ft) or less.

Quick-reference Table of Shrubs and Climbers

ABBREVIATIONS

Colour W white; Y yellow; O orange; R red; C crimson; Pl purple; P pink; B blue; M mauve; G green; Bl black.

Foliage E evergreen; D deciduous; Ac autumn colour; Yv yellow variegation; Wv white variegation; Pl purple; Gr grey or silver.

Soil A acid (no lime or chalk); L alkaline (with lime or chalk); O ordinary (suitable for most soils); D dry or well drained; M moist.

Prune H cut back hard each spring; F cut out flowering shoots when flowers fade; Tr trim lightly after flowering; Th thin moderately in Feb–Mar; S shorten side shoots in summer; Dh deadhead (remove faded flowers).

| Name | Colour | | Season | Foliage | Height | | Soil | Prune |
	Flower	Fruit			m	ft		
Azalea (deciduous)	Y O P R		May–June	D Ac	1·25–2·5	4–8	A	Dh
„ (evergreen)	W M P R		Apr–May	E	0·6–1·25	2–4	A	
Berberis darwinii	O	Pl	Apr–May	E	2–2·5	6–8	O	Tr
„ stenophylla	Y		Apr–May	E	2–2·5	6–8	O	Tr
„ thunbergii atropurpurea	Y	R	Apr–May	D Pl	1·25–2	4–6	O	Th
„ verruculosa	Y	Pl	May–June	E	0·6–1	2–3	O	Tr
„ wilsonae	Y	R	July	D Ac	1–1·25	3–4	O	Th
Broom: see Cytisus and Genista								
Buddleia alternifolia	Pl		July–Aug	D	2–3	6–10	O	Tr
„ davidii	W M Pl		July–Aug	D	2–3·5	6–12	O L	H
„ globosa	O		May–June	D	3–3·5	10–12	O	Tr
Calluna vulgaris	W P R Pl		Aug–Sept	E, Some Yv	0·6–1	2–3	A	Tr
Camellia japonica	W P R C		Mar–May	E	2–3	6–10	A	Tr
„ williamsii	W P		Mar–Apr	E	2–3	6–10	A	
Caryopteris	B		Sept–Oct	D Gr	0·6–1	2–3	O D	H
Ceanothus burkwoodii	B		July–Oct	E	1·5–2·5	5–8	O	S
„ dentatus	B		May	E	1·25–2	4–6	O	S
„ impressus	B		May	E	1·5–2·5	5–8	O	S
„ Gloire de Versailles	B		June–Oct	D	1·5–2·5	5–8	O	H
„ thyrsiflorus	B		May	E	3–3·5	10–12	O	S
Chaenomeles (cydonia)	W P R C	G	Mar–May	D	1·25–1·5	4–5	O	S
Choisya	W		May–June	E	1·5–2	5–6	O	Th
Cistus	W P C		May–July	E	0·6–1	2–3	O D	S
Clematis armandii	W		Mar–Apr	E	climber		O L	Tr
„ jackmanii	Pl		July–Aug	D	climber		O L	H
„ large flowered	W M B P R		June–Sept	D	climber		O L	H or F
„ macropetala	B P		May	D	low climber		O L	Tr
„ montana	W P		May	D	strong climber		O L	Tr
„ orientalis	Y		Aug–Sept	D	climber		O L	Tr
„ tangutica	Y		Aug–Sept	D	climber		O L	Tr
Cornus alba spaethii	W red stems		May–June	D Yv	1·5–2	5–6	O M	H

Name	Colour		Season	Foliage	Height		Soil	Prune
	Flower	Fruit			m	ft		
Cotinus Notcutt's variety	P		June–July	D Pl	2–2·5	6–8	O L	H or Th
Cotoneaster conspicuus decorus	W	R	June	E	1	3	O	
,,　　　dammeri	W	R	June	E	prostrate		O	
,,　　　franchetii	W	R	July	E	2	6	O	
,,　　　horizontalis	W	R	May	D Ac	0·3–2	1 or 6 on wall	O	Tr
,,　　　microphyllus	W	C	May–June	E	0·6	2	O	
,,　　　simonsii	W	R	June	D	2·5–3	8–10	O	Th
,,　　　wardii	W	R	June	D Ac	2–2·5	6–8	O	
Cytisus albus	W		May	D	1·5–2	5–7	O D	Tr
,,　battandieri	Y		June	D Gr	2·5–3·5	8–12	O D	Tr
,,　kewensis	Y		Apr–May	D	0·45	1½	O D	
,,　praecox	Y		Apr–May	D	1·5	5	O D	Tr
,,　scoparius hybrids	Y O P C		May–June	D	1·5–2	5–6	O D	Tr
Daphne burkwoodii	P		May	D	1	3	O	
,,　mezereum	W Pl		Feb–Mar	D	1	3	O M	
,,　odora marginata	Pl		Mar–Apr	E Yv	0·6–1	2–3	O	
Deutzia elegantissima	Pl		May–June	D	1·25–1·5	4–5	O	F
,,　scabra	W P Pl		June–July	D	2–2·5	6–8	O	F
Elaeagnus pungens maculata	W		Sept–Oct	E Yv	2·5–3	8–10	O	S
Erica arborea	W		Mar–May	E	2–2·5	6–8	A	F
,,　carnea	W P C		Dec–Mar	E	0·3	1	O	F
,,　cinerea	W P C		June–Aug	E	0·3–0·45	1–1½	A	F
,,　darleyensis	P		Nov–Apr	E	0·45	1½	O	F
,,　mediterranea	W		Mar–May	E	1·25–1·5	4–5	O	F
,,　stricta	P		June–Sept	E	0·6–1	2–3	O	F
,,　vagans	W P C		Aug–Nov	E	0·3–0·45	1–1½	A	F
Escallonia Apple Blossom	P & W		June–July	E	1·5–2	5–6	O	F
,,　　C. F. Ball	R		June–July	E	2–2·5	6–8	O	F
,,　　edinensis	P		June–July	E	2–2·5	6–8	O	F
Euonymus europaeus	R & O		Sept–Nov	D	2–2·5	6–8	O	F
,,　fortunei (radicans)				E Yv Wv	0·3–0·6	1–2	O	Th
Forsythia intermedia	Y		Mar–Apr	D	2–2·5	6–8	O	F
Fuchsia gracilis	R & Pl		June–Oct	D	0·6–1	2–3	O	H
,,　riccartonii	R & Pl		June–Oct	D	1–1·5	3–5	O	H
,,　hardy varieties	P R C Pl W		June–Oct	D	0·3–1·5	1–5	O	H
Garrya elliptica	Gr	Bl	Jan–Feb	E	2	6	O	Th
Genista aethnensis	Y		July	D	2·5–3	8–10	O D	Tr
,,　hispanica	Y		May–June	D	0·6	2	O D	Tr
,,　lydia	Y		May–June	D	0·6	2	O D	Tr
,,　tinctoria flore pleno	Y		June–July	D	prostrate		O D	
,,　virgata	Y		June–July	D	2·5–3·5	8–12	O D	Tr
Hamamelis mollis	Y		Dec–Feb	D	2·5–3·5	8–12	O	Th
Hebe (veronica)	W P R C Pl		July–Oct	E	0·6–3·5	2–12	O	Th Tr
Hedera (ivy)	G	Bl	Sept–Nov	E Yv Wv	climbing		O	Tr
Hibiscus syriacus	W B R Pl		Aug–Sept	D	2–2·5	6–8	O D	Th
Hydrangea arborescens	W		July–Aug	D	1–1·25	3–4	O	H
,,　macrophylla	W B P R Pl		July–Aug	D	1–2	3–6	O	Th
,,　paniculata	W		July–Aug	D	1–2	3–6	O	H
,,　petiolaris	W		June–July	D	climbing		O	
Hypericum calycinum	Y		June–Aug	E	prostrate		O L	
,,　patulum	Y		July–Aug	D	1–1·5	3–5	O	Th
Jasminum nudiflorum	Y		Nov–Feb	D	climbing		O	Tr
,,　officinale	W		June–Aug	D	climbing		O	Th

77

Name	Colour Flower	Fruit	Season	Foliage	Height m	ft	Soil	Prune
Kalmia latifolia	P		June	E	2–2·5	6–8	A	
Kerria japonica flore pleno	Y		Apr–May	D	climbing		O	Tr
Kolkwitzia amabilis	P		June	D	2–2·5	6–8	O	F
Lavandula (lavender)	B		July–Aug	E Gr	0·45–1	1½–3	O L	Tr
Leycesteria formosa	W & Pl	Pl	June–July	D	2	6	O	F (March)
Lonicera (honeysuckle)	Y O R C		June–Sept	D	climbing		O	Th
Magnolia stellata	W P		Mar–Apr	D	2–2·5	6–8	A	
Mahonia aquifolium	Y	Bl	Mar–May	E	1	3	O	Tr
,, japonica	Y		Feb–Mar	E	1·25–1·5	4–5	O	Tr
Olearia haastii	W		July–Aug	E	1·25–1·5	4–5	O	Tr
,, scilloniensis	W		May	E Gr	1·25–1·5	4–5	O D	Tr
Osmanthus delavayi	W		Mar–Apr	E	2–2·5	6–8	O	Tr
Passiflora coerulea	B W		June–Sept	D	climbing		O	H
Paeonia suffruticosa	P R Pl		May–June	D	1–1·25	3–4	O	
Pernettya mucronata	W W P R Pl M		May–June	E	1–1·25	3–4	A	
Perowskia	B		Aug–Sept	D	1–1·25	3–4	O D	H
Philadelphus	W W & Pl		June–July	D	1–4·5	3–15	O	F
Phlomis	Y		June–July	E Gr	1	3	O D	Th
Pieris	W		Mar–May	E	2–2·5	6–8	A	
Polygonum baldschuanicum	W		July–Oct	D	climbing		O	Th
Potentilla fruticosa	W Y O		June–Sept	D	0·6–1·25	2–4	O D	H or Th
Pyracantha	W	R Y O	June	E	2–2·5	6–8	O	S
Rhododendron	all		Mar–July	E	0·3–6	1–20	A	D
Rhus cotinus: see Cotinus								
Ribes sanguineum	P R C		Mar–Apr	D	2·5	8	O	F
Romneya	W & Y		July–Oct	D Gr	2	6	O D	H
Rosmarinus (rosemary)	B		Apr–May	E	0·3	1·5	O D	Tr
Rubus tridel	W		May–June	D	1·5–2·25	5–7	O	F
Santolina incana	Y		July–Aug	E Gr	0·6	2	O D	Tr (March)
Senecio laxifolius	Y		June–July	E Gr	1	3	O D	Th
Skimmia japonica	W	R	Mar–Apr	E	1	3	A	
Solanum crispum	B & Y		July–Sept	D	climbing		O D	Th
Sorbaria aitchisonii	W		July–Aug	D	2–3	6–10	O	H or Th
Spartium junceum	Y		July–Aug	D	2–2·5	6–8	O D	Tr
Spiraea Anthony Waterer	C		June–Aug	D	1	3	O	H
,, arguta	W		April	D	1·25	4	O	Tr
,, menziesii	P		July–Aug	D	1·5	5	O	H
,, van houttei	W		May	D	2–2·5	6–8	O	F
Symphoricarpos albus	W	W	Sept–Nov	D	2	6	O	Tr (March)
Syringa (lilac)	W M Pl		May–June	D	2–4	6–13	O L	D
Tamarix pentandra	P		July–Aug	D	1·5–3	5–10	O D	H
Viburnum bodnantense	P		Nov–Apr	D	2–2·5	6–8	O L	
,, carlesii	W		Apr–May	D	1·5	5	O L	
,, opulus sterile	W		May–June	D	2·5–3	8	O L	
,, ,, compactum	W	R	May–June	D	1	3	O L	
,, tinus	W & P		Nov–Apr	E	2·5–3	8–10	O L	Tr
,, tomentosum mariesii	W		May	D	2–2·5	6–8	O L	
,, ,, plicatum	W		May	D	2–2·5	6–8	O L	
Vitis coignetiae				D Ac	climbing		O	
,, quinquefolia				D Ac	climbing		O	
,, veitchii (inconstans)				D Ac	climbing		O	
,, vinifera purpurea		Pl		D Ac	climbing		O L	
Weigela	P R		May–June	D	2	6	O	F
Wistaria	M B W P		May–June	D	climbing		O	S
Yucca filamentosa	W		July–Aug	E	1	3	O D	

78

Clematis montana rubens

Popular Names of Shrubs and Climbers

Barberry = Berberis
Bachelor's Buttons = Kerria
Beauty Bush = Kolkwitzia
Blue Spiraea = Caryopteris
Broom = Cytisus, Genista, and Spartium
Calico Bush = Kalmia
Californian Tree Poppy = Romneya
Daisy Bush = Olearia
Dogwood = Cornus
Elder = Sambucus
Flowering Currant = Ribes
Golden Bells = Forsythia
Heather = Calluna, Daboecia, and Erica
Himalayan Honeysuckle = Leycesteria
Honeysuckle = Lonicera
Ivy = Hedera
Japanese Quince = Chaenomeles
Jasmine = Jasminum
Jerusalem Sage = Phlomis
Jew's Mallow = Kerria
Lavender = Lavandula
Lavender Cotton = Santolina
Laurustinus = Viburnum tinus

Lilac = Syringa
Mexican Orange Blossom = Choisya
Mock Orange = Philadelphus
Mountain Laurel = Kalmia
Oleaster = Elaeagnus
Passion Flower = Passiflora
Rock Rose = Cistus
Rose of Sharon = Hypericum
Rosemary = Rosmarinus
Russian Vine = Polygonum
St. John's Wort = Hypericum
Shrubby Cinquefoil = Potentilla
Silk Tassel Bush = Garrya
Smoke Tree = Cotinus
Snowball Tree = Viburnum
Snowberry = Symphoricarpos
Spindle Tree = Euonymus
Tree Mallow = Hibiscus
Tree Peony = Paeonia
Veronica = Hebe
Vine = Vitis
Wig Tree = Cotinus
Witch Hazel = Hamamelis

Lilacs

9 Trees

With the possible exception of the house itself, trees are often the tallest objects in or around a garden. Because of this they can play a dominating role in design, besides providing much of the shade and shelter that a garden requires. Columnar, or fastigiate, trees make a particularly dramatic effect and so do trees of very distinctive outline or colour, such as the flat topped Lebanon cedar, the weeping willow, blue spruce, copper beech, and purple Norway maple. All these need to be used with restraint and sited with care. Too many can destroy the effect of contrast or surprise which they can create so well when properly used.

All that has been said about the different types of shrub (evergreen and deciduous, coniferous and broad leaved) applies equally to trees. So do the recommendations about soil preparation, planting, and feeding and the advice to keep a good area of clear soil around each tree for some years, even if eventually the intention is to allow grass to grow to its base. It is also very important to stake young trees securely, for if they are rocked by wind their roots will be disturbed, or possibly broken, and they will be greatly checked or killed. Stakes should be strong and sufficiently long to be driven 45 cm (18 in.) into the ground and extend right up the main trunk of the tree. The stake should be driven into the centre of the planting hole before the tree is placed in it, then the tree can be secured to the stake before the soil is replaced around its roots. This prevents damage to the branches when driving in the stake and possible damage to the roots, which cannot be seen after planting; it also leaves the planter two hands free to return the soil. Special plastic tree ties are excellent since they do not chafe the bark readily. If strong twine is used a piece of sacking or rubber should be wrapped around the trunk, where the tie comes, to prevent damage. In any case ties should be examined at least once a year to make sure that they are still in good condition and are not cutting into the bark.

Most trees can be pruned but it needs to be done with great care if their natural habit and beauty are not to be destroyed. A good general rule is always to cut back to a fork, i.e. to a point where there is already a branch or stem that can approximately take the place and maintain the balance of the one that is being removed. November to March is the best period for pruning most trees.

It pays to spread manure, or a manure substitute, or peat with which some bone meal and hoof and horn meal has been mixed, for several feet round each tree each spring for some years after planting. Young trees need feeding and a surface mulch of this kind also helps to retain moisture in the soil.

SOME SPECIAL TREES

Acer (Maple). The Japanese maples, varieties of Acer palmatum, are very small deciduous trees, some little more than large shrubs, with deeply lobed leaves, cut into fern-like divisions in some varieties, purple in others. Almost all colour brilliantly before they fall in the autumn. They enjoy good well-drained soil and do specially well in light shade. A. negundo variegatum has light green and white leaves and grows about 6 metres (20 ft) high. It does well in town gardens. Most other maples are too large and too quick growing for any but large gardens, but A. platanoides Goldsworth Purple has shining purple leaves and is a fast growing tree, useful where this colour is required. The snake bark maples, of which A. grosseri and A. pensylvanicum are good examples, have green bark striped with light green and only grow 6–7 m (20–25 ft) high.

Cypress. These are evergreen conifers. There are many different kinds and varieties, some known as cupressus, some as chamaecyparis and one as cupressocyparis, but all have similar requirements. The Lawson Cypress, Chamaecyparis lawsoniana, is one of the most useful because of its numerous varieties, some light green, some blue-grey, some golden. All make fine conical trees clothed with branches to the base, but some are much narrower than others. Columnaris glauca, blue-green; pottenii, grey-green; ellwoodii, blue-grey; and erecta viridis, light green, are especially recommended as columnar forms. They are very suitable for small gardens.

The Leyland cypress, Cupressocyparis leylandii, is one of the fastest growing of all trees, adding 1 m (3 ft) or more each year and rapidly making a dark green column, 12–15 m (40–50 ft) high and 3–3·5 m (10–12 ft) through. The Arizona cypress, Cupressus arizonica conica (or pyramidalis), makes a narrow blue-grey column eventually 7–9 m (25–30 ft) high and 2 m (6–7 ft) through.

All these are quite hardy but the Monterey cypress, Cupressus macrocarpa, is not and is liable to be killed by frost or cold winds, even after years, except in mild or coastal districts. It is very fast growing.

Magnolia. There are a number of tree-like kinds, all deciduous except Magnolia grandiflora, which is rather too tender to be grown in the open and so is often trained like a climber against a sunny wall. It has large shining, laurel-like leaves and white bowl-shaped flowers produced a few at a time from July to September.

Magnolia soulangeana grows to about 6 m (20 ft), is wide spreading, and has large white, purple tinted

81

(top) Upright Cherry Ama-no-Gawa
(centre) Laburnum
(below) Flowering Almond

or all purple flowers in May. M. kobus is 4·5–6 m (15–20 ft) high, more erect in growth and has smaller but numerous flowers in April. M. sieboldiana is 3·5 m (12 ft) high and has hanging, cup-shaped, sweet scented, white flowers with a central boss of crimson stamens, produced from late May to July. All enjoy rather rich soil, preferably lime free for M. soulangeana and M. sieboldii, but M. kobus does not mind lime.

Malus (Crab Apple). These are among the showiest of flowering trees. All are deciduous, flower in April or May, and can be pruned in autumn or winter. Malus floribunda, rosy red and white, 5–6 m (16–20 ft), is one of the earliest, closely followed by M. lemoinei, purplish crimson, 6–7 m (20–25 ft). There are several others rather similar. Dartmouth Crab, Golden Hornet, and John Downie have white flowers followed by decorative crab apples, respectively red, yellow, and yellow flushed red. The fruits can be used to make jelly.

Prunus. The largest group of flowering trees which includes the ornamental almonds, peaches, cherries, bird cherry, and plums. All are deciduous. The almonds, Prunus communis (or amygdalus) and P. pollardii, have single pale pink flowers in March–April and grow about 6 m (20 ft) high. There are two good ornamental peaches, both bearing double flowers in April: Aurora, white to 6 m (20 ft) and Clara Meyer, deep pink to 4·5 m (15 ft). All these prefer rather warm, sheltered places and good well-drained soils.

The cherries are extremely numerous and varied, with single or double, white, greenish yellow or pink flowers, mostly in April–May. Some, such as Ama-no-gawa, are small and narrowly erect; others such as Kanzan, Pink Perfection, Sargentii, Tai-haku, and Ukon, are about as broad as high, eventually about 7 m (25 ft); yet others, such as Shirofugen and Shimidsu Sakara, are wide spreading. Cheal's Weeping is a small tree with small pink flowers and Prunus subhirtella autumnalis a tree of normal branching habit with small pink or near white flowers from November to March. There are many more and all will grow in any reasonably good soil and fairly light place. The bird cherries, varieties of P. padus, make large trees 9 m (30 ft) or more high with slender trails of white flowers in May–June. They are easily grown in sun or shade, but only suitable for large gardens.

The best ornamental plums are Prunus blireana, 1·6–6 m (16–20 ft) with coppery leaves and double pink flowers in March and

Special plastic tree ties are recommended. If twine is used, sacking or rubber should be wrapped around the stem to prevent chafing. Use sharp secateurs and a narrow pruning saw for pruning and paint all wounds with a good tree wound dressing.

82

P. cerasifera nigra or P. pissardii, 6–7 m (20–25 ft) with purple leaves and small pink flowers in February–March.

In general these various kinds of prunus do not like much pruning and when branches must be removed or shortened it is best done in spring or early summer immediately after flowering.

Robinia (False Acacia, Locust Tree, Rose Acacia). Deciduous trees with light elegant foliage. The false acacia or locust tree, Robinia pseudacacia, grows rapidly to 12–15 m (40–50 ft) and has trails of white flowers in June. It has a narrow column-forming variety, Fastigiata, and a golden leaved variety, Frisia, which is slower growing and very distinctive. All will grow in any soil and in sun or shade. The rose acacia, R. hispida, is only about 2·5 m (8 ft) high, little more than a shrub, has rose-pink flowers in June but needs a warm sunny place and well-drained soil.

Sorbus (Mountain Ash, Rowan, Whitebeam). Deciduous trees grown for their foliage and some kinds also for their fruits. The mountain ash, Sorbus aucuparia, is 6–8 m (20–25 ft) high, has elegant divided leaves, white flowers in June, and orange-scarlet berries. S. hupehensis and S. vilmorinii have white or pink berries and S. scopulina grows stiffly erect and has fine scarlet fruits. S. aria, the whitebeam, is 9–10 m (30–35 ft) high and is grown for its leaves, light green above and white below. It likes chalk soils.

(top) Malus eleyi
(centre) Magnolia soulangiana
(below) Acer palmatum

Japanese Cherry Kanzan

Quick-reference Table of Trees

ABBREVIATIONS

D deciduous; *E* evergreen.

Botanical name	Popular name	Type	Height m	ft	Special beauty
Acer grosseri and A. pensylvanicum	Snake Bark Maple	D	6–7	*20–25*	Green striped bark, autumn colour
,, negundo variegatum	Variegated Maple	D	6	*20*	Green and white leaves
,, palmatum	Japanese Maple	D	2–3·5	*6–12*	Graceful leaves, autumn colour
,, platanoides Goldsworth Purple	Purple Norway Maple	D	9–12	*30–40*	Purple foliage
Aesculus carnea	Pink Horse Chestnut	D	9–12	*30–40*	Pink flowers in May
,, briotii	Red Horse Chestnut	D	9–12	*30–40*	Red flowers in May
,, hippocastanum	White Horse Chestnut	D	12–18	*40–60*	White flowers in May
,, indica	Indian Horse Chestnut	D	12–18	*40–60*	Pink flowers in June
Ailanthus glandulosa	Tree of Heaven	D	12–18	*40–60*	Elegant compound leaves
Amelanchier canadensis	Snowy Mespilus	D	6–7	*20–25*	Small white flowers in May, autumn colour
Aralia chinensis	Chinese Angelica Tree	D	3·5–6	*12–20*	Elegant compound leaves
Betula papyrifera	Paper Birch	D	6–9	*20–30*	White bark
,, pendula youngii	Young's Weeping Birch	D	3·5–5	*12–16*	Pendulous branches
Catalpa bignonioides	Indian Bean Tree	D	6–9	*20–30*	White flowers in July–Aug
,, ,, aurea	,, ,, ,,	D	5–6	*16–20*	Large golden leaves
Cedrus atlantica glauca	Blue Atlas Cedar	E	18–30	*60–80*	Blue-grey foliage
,, deodara	Deodar	E	15–18	*50–60*	Pendulous branchlets
,, libani	Cedar of Lebanon	E	15–18	*50–60*	Dark leaves, horizontal branches
Cercis siliquastrum	Judas Tree	D	3·5–5	*12–16*	Purple flowers in May–June
Chamaecyparis lawsoniana columnaris glauca	Variety of Lawson Cypress	E	5–6	*16–20*	Dark green column
Chamaecyparis lawsoniana ellwoodii	Variety of Lawson Cypress	E	5–6	*16–20*	Blue-grey column
Chamaecyparis lawsoniana erecta viridis	Variety of Lawson Cypress	E	6–9	*20–30*	Bright green column
Chamaecyparis lawsoniana pottenii	Variety of Lawson Cypress	E	5–6	*16–20*	Grey-green column
Cornus kousa chinensis	Chinese Dogwood	D	3·5–5	*12–16*	White flowers in June
,, mas	Cornelian Cherry	D	3·5–5	*12–16*	Small yellow flowers in Feb–Mar
Crataegus carrierei	Thorn	D	5–6	*16–20*	White flowers, scarlet berries
,, oxycantha coccinea plena	Paul's Double Scarlet Thorn	D	5–6	*16–20*	Scarlet flowers in May
,, ,, rosea plena	Double Pink Thorn	D	5–6	*16–20*	Pink flowers in May
,, prunifolia	Thorn	D	5–6	*16–20*	White flowers, scarlet berries
Cryptomeria japonica elegans		E	5–6	*16–20*	Feathery green and russet foliage
Cupressocyparis leylandii	Leyland Cypress	E	12–15	*40–50*	Fast growing green column
Cupressus arizonica pyramidalis	Arizona Cypress	E	7–9	*25–30*	Blue-grey column
Fagus sylvatica cuprea	Copper Beech	D	12–18	*40–60*	Copper leaves
,, ,, fastigiata	Dawyck Beech	D	9–12	*30–40*	Green column
,, ,, purpurea	Purple Beech	D	12–18	*40–60*	Purple leaves
Gingko biloba	Maidenhair Tree	D	9–15	*30–50*	Elegant green leaves
Gleditschia Sunburst	Golden Honey Locust	D	5–6	*16–20*	Ferny golden leaves

84

Botanical name	Popular name	Type	Height m	ft	Special beauty
Juniperus communis hibernica	Irish Juniper	E	3–3·5	10–12	Grey-blue column
Laburnum alpinum	Laburnum	D	5–6	16–20	Yellow flowers in June
,, vossii	,,	D	5–6	16–20	Yellow flowers in May–June
Libocedrus decurrens	Incense Cedar	E	12–18	40–66	Tall green column
Liquidambar styraciflua	Sweet Gum	D	9–15	30–50	Rich autumn colour
Magnolia grandiflora	Laurel Magnolia	E	6–9	20–30	White flowers July–Sept
,, kobus		D	5–6	16–20	White flowers in April
,, sieboldiana		D	3·5–5	12–16	White and crimson flower in June–July
,, soulangeana		D	6	20	White or purplish flowers in May
Malus floribunda	Japanese Crab	D	5–6	16–20	Pink and white flowers in Apr–May
,, lemoinei	Red Crab	D	6–7	20–25	Crimson flowers in May
,, pumila (several varieties)	Crab Apple	D	6–7	20–25	White flowers and coloured fruits
Metasequoia glypto-stroboides	Dawn Redwood	D	12–18	40–60	Ferny foliage, autumn colour
Picea omorika	Siberian Spruce	E	12–18	40–60	Narrow Christmas tree
,, pungens glauca	Blue Spruce	E	9	30	Blue-grey foliage
Populus alba pyramidalis	Columnar White Poplar	D	12–18	40–60	Silvery white column
,, nigra italica	Lombardy Poplar	D	12–18	40–60	Green column
Prunus blireana		D	5–6	16–20	Pink flowers, copper leaves
,, cerasifera nigra	Purple-leaved Plum	D	6–7	20–25	White flowers, purple leaves
,, communis	Almond	D	6	20	Pink flowers in Mar–Apr
,, padus	Bird Cherry	D	9	30	White flowers in May–June
,, persica (several varieties)	Peach	D	5–6	16–20	Pink or white flowers in April
,, serrula		D	6	20	Polished red bark
,, serrulata (many varieties)	Japanese Cherry	D	3–7	10–25	White, lemon or pink flowers in Apr–May. Trees of many shapes
,, subhirtella autumnalis	Autumn Cherry	D	5–6	16–20	Pink flowers in Nov–Mar
Pyrus salicifolia	Willow-leaved Pear	D	5–6	16–20	Silver leaves, weeping
Quercus coccinea	Scarlet Oak	D	12–18	40–60	Autumn colour
,, robur fastigiata	Fastigiate Oak	D	6–9	20–30	Green column
Robinia hispida	Rose Acacia	D	2–2·5	6–8	Pink flowers in June
,, pseudoacacia frisia	Golden False Acacia	D	9–12	30–40	Golden ferny foliage
,, ,, inermis	Mop-headed False Acacia	D	4·5–6	15–20	Round head of ferny leaves
,, ,, pyramidalis	Fastigiate False Acacia	D	12–15	40–50	Column of ferny foliage
Salix alba tristis	Golden Weeping Willow	D	12–15	40–50	Golden young stems, weeping habit
Sorbus aria	Whitebeam	D	9–10	30–35	Leaves white below
,, aucuparia	Mountain Ash, Rowan	D	7–9	25–30	White flowers, scarlet berries
,, hupehensis		D	7–9	25–30	White flowers, white berries
,, scopulina		D	7–9	25–30	White flowers, scarlet berries
,, vilmorinei		D	7–9	25–30	White flowers, pink berries
Tilia platyphyllos rubra	Red-twigged Lime	D	18–24	60–80	Suitable for pleaching
Taxodium distichum	Swamp Cypress	D	12–15	40–50	Ferny leaves, autumn colour
Taxus baccata fastigiata	Irish Yew	E	3–5	12–16	Dark green column
,, ,, ,, aurea	Golden Irish Yew	E	2·5–3	8–10	Golden column

10 Rock and Water Features

Most rock plants are both small and permanent. They are little shrubs, hardy plants or bulbs that have adapted themselves to live in stony places, and because of their small size it is possible to grow a lot of them in quite a limited space. They can be planted in rock gardens, but equally well many of them can be grown in raised beds, double walls with a core of soil between, or in stone troughs.

A well made rock garden can be an attractive feature in itself, quite apart from the plants with which it is stocked. Any stone can be used, but rather porous stones, such as limestone and sandstone, are the most suitable. Rock gardens can be made on banks, on ground thrown into irregular mounds, or on completely flat ground. The position should be reasonably open, since many rock plants like sun. It should not be overhung with trees, because falling leaves in autumn may smother and kill many plants.

Wherever rock gardens are made each rock should be laid on its broadest side, not cocked up on end like a tombstone, and should be well buried into the soil. It is wise to give each rock a slight backward and downward slope so that water, falling on to it, flows backwards into the soil and is not shot off forwards, as from a roof. If the same angle of inclination is followed throughout a construction it will give it unity and a feeling of cohesion. The effect to be aimed at is of a natural outcrop of stratified rock such as can be seen on many hillsides.

The rocks should be set to form level terraces or pockets of irregular breadth and outline. Steep slopes of soil should be avoided because rain will rush down them and wash the surface soil away.

Many rock plants will grow well in ordinary garden soil, but some are more exacting, so it will be wise to decide what plants are going to be grown before making the rock garden and prepare the soil accordingly. In any case there is much to be said for adding peat and coarse sand or grit quite generously to the existing soil as most rock plants grow best in a soil that, while not being dry, permits free passage for surplus water.

Raised beds are made by building stone or brick walls around a rectangle of any convenient size and to a height of 60–90 cm (2–3 ft). No mortar is used but soil is rammed between the stones and the bed is filled level with soil or a mixture of soil, peat, and sand or grit. Rock plants are then grown on top of the bed and also in the wall crevices.

Double walls are really narrow raised beds. They are built in exactly the same way and the inner faces of the two walls should be at least 30 cm (1 ft) apart so that there is a good core of soil between them into which plants can root and feed. Both raised beds and double walls will require liberal watering in hot weather.

Stone troughs for rock plants must have drainage holes so that surplus water can escape. They are filled with a similar soil mixture, a few small stones are half buried in the surface, and small rock plants are planted around them. Troughs must also be well watered in summer. It is best to stand them on stones or bricks

so that they are raised above the ground, otherwise drainage holes may become blocked. Troughs make excellent showpieces for terraces and patios. Some small creeping rock plants can also be grown in the crevices between the paving slabs in such places.

Yet another way to grow some rock plants is in peat beds or walls. These are constructed in very much the same way as rock gardens or double walls, but blocks of peat are used instead of rock. The kind of peat blocks sold as fuel will do well. If the space retained by the blocks is then filled with a mixture of peat and sand many plants that like rather acid soil conditions can be grown. It is often best to make peat beds in a moderately shady place since this is what many of these acid soil plants enjoy.

Rock plants are usually sold in pots or other small containers from which they can be planted at almost any time of the year. Small plants are best for planting in crevices between rocks, or they may be built into place as the rock garden or wall is made.

Many rock plants can be readily raised from seed sown in a cool greenhouse or frame in March–April or outdoors in May–June. Many can also be increased by division in spring or immediately after flowering, and shrubby kinds also by cuttings in a propagating box or frame in summer.

Water can be used in conjunction with a rock garden or separately as a feature on its own. If the former a pool of irregular outline is best, since a rock garden is essentially an informal feature. Rectangular, circular or oval pools are more appropriate in rose gardens or formal bedding schemes or entirely on their own in paving or mown grass.

Pools can be lined with concrete, or with plastic or rubber sheets, or they can be purchased ready made in fibre glass, in which case it is only necessary to dig a hole of the correct size to contain the pool. If concrete is used it should be prepared with a waterproofing compound and be at least 10 cm (4 in.) thick. The edges of all pools can be camouflaged with turf, rock or flagstones and if plastic sheeting is used these will help to secure it in place.

If water lilies are to be grown pools should be at least 30 cm (1 ft) deep as there are only a few

(top) Aubrieta, Dianthus, and Cytisus kewensis

(centre) Helianthemums

(right) Erythroniums, miniature Narcissi, Crocuses, Iris reticulata, and Anemone blanda

Large blocks of stone can be levered into position. Place stones to form natural looking outcrops with fairly level shelves of soil for plants. Construct rock gardens and dry walls (centre) so that plants can root freely down into the soil below.

kinds which will thrive in shallower water. However, many aquatic plants prefer shallow water, so it is a good plan to make pools with a ledge around the edge so that some plants can be grown with no more than 5–8 cm (2–3 in.) of water over their roots.

If water is required primarily for the delightful reflections it can give, and for its smooth gleaming surface, it may be better to have no plants at all and in this case the pool need be no more than 15 cm (6 in.) deep. The water can then be treated chemically to keep it clear or it can be changed frequently, neither of which is desirable if plants are being grown.

Moving water can be as delightful as still water, bringing a constantly changing play of light and many pleasant sounds. Fountains, streams, and cascades are all quite easily installed. Small electrically operated pumps are available to circulate the water in the pool and some of these can simply be submerged in the pool and attached direct to the fountain or to a plastic pipe taking the water to the head of the stream or cascade. Water may be fed direct from the mains or a reservoir and allowed to flow away, but this is not desirable if there are plants or fish because of the constant change of temperature, the removal of food, and the chemical treatment of much mains water.

Water plants are often most conveniently grown in plastic baskets made specially for the purpose. The baskets are partly filled with good garden soil to

Pools can be lined with plastic sheets which will last for years. Stones or slabs can be used to hold the sheet in place. Water plants can be grown in plastic buckets and a pump to operate a fountain and cascade can also be placed in the pool.

which a sprinkling of bone meal has been added. The plants are then placed in position, one in each basket, more soil is put around and just over them, and the basket is then sunk in the pool where it is required. Baskets can be raised on bricks to bring plants to the best level for each kind.

Some plants float in the water and do not root into soil at all. Some of these are valuable because they help to keep the water fresh and provide cover for fish. They can simply be dropped into the pool or a small stone can be tied to the bottom of each piece to sink it in position. They are known as oxygenating plants because of the oxygen they give off and they are essential in a pool in which fish are to be kept. However, some kinds, especially Elodea, can increase rapidly and may have to be pulled or raked out if they take up too much room.

There are also weeds that establish themselves in water, one of the most troublesome being blanket weed. This is a form of alga, related to the green scum that forms on the surface of still water and on wet surfaces. It can clog a pool with dense masses of growth like green cotton wool and is likely to be most troublesome in warm weather and in pools fully exposed to strong sunshine. The best preventives are to keep pools well stocked with fish, which eat the weed, and to provide moderate shade from the hottest sun. If blanket weed does appear it should be immediately raked out. Both green scum and blanket weed can be killed with copper sulphate at about 25 grammes for every 5,000 litres (1 oz per 1,000 gallons) of water, but this is a remedy best confined to pools containing neither fish nor plants.

If mains electricity is installed near a pool to operate a pump, water heater, or lamps it is essential that all fittings, plugs, etc., are fully waterproof. Water has a most insidious way of penetrating where it is not wanted and can short-circuit electricity with disastrous results. Installations should be made by professionals with experience of this type of work.

A charming small water garden

Quick-reference Table of Rock Plants

ABBREVIATIONS

Type   *Tft* tufted; *Bsh* bush; *Ert* erect; *Mt* mat forming; *Tr* trailing; *Rst* rosette; *Csh* cushion.
Place *Lv* level pockets or shelves; *Vc* vertical crevices or walls; *Pv* paving or flat crevices.
       * Dislikes lime.
       † Readily raised from seed.

Name	Type	Place	Special beauty	Season
Acaena	Mt	Pv Lv	Small green or grey leaves	all year
Acantholimum	Csh	Lv	Narrow leaved hummocks, pink flowers	July–Aug
Achillea ageratifolia	Mt	Lv	Grey leaves, white flowers	May–June
,, tomentosum	Mt	Lv	Yellow flowers	May–June
†Aethionema	Bsh	Vc	Pink flowers	May–June
Ajuga reptans	Mt	Lv Pv	Coloured leaves, purple flowers	May–June
†Alyssum saxatile	Tft	Lv Vc	Yellow flowers, grey leaves	Apr–June
Androsace	Csh	Lv Vc	Pink flowers, grey leaves	June–July
Antennaria dioica	Mt	Lv Pv	Silvery leaves, pink flowers	May–June
†Arabis	Tr	Lv Vc	White or pink flowers, grey leaves	Mar–May
Arenaria balearica	Mt	Lv Pv	Tiny green leaves and white flowers	all year
†Armeria maritima	Csh	Vc Pv	Pink flowers, grassy leaves	May–June
†Aubrieta	Tr	Lv Vc	Purple, lavender, pink or crimson flowers	Mar–June
†Campanula carpatica	Tft	Lv	Lavender or white flowers	July–Aug
† ,, garganica	Tr	Lv Pv	Violet-blue flowers	June–July
† ,, muralis	Tr	Lv Vc	Violet-blue flowers	June–July
† ,, pusilla	Tft	Lv Pv	Blue or white flowers	June–July
Cheiranthus Harper Crewe	Bsh	Lv Vc	Double yellow flowers	Mar–May
,, Moonlight	Bsh	Lv Vc	Lemon-yellow flowers	Apr–June
Convolvulus cneorum	Bsh	Lv Vc	Silver leaves, white flowers	May–June
Cotyledon simplicifolia	Rst	Vc	Yellow flowers	July–Aug
†Dianthus alpinus	Tft	Lv Vc	Rose-pink flowers	May–June
† ,, caesius	Tft	Lv Vc	Pale pink flowers, grey leaves	May–June
† ,, deltoides	Tr	Vc Pv	Pink or carmine flowers	July–Aug
† ,, neglectus	Csh	Lv	Rose and buff flowers	June–Aug
Dryas octopetala	Mt	Lv	White flowers, evergreen leaves	May–June
†Erinus alpinus	Tft	Vc Pv	Soft purple flowers	Apr–June
Erodium corsicum	Mt	Lv Pv	Grey leaves, pink flowers	May–Oct
,, reichardii roseum	Mt	Lv Pv	Green leaves, pink flowers	May–Oct
†Gentiana acaulis	Mt	Lv	Deep blue trumpet flowers	Apr–June
† ,, asclepiadea	Ert	Lv	Sprays of deep blue trumpets	June–Sept
† ,, lagodechiana	Tr	Lv	Deep blue flowers	July–Sept
*† ,, sino-ornata	Tr	Lv	Bright blue flowers	Aug–Nov
† ,, verna	Tft	Lv	Brilliant blue flowers	Apr–May
Geranium sanguineum	Mt	Lv Pv	Magenta or pink flowers	June–Sept
,, subcaulescens	Tft	Lv	Carmine flowers	May–July
†Gypsophila repens	Tr	Lv Vc	Grey leaves, pink or white flowers	May–July
†Helianthemum	Bsh	Lv Vc	White, yellow, orange, pink, scarlet or crimson flowers, grey or green leaves	May–June
†Hypericum coris	Tft	Lv Vc	Yellow flowers	June–Aug
† ,, olympicum	Tft	Lv	Yellow flowers	June–July
† ,, polyphyllum	Mt	Lv Pv	Yellow flowers	July–Sept
† ,, repens	Mt	Lv Pv	Yellow flowers	July–Sept
†Iberis gibraltarica	Bsh	Lv Vc	Lilac flowers	May–July
† ,, saxatilis	Bsh	Lv Vc	White flowers	May–June
† ,, sempervirens	Bsh	Lv Vc	White flowers	May–June

Name	Type	Place	Special beauty	Season
†Leontopodium alpinum	Mt	Vc	Grey woolly leaves, white flowers	June–July
Lewisia	Rst	Vc	Fleshy leaves, pink, salmon or apricot flowers	May–June
Linaria aequitriloba	Mt	Pv	Tiny leaves, purple flowers	June
† ,, alpina	Tft	Lv Pv	Purple or shrimp-pink flowers	June–Sept
Linum arboreum	Bsh	Lv Vc	Yellow flowers, evergreen leaves	June–Sept
,, flavum	Bsh	Lv Vc	Yellow flowers	June–Sept
† ,, narbonnense	Ert	Lv	Blue flowers	June–Sept
† ,, perenne	Ert	Lv	Sky blue flowers	June–Sept
,, salsoloides	Ert	Lv	Pearl white flowers	June–July
*Lithospermum diffusum	Tr	Lv Vc	Bright blue flowers	May–June
Morisia hypogea	Rst	Lv Vc	Green rosettes, yellow flowers	May–June
Omphalodes cappadocica	Mt	Lv	Sky blue flowers	Apr–May
Onosma tauricum	Tft	Vc	Yellow flowers, grey leaves	May–June
Oxalis adenophylla	Csh	Lv	Grey-green leaves, pink flowers	May–June
,, enneaphylla	Csh	Lv	Grey-green leaves, white flowers	May–June
Penstemon rupicola	Mt	Lv Pv	Crimson flowers	June–July
,, scouleri	Bsh	Lv Vc	Lavender flowers	Apr–July
Phlox subulata	Mt	Lv Vc	White, pink, carmine or mauve flowers	May–June
Polygonum affine	Mt	Lv Vc	Rose-red flowers	Aug–Oct
,, vaccinifolium	Mt	Lv Vc	Pink flowers	Aug–Oct
Potentilla nitida	Mt	Lv Pv	Pink flowers	May–June
,, tonguei	Mt	Lv Pv	Apricot flowers	June–Sept
,, verna	Mt	Lv Pv	Yellow flowers	May–June
†Primula denticulata	Ert	Lv	Lavender, pink or white flowers	Mar–May
,, juliae	Mt	Lv	Magenta flowers	Mar–Apr
,, juliana	Ert	Lv	Ruby to purple flowers	Mar–Apr
,, marginata	Rst	Lv Vc	Lavender-blue flowers, grey-green leaves	Apr–May
,, pubescens	Rst	Lv Vc	Leathery leaves, white to crimson flowers	Mar–May
Ramonda myconi	Rst	Vc	Leathery leaves, lavender or white flowers	May–June
Raoulia australis	Mt	Lv Pv	Tiny silvery leaves	all year
†Saponaria ocymoides	Tr	Lv Vc	Rose-pink flowers	June–Aug
†Saxifraga aizoon	Rst	Lv	Silver edged leaves, white, pink or yellow flowers	June–July
† ,, apiculata	Csh	Lv	Close hummocks studded with yellow flowers	Mar–Apr
† ,, burseriana	Csh	Lv	Close hummocks, white flowers	Mar–Apr
† ,, cochlearis	Csh	Lv Vc	Silvery hummocks, white flowers	June–July
† ,, cotyledon	Rst	Lv Vc	Silver edged leaves, white or crimson spotted flowers	May–June
,, elizabethae	Csh	Lv	Close hummocks, yellow flowers	Mar–Apr
† ,, griesbachii	Rst	Lv Vc	Silver leaves, crimson flower spikes	Mar–Apr
,, jenkinsae	Csh	Lv	Close hummocks, pink flowers	Mar–Apr
,, (mossy varieties)	Mt	Lv	Soft green foliage, white, pink or red flowers	Apr–May
,, oppositifolia	Mt	Lv Pv	Purple flowers	Mar–May
,, umbrosa	Rst	Lv Vc	Large green rosettes, pink flowers	June–July
Sedum cauticola	Ert	Lv	Grey leaves, purple flowers	Sept–Oct
,, hispanicum	Mt	Lv Pv	Small blue-grey leaves	all year
,, spathulifolium	Mt	Lv	Fleshy grey or purplish leaves, yellow flowers	all year
,, spurium	Mt	Lv Pv	Green leaves, pink or purple flowers	Sept–Oct
†Sempervivum arach-noideum	Rst	Lv Vc	Cobweb-like filaments over fleshy rosettes	all year
† ,, calcareum	Rst	Lv Vc	Fleshy green, purple tipped rosettes	all year
† ,, tectorum	Rst	Lv Vc	Large, fleshy green rosettes	all year
Silene acaulis	Csh	Lv	Small pink flowers	Apr–June
,, alpestris	Csh	Lv	Single or double white flowers	May–June
† ,, schafta	Tft	Lv	Carmine flowers	June–Oct
†Thymus serpyllum	Mt	Lv Pv	Tiny, fragrant leaves, purple or white flowers	June–Aug

Name	Type	Place	Special beauty	Season
Veronica cataractae	Bsh	Lv Vc	White flowers	June–Sept
,, prostrata (rupestris)	Mt	Lv Pv	Blue or pink flowers	June–July
†Viola cornuta	Tr	Lv	White or blue or purple flowers	Apr–Aug
,, gracilis	Tr	Lv	Purple or yellow flowers	Apr–Aug

Quick-reference Table of Water and Bog Plants

ABBREVIATIONS

Colour   *W* white; *Y* yellow; *O* orange; *R* red; *C* crimson; *P* pink; *B* blue; *G* green; *Br* brown.

Place   *Dw* deep water, i.e. 30–60 cm (1–2 ft); *Sw* shallow water, 8–30 cm (3–12 in.); *M* marginal, 2–7 cm (1–3 in.) of water; *B* bog, wet ground not covered with water.

*Readily raised from seed.

Botanical name	Popular name	Colour	Season	Place	Special features
Aponogeton	Water Hawthorn	W	Apr–Oct	Sw Dw	Floating leaves, scented flowers
Butomus	Flowering Rush	P	July–Sept	M	Reed-like leaves
Calla palustris	Bog Arum	W & G	June	B	Like a small arum lily
Caltha	King-cup, Marsh Marigold	Y	Apr–May	B	Large buttercup-like flowers
Iris kaempferi	Japanese Iris	W–Pl	June–July	B	Very showy flowers
,, laevigata	Water Iris	W–Pl	June–July	M B	Very showy flowers
,, pseudacorus	Yellow Flag	Y	May–July	M B	Too vigorous for small gardens
Lysichitum	Skunk Cabbage	Y W	Apr–May	M B	Large arum-like flowers
Menyanthes	Bog Bean	W & P	May–July	Sw	Floating leaves
*Mimulus	Musk, Monkey Flower	Y & R	July–Sept	B	Pouched, spotted flowers
Nymphaea	Water Lily	W Y P C	July–Sept	Sw Dw	Many different varieties
Pontederia	Pickerel Weed	B	July–Sept	M	Spikes of flowers
*Primula florindae	Giant Cowslip	Y	July	B	Nodding, scented flowers
,, helodoxa	Candelabra Primrose	Y	May–June	B	Whorls of bloom
* ,, japonica	,, ,,	C P W	June	B	Green leaves and stems
* ,, pulverulenta	,, ,,	C P W	June	B	Mealy stems
* ,, sikkimensis	Thibetan Cowslip	Y	July	B	Nodding flowers
Sagittaria	Arrowhead	W	July–Aug	Sw	Arrow-shaped leaves
Scirpus zebrinus	Porcupine Quill, Zebra Rush	foliage only		B M	Leaves banded green and white
Typha minima	Small Reed Mace	Br	Aug–Oct	M	Cigar-like flower heads

11 Greenhouse and Frame

A greenhouse enables a gardener to create the climate required to grow whatever plants he is interested in. Unless it is to be used solely for hardy plants or is only to be used from about April to October, some kind of heating will be necessary, at least to exclude frost and possibly to maintain higher temperatures. Also unless the greenhouse is to be used exclusively for tropical plants, it will require good ventilation so that temperatures can be kept down to an acceptable level in summer. Some shading may be necessary for the same purpose and also to protect those plants that do not like hot sunshine. The shading can be provided by spraying or painting the glass with limewash or a shading compound but it is more convenient to have blinds that can be raised or lowered at will.

For all these reasons it is wise to have some idea at the outset what plants are to be grown and to choose and equip the greenhouse accordingly. As far as temperature is concerned four levels are commonly recognized and referred to as cold house, cool house, intermediate house, and warm house.

The *cold house* is entirely unheated and in winter the temperature inside it may often be below freezing, so at that season it will only be suitable for hardy plants such as alpines, daffodils, tulips, and hyacinths.

The *cool house* will have a minimum night temperature, even in winter, of 7 °C (45 °F). Many popular greenhouse plants can be grown in such a house, and artificial heat is only likely to be required between late November and early April, and then by no means all the time. This is therefore a very economical kind of house to run. In spring and summer the aim will be to maintain a temperature between 13 °C and 18 °C (55–65 °F) by sunheat and when the outside temperature is above this upper limit the house will be kept as near as possible to it by ventilation, shading, and damping down (*see* page 96).

The *intermediate house* has a winter minimum of 13 °C (55 °F) and in summer the level will be between 16 °C and 21 °C (60–70 °F). Plants from warmer regions of the world can be grown in such a house, as well as most of those grown in a cool house, in fact some of these will respond better to the higher winter temperature, but the cost of heating can be two or three times that of a cool house.

Span roofed greenhouses are designed to stand in the open, lean-to houses (right) to be placed against a house or wall. Glazing to ground level is recommended for tall plants, half-walling and staging for seedlings and small pot plants. The two can be combined (centre).

Finally in the *warm house* a winter minimum of 18 °C (65 °F) is maintained and in summer temperatures will range between 21 °C and 27 °C (70–80 °F). Tropical plants, including some tropical orchids, require such temperatures but they are costly to maintain.

Special soil mixtures, or potting composts, are required for a few plants but most can be grown in one or other of the standard soil or no-soil composts. The soil composts are usually based on the John Innes formula of 7 parts by loose bulk of medium loam, 3 parts fibrous or granulated peat, and 2 parts clean, relatively lime-free sand. It is recommended that the loam, but not the other ingredients, is sterilized before use. To these ingredients ground chalk (or ground limestone) and the John Innes base fertilizer are added. The base fertilizer itself is prepared with 2 parts by weight hoof and horn meal, 2 parts superphosphate of lime, and 1 part of superphosphate of potash. For what is known as John Innes Potting Compost No. 1 (or for short J.I.P.1) 30 grammes of this base fertilizer and 5 grammes of ground chalk are added to each 10 litres of compost (4 oz of fertilizer, $\frac{3}{4}$ oz of chalk per bushel). For J.I.P.2 the quantities are doubled, and J.I.P.3 has a triple dose of fertilizer and ground chalk.

John Innes Potting Compost can be purchased ready for use, but unless stated otherwise, it will be J.I.P.1, so if richer compost is required more base fertilizer and more ground chalk will have to be added. Both can be purchased.

John Innes Seed Compost is used for germinating seed and very often for growing on the seedlings until they are large enough to go singly into pots. It is prepared with 2 parts by loose bulk of loam, 1 part peat, and 1 part sand, all similar to that used for potting, plus 10 grammes of superphosphate of lime and 5 grammes of ground chalk per 10 litres (1½ oz of fertilizer and $\frac{3}{4}$ oz of chalk per bushel). Again this J.I.S. compost, as it is called, can be purchased ready for use.

No-soil composts are usually based on peat and fertilizers, sometimes with the addition of sand, clay or other ingredients. There are a number of different brands available, some claimed as suitable for both seed raising and growing on, some in separate packs for seed and potting. Advantages of no-soil composts are greater uniformity, lightness, and ease of handling. Many plants do well in them and they are being increasingly used by gardeners.

Small plants are not, as a rule, put straight into large pots but are moved into larger pots as they fill the smaller ones with roots.

Automatic ventilation is possible with a piston type ventilator lifter (top) or thermostatically controlled fan and gravity louvres. Paraffin radiators provide simple, cheap heating, but electric radiators are easier to control. They can be low temperature tubular, permanently mounted, or fan assisted and portable (bottom).

94

Greenhouse Calceolaria Carters Victoria Prize

Usually young plants are started in pots about 6 cm (2½ in.) in diameter, go from these to 10–12 cm (4–5 in.) diameter pots, and then to 15–18 cm (6–7 in.) diameter pots, a process known as potting-on.

When potting or potting-on plants they must be kept at the correct depth, the uppermost roots, or the ball of soil and roots, just covered with compost. The compost is filled in evenly all round the plant and if it is soil compost is made firm with the fingers. No-soil composts usually require no such firming, it being sufficient to rap the pot two or three times on a firm surface, such as a wooden potting bench, to settle the compost in. Whichever type of soil is used the plants should be well watered, after potting, from a watering can fitted with a coarse rose, and this will help to settle the compost still more closely around the roots. Pots are never filled quite full but a little space is left to hold water.

Once plants are established in pots, it is better to water them directly from the spout of a watering can rather than through a rose, which is apt to give a deceptive appearance of wetness when really the water has not penetrated very far. It is always best to apply sufficient water to moisten the soil right through the pot and start to trickle out at the bottom. Then no more need be applied until the soil begins to get dry. Seedlings and newly potted plants are watered through a rose so as not to wash the soil about and possibly dislodge the plants.

Most plants require far less water from October to March than they do from April to September, but there are exceptions, particularly among bulbs and tubers, many of which rest in summer and need to be almost dry in July and August. However, in general it is wise to look plants over daily for watering in spring and summer, but only once or twice a week in autumn and winter.

An alternative to overhead watering is the capillary bench or bed, a layer of sand kept constantly moist. Pot plants are placed on this and draw water up from the bench through the drainage holes as the soil in the pots dries. Various devices

Repot plants when the soil is full of roots. Steady plants as shown when inspecting them. Use a pot one or two sizes larger and either John Innes or peat potting compost. Firm the former well, using a stick around the edge for larger plants.

are available for keeping the sand sufficiently moist automatically, or it can simply be flooded once or twice daily, the surplus being allowed to drain away. Plastic pots are more suitable than clay pots for capillary bench watering since they are thinner and permit the soil in the pot to come more readily in contact with the moist sand. When plants are first placed on a capillary bench they must be well watered to start the capillary action.

Pot plants can usually be fed most conveniently by adding fertilizer to the water (but not to the water used to supply a capillary bench). It is most important not to use too much as this will simply scorch the leaves and possibly kill the plants. Always read the label instructions and if anything give less than advised. Plants grown in J.I.P.1 and no-soil composts may need feeding after six or eight weeks. In general, feeding, once started, should be continued at intervals of two to three weeks until about September, or until growth ceases, whichever is earlier.

Some plants like to be syringed with water when they are growing and a great many appreciate a rather moister atmosphere than would be normal in Britain. To obtain this the paths, walls, and stages on which the plants are growing are thoroughly wetted several times a day, a process known as damping down, or shallow trays of water are placed in the house to evaporate. One of the advantages of capillary bench watering in summer is that the moist sand gives off plenty of water vapour to keep the air moist. Evaporation in the greenhouse also helps to keep the air cool in hot weather, but the two principal controls over summer temperature are shading and ventilation. The first prevents sunshine from warming up the house, the second allows the hot air to escape and be replaced by cooler air from outside. Shading at some period is beneficial to most plants except succulents (including cacti) and some bulbs and tubers which like to be well baked in summer. It is likely to be needed most between May and September and only a few plants require shading at other times of the year. Even in summer many plants appreciate light so long as it is not accompanied by scorching heat. Shading, therefore, will be most necessary on the sunny side of the house and may not be required at all on the north-facing side. Greenhouses should be sited in reasonably light places, not under trees or on the north side of a high building, unless they are intended for shade loving plants.

Most greenhouses have flap ventilators in the roof and the more there are the better, since it is these that allow the rapid exit of hot air. They can be made to open automatically with a simple piston and lever device which can be set to commence lifting the ventilator at a predetermined temperature. Alternatively extractor fans can be fitted and connected to a thermostat, which can be set to start the fan working at any desired temperature. Side ventilators may also be fitted and are useful in summer to permit a quick flow of air.

One advantage of hand ventilation is that ventilators can be closed in good time so as to allow the temperature to rise a few degrees and trap heat for the night. Considerable saving in artificial heat can be effected in this way, especially in spring and autumn.

In winter very little ventilation will be needed, except on mild sunny days, but artificial heat will be most useful both to warm and dry the atmosphere, which at this season is often too damp. At this period little or no damping down is required and hand watering is better than a capillary bench, which may be allowed to remain dry from October to March.

It does not matter what form of heat is used provided it is well distributed throughout the greenhouse and does not produce any harmful fumes in the house. If it can be controlled by a thermostat so much the better as this will economize fuel and at the same time ensure against damage caused by too high or too low temperatures.

Pests and diseases in greenhouses can usually be most readily controlled by fumigation with smoke canisters or pellets containing an appropriate insecticide or fungicide. Pre-packed aerosols are also convenient. In autumn and winter various moulds may be troublesome, especially in rather inadequately heated houses. All decaying leaves should be picked off and burned, decayed stems removed, and susceptible plants dusted occasionally with flowers of sulphur or thiram. It is possible to obtain vaporizing strips which can be suspended in a greenhouse to kill many pests or small electrically operated vaporizers may be installed.

Frames can perform many of the functions of a greenhouse and have one notable advantage over them: the protective lights can be removed completely, so exposing the plants to the open air. This can be most useful in spring when plants reared under glass are being prepared for planting outdoors. Even with the most generous ventilation in a greenhouse, the change of

(above) Begonia Crown Jewels
(centre) Achimenes Longiflora major (top) and Little Beauty
(below) Petunia Cherry Tart

temperature when the plants do go outside can be too much for them. But if they can be transferred to a frame for two or three weeks as an intermediary stage, and the lights are fully opened on all fine days, they will become more thoroughly acclimatized and suffer far less check. This is the process known as hardening off.

Frames are particularly useful for germinating seed, rooting cuttings, and rearing small plants. Lettuces, cucumbers and melons, bush tomatoes, and other small crops can be grown in them and in late summer they come in very useful for drying off bulbs, including onions, shallots, and garlic.

Frames can be heated if desired and this will extend their usefulness just as it extends the usefulness of greenhouses. One convenient and popular method of frame heating is by soil-warming electric cables buried in sand about 15 cm (6 in.) beneath the surface of the soil. The soil is then slightly warmer than the air, which suits many young plants well, and the heat is also well distributed. Another possibility is to install similar cable around the sides of the frame, so heating the air directly.

A propagator is really a small frame made to stand inside a greenhouse. It is useful for germinating seeds, rooting cuttings, and starting some bulbs and tubers into growth, since it is easier to maintain a higher temperature within the propagator and also have very still moist air, which is particularly important for cuttings.

SPECIAL GREENHOUSE PLANTS

Aphelandra. The kind commonly grown, Aphelandra squarrosa louisae, is a perennial with shining green leaves striped with ivory and stiff spikes of yellow flowers in spring. It likes intermediate house conditions and shade in summer. Grow in J.I.P.3 and keep moderately moist even in winter.

Begonia. The double flowered, tuberous rooted varieties described on page 24 make splendid pot plants for a cool greenhouse, though the higher temperatures of intermediate house or propagator will be useful for seed germination and starting the tubers. There are also pendulous varieties which require exactly the same treatment but are best grown in hanging baskets suspended from the rafters or ridge plate.

Rex begonias are grown for their handsome heart-shaped or kidney-shaped leaves richly coloured and mottled in shades of green, purple, crimson, bronze, and silver. They enjoy shade and can be grown under the greenhouse staging, preferably in intermediate house conditions though they can be grown in a cool house. They should be watered moderately in winter as they do not make tubers and so have no dormant season. They can be increased by seed, division or leaf cuttings and are best grown in peat compost or J.I.P.1 with some extra peat.

Some winter flowering begonias, such as the Lorraine and Hiemalis groups, need the warmer temperatures of an intermediate house, but Begonia fuchsioides, B. haageana, B. manicata, and B. socotrana can be grown in cool or intermediate houses and so can the many varieties of B. semperflorens (*see* page 24), which under glass flower most of the year. All like J.I.P.2 compost and should be watered moderately in winter. Gloire de Lorraine is grown from cuttings, B. semperflorens from seed, other species by division, cuttings, or seed.

Beloperone guttata (Shrimp Plant). A perennial 30 to 45 cm (12 to 18 in.) high with arching spikes of white and shrimp pink flowers in summer. It is suitable for a cool house in J.I.P.1 compost and can be increased by cuttings.

Bougainvillea. Showy and vigorous climbers for a cool or intermediate house. The flowers are enclosed in purple, pink, or orange bracts. Best planted directly in a bed of soil on the floor of the house and trained under the rafters. Each winter cut back the stems made the previous summer. Increase by cuttings.

Caladium. Perennial plants grown for their variously coloured, broadly arrow-shaped leaves. They need warm house conditions and J.I.P.2 compost. The leaves die down in autumn, when little water should be given until March. Shade from strong sunshine. Increase by division in spring.

Calceolaria. The greenhouse varieties, such as Victoria Prize, which have large pouched flowers in various colours, often splashed or spotted with one colour on another, are biennials. Seed is sown in May or June in J.I.S. in an unheated greenhouse or frame, the small seed barely covered with fine sand. Seedlings are pricked off into similar compost and later potted singly in 6 cm ($2\frac{1}{2}$ in.) pots in J.I.P.1. They are grown until late September in a frame and are then brought into a cool greenhouse. Pot on into 12 cm (5 in.) pots and J.I.P.2 in October and, if necessary, move on again into 15–18 cm (6–7 in.) pots and similar compost in early March. Water moderately in autumn and winter, keeping water off the leaves and crowns. Give all the light and air possible, but maintain a minimum temperature of 7 °C (45 °F). Plants will flower in May and June and are discarded afterwards.

Carnation. It is the perpetual flowering varieties that are commonly grown as greenhouse pot plants, usually from cuttings rooted in winter and early spring, though plants can also be grown from seed. They need cool house conditions, with plenty of ventilation in spring and summer, when temperatures should be kept below 21 °C (70 °F) if possible. If preferred, plants can be grown in a frame from June to September. Grow in J.I.P.2 compost. Pinch out tips of young plants when they have six to eight pairs of leaves. Do not shade plants at any time. Stake and tie the stems as they grow and for best results remove side flower buds, only retaining the terminal bud on each stem. Discard plants after the second or third year.

Coleus   Carnation Giant Grenadin

Celosia. Both the crested or cockscomb variety and the plumed variety are excellent greenhouse pot plants. They are annuals grown from seed sown from March to May and later pricked out into boxes and finally potted singly in 10 or 12 cm (4 or 5 in.) pots in J.I.P.1 compost. Grow in a sunny unheated greenhouse, water freely, and discard after flowering.

Chrysanthemum. There are a great many varieties of chrysanthemum, differing not only in colour but also in the form of their flowers and the time at which they are produced. Those that normally flower before 1 October are known as Early Flowering and can be planted outdoors from about April to November. Those that flower after 1 October are grown in pots and brought into a greenhouse to flower, though they can with advantage stand outdoors from June to September.

Chrysanthemums with a lot of incurling petals, making ball-like flowers, are known as Incurved, those with outward curling petals as Reflexed, and those in which the petals go each way as Intermediate.

Singles have up to five rows of petals and a button-like disc in the centre; Anemone-centred varieties have a pad of short petals in the centre; Pompons have flowers like small balls; and Spoon-petalled have spidery flowers with petals broadening at the ends. There are other special types.

All are best renewed annually from cuttings taken between January and April and rooted in a cool greenhouse. They can also be grown from seed sown in a cool greenhouse in February–March, but seedlings often show considerable variation. However, seed provides an excellent means of rearing the single flowered Charm and Cascade varieties for use as autumn flowering pot plants, the latter to be trained downwards instead of upwards to make trailing specimens.

Chrysanthemums are nearly hardy and only require protection from frost. Greenhouse varieties are first potted in 6 cm ($2\frac{1}{2}$ in.) pots in J.I.P.1, moved on to 12 cm (5 in.) pots in J.I.P.2, and finally in May or June into 18–25 cm (7–10 in.) pots and J.I.P.3.

In early June plants are stood outdoors in a sunny but sheltered place, preferably on a cinder or gravel base. They are returned to the greenhouse in late September but no artificial heat is usually required before November, and then only to dry

Pot plants can be automatically watered by standing them on a capillary bench (top left). Seed pans and very small plants are often best watered by standing them in water for a minute or so. Established plants are best watered direct from the spout.

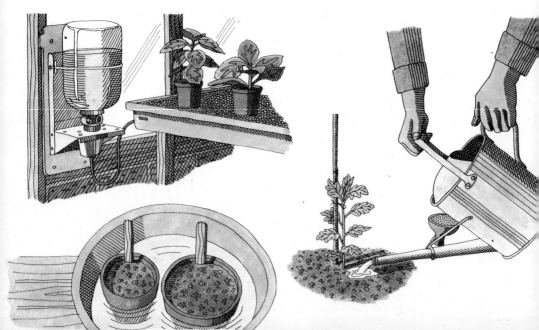

the air a little and keep out frost.

The tips of shoots may be pinched out when the plants are 20 cm (8 in.) high and again when side branches are about 20 cm (8 in.) long, though different methods of stopping may be required for exhibition purposes. Plants must be well staked and tied. If fine specimen blooms are required the side flower buds on each stem are removed as soon as they can be seen, only the top bud being retained. If sprays of smaller flowers are required the top bud is removed and the side buds allowed to develop.

Throughout their growing period chrysanthemums must be well watered, and from about early July until flower buds commence to show petal colour they should be fed every ten to fourteen days with a good chrysanthemum fertilizer.

After flowering, a few good plants of each variety are cut down almost to the soil and reserved as stock plants in a cool house or frame to provide cuttings. The rest are discarded.

Cineraria. Bushy biennials with abundant daisy flowers in many different colours from November to May. Seed can be sown in batches from April to June, to give a long flowering season. Treatment is similar to that for greenhouse calceolarias (*see* page 99) and, as with them, the plants are discarded after flowering. There are large flowered varieties and smaller flowered varieties such as the Intermediate Multiflora type.

(top) Cineraria Dwarf Large Flowered
(centre) Torenia fournieri

(below left) Zonal Pelargonium or Geranium Carefree F$_1$ Hybrid; (below right) Gloxinia Carters Prize Strain

Many plants appreciate a moist atmosphere especially in summer, so paths, staging, and the soil below can be well watered daily. To prevent too high a temperature in sunny weather shading will be required. Blinds that can be lowered or raised at will are ideal.

Coleus. Perennial plants grown for their nettle-shaped leaves in various colours, often zoned in several different colours on the same leaf. They are readily grown from seed in a cool house, or even in a cold house if seed can be sown in March or April in a propagator with a temperature 15 to 18 °C (60–65 °F). In winter they prefer intermediate house conditions and so for economy are often treated as annuals and not kept over the winter. Raise in J.I.S. compost and transfer seedlings singly to 8 cm (3 in.) pots and then to 12 to 15 cm (5 to 6 in.) pots in J.I.P.2 compost. Water fairly freely in spring and summer, rather sparingly if kept over the winter. Pinch out the tips when plants are about 15 cm (6 in.) high.

Crossandra undulifolia. A perennial with dense spikes of orange-scarlet tubular flowers in summer. It needs an intermediate or warm greenhouse and can be grown from seed in March–April in a temperature of 18–21 °C (65–70 °F) and not covered. Grow plants in J.I.P.1 with some shade in summer.

Cyclamen. Tuberous rooted perennials flowering from about November to April. They are grown from seed sown between August and January in J.I.S. or peat seed compost in a cool greenhouse. Seed is often slow and erratic in germination, so seedlings should be lifted carefully as they appear and be transferred singly to 6 cm (2½ in.) pots in J.I.P.1 compost. Later they can be moved to 10 cm (4 in.) pots and finally to 12–15 cm (5–6 in.) pots in the same compost. From June to September plants do best in a shaded frame; from October to May in a cool greenhouse. Water fairly freely while in growth but after flowering gradually reduce the supply and keep almost dry in a shady frame in June and July. Repot in August and return to the greenhouse in October. Always keep the tubers just on the surface of the soil when repotting.

Didiscus coeruleus (Blue Lace Flower). An annual with heads of small lavender flowers on 45 cm (18 in.) stems in summer. It is almost hardy and can be grown in a cold or cool house from seed sown between March and May. Grow in J.I.P.1 compost. It is also known as Trachymene coerulea.

Euphorbia (Poinsettia, Crown of Thorns). Perennial plants for intermediate or even warm greenhouses. Euphorbia pulcherrima, the poinsettia, is grown for its head of large scarlet or pink bracts in winter; E. fulgens for its arching stems of small scarlet flowers, also in winter; E. splendens, the crown of thorns, for its strange spiny growth and its scarlet flowers in summer. The poinsettia and E. fulgens are best grown in J.I.P.3, the crown of thorns in J.I.P.1 with a little extra sand or grit. It also needs a drier atmosphere and less water, especially in winter, than the other two. The poinsettia is often renewed annually from spring cuttings.

102

Exacum affine. A bushy annual with lilac blue and yellow sweetly scented flowers in summer and autumn. It can be grown in a cold house from seed sown in March or April or in a cool house from seed sown in September. Grow in J.I.P.2 compost in 10 or 12 cm (4 or 5 in.) pots and shade only from strong sunshine.

Ficus (Rubber Plant). A shrubby plant grown for its large leathery dark green leaves. It will grow in quite dense shade in cool, intermediate, or warm greenhouse or in a living room in J.I.P.2 compost and enjoys a moist atmosphere.

Fuchsia. Shrubby plants flowering more or less continuously from spring to autumn. They can be grown in cool house conditions in J.I.P.2 compost, bushy varieties in pots, and the more pendant cascade varieties in baskets hanging from the rafters. Some varieties can also be trained as climbers. Water fairly freely in spring and summer, moderately in autumn, sparingly in winter. Shade from strong sunshine but grow in a light place. Feed plants every ten to fourteen days from May to September. Fuchsias are easily raised from cuttings in spring and summer and can also be grown from seed sown in spring in a temperature of 15–18 °C (60–65 °F).

Gardenia jasminoides (Cape Jasmin). A small evergreen shrub with very fragrant single or double white flowers at various times of the year. It needs intermediate or warm house conditions and can be grown in J.I.P.2 with a little extra peat. Feed every 10–14 days from May to September. Shade from strong sunshine and maintain a moist atmosphere in spring and summer.

Grevillea robusta (Silk Oak). An Australian tree grown as a greenhouse pot plant for its finely divided, almost fern-like leaves. It can be raised from seed sown in a temperature of 15–18 °C (60–65 °F), but the seedlings can be grown on in a cool or intermediate house. Grow in J.I.P.1 with shade from strong sunshine. Discard plants when they get too large.

Hibiscus rosa-sinensis (Rose Mallow). A shrubby plant with showy single or double scarlet, crimson, rose, or yellow flowers in summer. It needs an intermediate or warm greenhouse and a moist atmosphere in spring and summer. Prune plants to shape each February. Feed from May to August and water freely in spring and summer. Increase by cuttings.

Hoya (Wax Plant). Two kinds are grown, Hoya carnosa, a twiner with pale pink flowers and H. bella, a trailer with white and pale purple flowers, very sweetly scented. Both flower in summer. H. carnosa can be grown in a cool house, but H. bella prefers an intermediate house. Grow in J.I.P.1 compost with some extra peat. Syringe plants frequently with water in summer. Allow H. carnosa to climb up wires under the rafters and grow H. bella in hanging baskets.

Humea elegans (Incense Plant). A biennial with tall arching sprays of small reddish-brown incense scented flowers in summer. Grow from seed sown between May and July in an unheated greenhouse or frame. Pot seedlings in J.I.P.1 compost and from October onwards grow in a cool house. Water moderately throughout and be careful not to break the roots when repotting.

Hydrangea. The many varieties of Hydrangea macrophylla (*see* page 73) make excellent pot plants for a cold or cool greenhouse. Grow from spring cuttings potted when well rooted in 12–15 cm (5–6 in.) pots in J.I.P.2 compost. Grow in a frame or sheltered place outdoors until October and then bring into the greenhouse and keep moderately watered. Application of a proprietary 'blueing' compound according to the label instructions will ensure blue or purple flowers from coloured varieties.

Maranta. Perennials grown for their handsome leaves, splashed or veined dark green on a lighter green base. They enjoy warm house conditions, but can be grown in an intermediate house and should be well shaded in summer and the air kept moist. Grow in J.I.P.1 with a little extra peat and sand.

Monstera. Evergreen climbing plants with large perforated dark green leaves. They will grow in quite dense shade in a cool, intermediate, or warm greenhouse and are much used as house plants. Grow in J.I.P.2 compost and maintain a moist atmosphere.

Nerium (Oleander). Rather large shrubby plants with showy pink or white flowers all summer. They are easily grown in a cool house without shading in J.I.P.2 compost, and flowering stems can be shortened almost to the base after flowering.

Passiflora (Passion Flower). Vigorous climbers with variously coloured flowers in summer. Passiflora coerulea, blue or white, and P. antioquiensis, rose red, will grow in a cool house, but most other kinds prefer an intermediate house. They are best planted in a border of good soil and permitted to climb up wires strained against a wall or beneath the rafters. They can be grown from seed or cuttings.

Pelargonium (Geranium). There are several quite different types of pelargonium, such as the zonal-leaved pelargonium or bedding geranium with white, scarlet, pink or crimson flowers for the greater part of the year; the regal pelargonium with larger flowers often blotched with one colour on another and produced mainly in May and June; the ivy-leaved pelargonium, a sprawling plant which can be trained up a wall, grown in hanging baskets or allowed to hang over the staging, with pink, lilac, or scarlet flowers; and the scented-leaved pelargoniums, mostly with insignificant flowers and grown for their variously shaped aromatic foliage, which may sometimes be velvety.

104

All can be grown very easily in cool or intermediate greenhouses in J.I.P.1 compost and without
shading in summer. They should be watered rather
sparingly from November to February. They can
be raised from seed sown from February to April
or from cuttings rooted in spring or summer, and
plants can be cut back quite severely after flowering
to keep them shapely and within bounds.

Primula. Four kinds of primula are commonly
grown in greenhouses and all will give winter
flowers under cool house conditions. Primula obconica will often continue to flower on and off
throughout the year, but it is from October to
April that it is most valuable. The flowers are large
and carried in clusters on 30 cm (12 in.) stems. The
colour range includes white, blue, pink, carmine,
and crimson. It is wise to make at least two sowings,
one in March for autumn and winter flowering and
one in June–July for spring. Seed will germinate
and seedlings grow well in a temperature of 13–
16 °C (55–60 °F). Sow and prick out in J.I.S.
compost, pot into 6 cm (2½ in.) pots in J.I.P.1, and
pot on into 10–12 cm (4–5 in.) pots in J.I.P.2. Keep
plants in a shaded frame from June to September,
then bring into a light, well ventilated greenhouse.
Water rather sparingly in cold weather.

Primula malacoides, the Fairy Primrose, has
larger, looser sprays of smaller flowers also in a
good colour range, but without such good blues.

(top) Molucella laevis; (centre) Cyclamen Rex strain;
(below left) Schizanthus Carters Butterfly;
(below right) Gerbera F₁ Hybrid strain

It flowers from January to March, should be sown successively from April until July, and is grown in the same way as P. obconica.

Primula sinensis has two forms, one with clusters of large round flowers with waved petals, the other with taller, looser sprays of more star-shaped flowers. Both have a good colour range, including orange as well as pink, red, and blue, and flower from December to March. Sow from May to July and treat in the same way as the previous two.

Primula kewensis has yellow flowers, also in winter, is sown in March or April and grown like the others except that it is hardier and will not mind temperatures as low as 5 °C (40 °F).

Saintpaulia (African Violet). Perennial plants with rosettes of dark green, velvety leaves and intense violet-blue or pink, single or double flowers on 10–15 cm (4–6 in.) stems, more or less throughout the year. It requires intermediate or warm house conditions with shade from direct sunshine and a moist atmosphere. It can be grown from seed sown in March–April in a temperature of 18–21 °C (65–70 °F) or from leaf cutting in summer. Grow in peat compost or J.I.P.1 with some additional peat. Water carefully at all times, avoiding wetting the leaves unnecessarily.

Schizanthus (Butterfly Flower). Annuals with large sprays of small butterfly-like flowers in a wonderful range of colours, often marked in the most attractive way. They will grow well in a cool greenhouse and may be had in flower in April–May from a sowing made in August–September or in summer and autumn from sowings made successively between January and May. Sow in J.I.S. compost and grow on in J.I.P.1. The small 30 cm (12 in.) high varieties can be flowered in 10 cm (4 in.) pots; the larger 60–75 cm (24–30 in.) high varieties may need 15–18 cm (6–7 in.) pots. Shade lightly from strong sunshine. Plants may be kept in a frame from June to September.

Smithiantha (Temple Bells). Plants with velvety leaves and 40 cm (16 in.) sprays of tubular flowers in a variety of colours, including cream, yellow, apricot, pink and red. Plants sold as gesneria and naegelia belong here or require identical treatment. Plant tubers in March, 1 cm ($\frac{1}{2}$ in.) deep, one in each 10 cm (4 in.) pot in peat potting compost. Start in a temperature of 15 °C (60 °F), water sparingly at first, freely when roots are well developed. Feed every ten days from the time the flower buds appear. Gradually reduce the water supply after flowering and keep quite dry with the pots on their sides from November to February. Grow throughout in a cool or intermediate greenhouse. *See also* Table, p. 52.

Frames can do much of the work of a greenhouse and are invaluable for acclimatizing greenhouse raised plants to outdoor conditions. Heated propagators inside the greenhouse are excellent for seeds and cuttings and allow the higher temperatures and damper atmosphere required to be maintained at minimum cost.

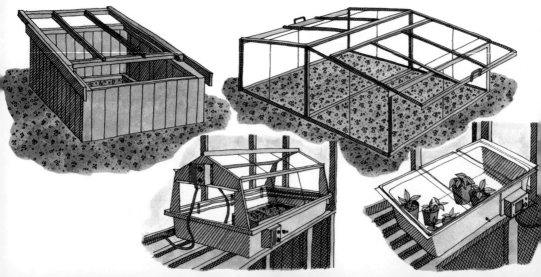

House plants often suffer from the dry atmosphere of rooms. This can be countered to some extent by plunging pots in containers filled with moist peat. Even better conditions exist in the almost completely closed environment of the bottle garden.

Solanum capsicastrum (Winter Cherry). A bushy perennial grown for its orange-scarlet cherry-like fruits in winter. Sow in March in a temperature of 15·5–18 °C (60–65 °F) in J.I.S. compost, prick out in J.I.P.1, and later pot in 10–12 cm (4–5 in.) pots in J.I.P.3. Pinch out the tips of stems occasionally to produce plenty of short branches. Stand plants outdoors from May to September and syringe daily with water while they are in flower. Return to a cool or intermediate greenhouse at the end of September.

Statice suworowii. An annual with slender branched spikes of pink 'everlasting' flowers in summer. It is easily raised from seed sown in March–April and grown in J.I.P.1 compost in a cool greenhouse without shading. From June onwards it can be placed in a sunny frame if preferred and should be discarded after flowering.

Stephanotis floribunda (Madagascar Jasmine). An evergreen twining plant with white, richly scented flowers which may be produced at any time according to the warmth available. It requires intermediate or warm house conditions and should be grown in J.I.P.3 compost in a large pot or a bed on the floor of the house. Shade in summer and maintain a very moist atmosphere.

Strelitzia reginae (Bird of Paradise Flower). A perennial with large leaves and extraordinary orange and blue flowers shaped like the crested head of a bird and borne in May and June on stout stems. It can be grown in J.I.P.1 compost in large pots or a bed on the floor of the house. Plants can be divided or raised from seed, but a temperature of about 21 °C (70 °F) is required for germination.

Streptocarpus (Cape Primrose). The popular name is misleading since the trumpet-shaped blue, pink, red, or white flowers do not in any way resemble primroses. Streptocarpus is a perennial readily raised from seed and suitable for a cool or intermediate greenhouse. Sow in February and July in J.I.S. compost covering the small seeds very lightly. Prick out in J.I.P.1 compost and grow on in J.I.P.2 with a little extra peat. Shade from May to September and maintain a moist atmosphere during this period. Good plants can be obtained in 10 cm (4 in.) pots.

Streptosolen jamesonii. A climber with clusters of light orange flowers in June and July. It can be grown in a cool greenhouse in J.I.P.1 compost in pots, the stems trained up canes or over a wire frame. No shading is required. Long stems can be cut back each February.

107

Thunbergia alata (Black-eyed Susan). An annual with slender twining stems and orange, buff, or white flowers with black centres. Sow directly in 8 cm (3 in.) pots of J.I.P.1 compost in March in a temperature of 15–18 °C (60–65 °F), reduce seedlings to about three per pot, and later transfer bodily to 15 cm (5 in.) pots. Place three thin canes in each pot for the stems to twine around or alternatively grow in baskets and allow the stems to hang down. No heat is required after April. Discard plants after flowering.

Tibouchina semi-decandra. An evergreen shrub with long stems often trained as a climber. It has soft green leaves and large violet-blue flowers produced most of the year. It thrives in a cool or intermediate house in J.I.P.2 in large pots or planted in a bed. Plants can be pruned quite hard to tidy them.

Torenia fournieri. A slender annual with flowers in two shades of blue plus yellow. It needs intermediate house conditions, can be sown from February to June, and should be shaded from direct sunshine. If grown in pots some small sticks should be provided for support, alternatively grow in hanging baskets and allow to hang down. J.I.P.2 will suit it.

Trachelium caeruleum. A dainty plant with tiny lavender-blue flowers carried in cloud-like clusters. It is a perennial usually grown as an annual or biennial, i.e. sown in February–March to flower from July onwards or in July–August to flower from the following May. Give it cool house treatment throughout and flower in 7–12 cm (3–5 in.) pots of J.I.P.2 compost.

Tradescantia fluminensis (Wandering Jew). Sprawling plants with green leaves with white, cream, or pink variegations. Zebrina pendula is very similar and both plants are excellent for baskets, the edges of staging or even growing under the staging since they do not mind shade. They will thrive in J.I.P.1 compost in any place from which frost can be excluded and are readily increased by cuttings.

Vinca rosea (Madagascar Periwinkle). A greenhouse creeping perennial often grown as an annual from seed sown in February–April. It enjoys intermediate or warm house conditions, with shade in summer, will thrive in J.I.P.2 compost, and flowers most of the year. The flowers are rose pink or rose and white.

OTHER GROUPS

Bromeliads. A group or family name for a number of handsome plants many of which make large rosettes of stiff, variegated or banded leaves surrounding a central cup or 'vase'. Popular kinds are aechmea, billbergia, cryptanthus, neoregelia, nidularium, and vriesia. Most like intermediate or warm house conditions with shade in summer and a moist atmosphere. The central 'vase' of those varieties that form one should be kept full of water. Grow in the smallest pots that will contain them in peat compost or a mixture of equal parts of peat, sand, and osmunda fibre. Billbergia nutans can be grown in J.I.P.1 in a drier and cooler atmosphere.

Cacti. These are leafless plants with thickened stems which serve the purpose of leaves. They are of many strange and sometimes beautiful shapes, sometimes covered in spines or grey hairs. Many kinds also produce showy flowers. All are succulents accustomed to growing in hot, dry places. They are excellent pot plants for cool or intermediate houses, grown in J.I.P.1 with some extra sand, grit, or powdered brick. They require no shading in summer and should be watered sparingly in winter, fairly freely in summer, moderately at other times. They can

Bletia striata
　　　　　　　　　　　　　　　Salpiglossis Carters Mammoth strain

be grown from seed in J.I.S. compost with extra sand, grit or powdered brick, or in peat compost, in a temperature of 18–26 °C (65–70 °F). Seeds often germinate irregularly, so seedlings should be carefully lifted and pricked off as they become large enough to handle, the compost being disturbed as little as possible in the process so that the remaining seeds have a chance to grow. Many cacti also produce offsets which can be separated from the parent plant when repotting.

Ferns. A number of ferns make excellent pot plants for a cool shady greenhouse. They can be grown in peat potting compost, in the smallest pots that will hold their roots, and can be increased by division in spring, the best repotting season, or by spores. Sow these very thinly on the surface of moist peat seedling compost in a pot or pan, cover with a sheet of glass, and place in a shady frame or greenhouse. When more water is needed give it by holding the container almost to its rim in water. Water ferns freely in spring and summer, moderately in autumn and winter.

Among the best kinds for greenhouse or room cultivation are Adiantum cuneatum, Asplenium bulbiferum, Blechnum gibbum, Cyrtomium falcatum, Davallia canariensis, Nephrolepis exaltata, N. todeoides, Polypodium aureum, P. vulgare and its several varieties, Pteris cretica, P. serrulata, and P. tremula. The Elk's Horn Fern or platycerium is peculiar in that it grows well bound to a block of wood with sphagnum moss and peat packed around its roots, and then suspended so that it is growing on its side.

Orchids. A great family of plants with many different species and a fantastic range of flower forms and colours. Many of the greenhouse kinds are epiphytic, i.e. they obtain most of their food from the air and like to grow in a mixture of osmunda fibre and sphagnum moss, a good general mixture being three parts of the former to one of the latter. Some kinds, such as the popular cypripediums or slipper orchids (now known as paphiopedilum) like two parts of loam added to the above mixture, and cymbidiums do well with either type of compost.

There are orchids for cool house, intermediate house, and warm house conditions. All need to be shaded from direct sunshine and many like quite a lot of shade from May to September. All enjoy a very moist atmosphere. Many rest for a few weeks after flowering, and require little water then, but should be watered fairly freely at other times. They are generally repotted as growth restarts, after this resting period. Many make bulb-like structures, known as pseudo-bulbs, above the compost in which they are growing and when repotting the older pseudo-bulbs should be removed and discarded.

Among the most popular kinds are cattleya, coelogyne, cymbidium, cypripedium, dendrobium, epidendrum, laelia, lycaste, masdevallia, miltonia, odontoglossum, oncidium, pleione (suitable for a cold or cool house), sophronitis, vanda, and zygopetalum.

Bletilla striata, also known as Bletia hyacinthina, is hardy enough to be grown outdoors in sheltered gardens in a shady place in equal parts peat and loam or can be grown in pots in a frost-proof greenhouse. It has rose-pink or white flowers on 30 cm (12 in.) stems in summer.

Succulents. Fleshy plants which are able to withstand periods of considerable drought or heat. Cacti (*see* page 108) are a particular family of succulents, leafless or nearly so, but some other kinds, such as agave, aloe, echeveria, and haworthia, are grown primarily for their stiff or strangely coloured leaves, and others, such as mesembryanthemum, kalanchoë, and rochea, for their flowers. Nearly all enjoy plenty of light, need no shading, like well drained rather gritty soil, such as J.I.P.1 with some extra sand, and should be watered very sparingly in winter. Many can be raised from seed in the same way as cacti and some can be in increased by divisions or cuttings.

HOUSE PLANTS

These are plants that are commonly grown in living rooms. In the main they are greenhouse plants that will grow in poor light. They are included in the quick-reference table at the end of this chapter and are distinguished from other greenhouse plants by asterisks and daggers before their names. Those with an asterisk only need to be kept fairly near to windows, but those with a dagger can be grown satisfactorily in shadier parts of rooms. It will be observed that most of the latter are plants grown for their handsome leaves rather than for their flowers. Many of them grow wild in forests where they are constantly in the shade. In addition many ferns make excellent room plants, particularly Adiantum cuneatum, Cyrtomium falcatum, Nephrolepis exaltata, Platycerium bifurcatum, and several kinds of pteris (*see* page 109).

Soils for potting, methods of potting, and propagation are all the same as if the plants were grown in a greenhouse. Up to a point so is watering, but the air in rooms is usually much drier than that in greenhouses and this causes special problems. Soil may dry out more rapidly and this may necessitate more frequent watering than would be required in a greenhouse. However, it is just as necessary when watering to give sufficient to wet the soil right through and then not to water again until the soil shows signs of drying out. It is often easier and more efficient to water house plants by standing the pots for about a minute in a bucket of water than to water from a can or jug, but either will do.

The greatest problems are usually the dryness of the air and the considerable temperature fluctuations that can occur in rooms that are not centrally heated. Air dryness causes leaves to turn yellow and drop off and also encourages some pests, particularly red spider mites. It helps to sponge leaves daily with water or to spray plants with water from an atomizer. Pots can be stood on gravel in special trays containing water, but not so much as to flood over the gravel and flow into the pots via the drainage holes. House plants are often arranged in ornamental troughs and these can be filled with peat or sphagnum moss kept constantly moist, so that there is evaporation around the leaves. Climbing plants can be trained around wire cylinders packed with sphagnum moss kept moist.

Plants grow towards the light and so it is desirable to turn pots round every few days so that there is proper balance of growth.

House plants need to be fed, but rather less than similar plants growing in greenhouses since they have not so much light to enable them to make use of the food. Liquid feeding is usually most satisfactory and complete plant foods such as Phostrogen can be used or 'natural' fertilizers such as seaweed extracts.

Repotting should be done in spring when pots become overcrowded with roots. Although in the reference table John Innes composts are suggested, many growers of house plants will prefer to use peat composts as being cleaner, lighter, and easier to handle. There is no disadvantage in this but feeding may be required rather sooner because of the smaller food reserve in some of these composts.

Many house plants can be divided when they are repotted and some can be thinned or cut back if they are growing too large. Always cut back to new shoots or growth buds.

PALMS

Some kinds make good plants for a cool or intermediate greenhouse and a few can even be grown in rooms for months at a time, though they usually appreciate periods of recuperation in a moister atmosphere. They can be grown in J.I.P.2 or peat potting compost in the smallest pots that will accommodate their roots comfortably. Water freely in spring and summer, moderately in autumn and winter. Shade from direct sunshine from May to September. Syringe frequently with

Impatiens or Busy Lizzie

Mixed Cacti

water in summer or indoors sponge leaves daily with water. Neanthe bella and Cocos weddelliana are quite small palms, Kentia belmoreana and Phoenix roebelenii are larger kinds. Kentia is particularly tough and hard wearing.

BOTTLE GARDENS

Many house plants can be grown most successfully inside glass carboys or very large bottles. These bottle gardens not only make highly decorative and novel ornaments for a room but they are also a very practical way of overcoming the dry atmosphere, fluctuating temperature, and draughts which are the major hazards in growing plants in living rooms. Inside a bottle the plants create their own atmosphere, the moisture they transpire being mostly trapped inside the bottle, eventually condensing and running back into the soil. Plants in a bottle garden need very little watering, perhaps no more than three or four times a year, and no other attention beyond the removal of dead or decaying leaves.

Either J.I.P.2 or peat potting compost may be used, but add some crushed charcoal to it to keep it sweet. Also put in a 5 cm (2 in.) layer of small pebbles in the bottom of the bottle for drainage. Then put 8–10 cm (3–4 in.) of compost on top of this, pouring all in through a funnel. The compost must be nicely moist.

Plants must be obtained sufficiently small to be passed through the neck of the bottle. Some home-made tools will be needed to plant them—something like a teaspoon, small fork, and a cotton reel attached to canes long enough to reach easily to the bottom of the bottle. The cotton reel enables the compost to be made firm around the plant.

Choose slow growing plants such as cryptanthus in variety, Ficus pumila, fittonias, small leaved ivies, maranta, peperomia, Pteris cretica, Cocos weddelliana, and Neanthe bella and do not overcrowd. Water the plants in lightly; then stand the bottle in a light place but not where the sun will shine directly on it and, perhaps, heat it up too much. The plants will need no feeding or syringing and are only watered when the compost begins to look dry, which may not be for months.

PLANT CABINETS AND WARDIAN CASES

These are other devices for overcoming the atmospheric disadvantages of rooms and creating mini-climates to suit particular plants. The Wardian case is really a tiny ornamental greenhouse or frame which can stand in a room and in which plants can be grown either in a bed of compost or in pots. It is completely enclosed and has all the merits of a bottle garden with the advantage that it can be opened up occasionally to make it much easier to fill it with plants, remove decaying leaves, water when necessary, and replace plants when they get too large.

Plant cabinets are a modern development of the Victorian Wardian case. They, too, are miniature indoor greenhouses, but more elaborate and often fitted with their own thermostatically controlled heating and also fluorescent lighting to compensate for the lack of daylight. There are numerous models differing greatly in design and complexity and each must be operated according to the manufacturer's instructions. The best do greatly extend the range of plants that can be grown and may make it possible to include small flowering plants such as saintpaulias.

Quick-reference Table of Greenhouse Plants

Type   *An* annual; *Bn* biennial; *Bb* bulb or tuber; *Pr* perennial; *Sh* shrub; *Cr* climber; *Tr* trailer.
Colour   *W* white; *Y* yellow; *O* orange; *P* pink; *R* red; *C* crimson; *Pl* purple; *B* blue; *M* mauve; *G* green.
House   *Cd* cold house, no heating at any time of the year.
           Cl cool house, winter minimum 7 °C (45 °F), summer average 13–18 °C (55–65 °F).
           In intermediate house, winter minimum 13 °C (55 °F), summer average 16–21 °C (60–70 °F).
           Wm warm house, winter minimum 18 °C (65 °F), summer average 21–27 °C (70–80 °F).
Soil   *J.I.P.1* John Innes Potting Compost No. 1; *J.I.P.2* John Innes Potting Compost No. 2; *J.I.P.3* John
           Innes Potting Compost No. 3.
           These are the recommendations for mature plants. Seedlings or cuttings are normally started in
           John Innes seed compost and moved on into J.I.P.1 before going to a richer compost, if this is
           required. For most plants the commercial no-soil (peat) composts can be substituted for these
           John Innes soil composts and should be used according to manufacturer's instructions.
Water   *N* normal watering, freely April to September, moderately October to March.
           WR winter rest, keep quite dry from about November to February.
           PWR partial winter rest, water very sparingly in winter.
           SR summer rest, keep quite dry from about midsummer until August.
           PSR partial summer rest, water very sparingly from about midsummer to August.
Increase *Sd* from seed; *Ct* from cuttings; *Lc* leaf cuttings; *Dv* division or from offsets.
           Months for propagation in brackets: (1) January; (2) February, etc.
           * These plants can be grown indoors in a very good light, e.g. on a window ledge.
           † These plants can be grown as house plants, even out of direct light.

Name	Type	Colour	Season	House	Soil J.I.P.	Water	Increase
Abutilon	Sh	W Y P C	all year	Cl In	2	N	Sd (2–3), Ct (3–8)
Acacia	Sh	Y	spring, autumn	Cl In	2	N	Sd (2–3), Ct (7–8)
Achimenes	Bb	P R Pl B	June–Sept	Cl In	1	WR	Sd (1–2), Dv (2–3)
†Aechmea	Pr	R & B and foliage		In Wm	*see* page 108		Dv (3)
Agapanthus	Pr	B W	June–Aug	Cl	3	N	Sd (3–4), Dv (3–4)
†Aglaonema	Pr	foliage only		In	2	N	Dv (3–4)
Aichryson domesticum	Pr	foliage only		Cl In	1	PWR	Ct (3–8)
Allamanda	Cl	Y	Apr–Sept	In Wm	2	N	Ct (3)
†Aloe variegata	Pr	O	May–June	Cl In	1	PWR	Dv (3–4)
*Anthurium	Pr	R P	May–Sept	In Wm	2	N	Dv (2–3)
†Aphelandra	Pr	Y	any time	In Wm	3	N	Ct (5–8)
Aralia: *see* Dizygotheca and Fatsia							
†Araucaria excelsa	Sh	foliage only		Cl	1	N	Sd (3–4)
Arum Lily: *see* Zantedeschia							
Asclepias currassavica	Pr	O & Pl	June–Oct	In	2	N	Dv (3–4), Sd (2–3)
Asparagus plumosus	Cr	foliage only		Cl	2	N	Sd (2–3)
,, sprengeri	Cr Tr	foliage only		Cl	2	N	Sd (2–3)
†Aspidistra	Pr	foliage only		Cl	2	N	Dv (3–4)
Azalea, Indian	Sh	P R W	Dec–Apr	Cl	1	N	Ct (6–7)
†Begonia rex	Pr	foliage only		Cl In	1	N	Sd (2), Dv (3), Lc (7)
,, semperflorens	Pr	W P R C	Apr–Nov	Cl In	2	N	Sd (2–5)
,, , tuberous rooted	Bb	W Y O R C P	June–Sept	Cl	2	WR	Sd (1–2), Dv (2–3)
,, , winter flowering	Pr	W P O R	Nov–Feb	In	2	N	Ct (3–4)
*Beloperone	Pr	P & W	June–Aug	Cl In	1	N	Ct (4)
†Billbergia	Pr	G & P	June–Aug	Cl In	1	PWR	Dv (3–4)
Bougainvillea	Cl	Pl P O	July–Sept	Cl In	2	N	Ct (7–8)

113

Name	Type	Colour	Season	House	Soil J.I.P.	Water	Increase
Bouvardia	Sh	W P R	Oct–Feb	In	2	N	Ct (3–4)
Browallia	An	B	July–Dec	Cl In	1	N	Sd (2–5)
Brunfelsia calycina	Sh	B	all year	In	2	N	Ct (6–7)
Caladium	Bb	foliage only		Wm	2	WR	Dv (3)
†Calathea	Pr	foliage only		In Wm	2	N	Dv (3–4)
Calceolaria	Bn	Y O R C	May–June	Cl	1	N	Sd (5–6)
Camellia	Sh	W P R	Dec–Apr	Cd Cl	1	N	Ct (6–7)
Campanula pyramidalis	Bn	B W	July–Aug	Cd Cl	2	N	Sd (3–4)
Carnations, perpetual	Pr	W P R O Y Pl	all year	Cd Cl	2	N	Ct (12–3)
Cassia	Cl	Y	June–Oct	Cl In	1	N	Ct (3–6)
Celosia	An	Y R	July–Sept	Cd Cl	1	N	Sd (3)
Celsia arcturus	An Bn	Y & B	Apr–Oct	Cl	1	N	Sd (3 or 7)
†Chlorophytum	Pr	foliage only		Cl In	2	N	Dv (3–4)
Chrysanthemum	Pr	W Y O R Pl C P	Oct–Jan	Cl	3	N	Ct (1–4)
Cineraria	Bn	B P R C & W	Nov–May	Cl	1	N	Sd (4–6)
†Cissus	Cl	foliage only		Cl In	2	N	Ct (4–7)
*Citrus	Sh	W	Oct–Apr	Cl In	2	N	Sd (3–4), Ct (6–7)
Clianthus	Sh	R W	May–June	Cl	1	N	Sd (3–4)
Clivia	Bb	Y O	Mar–May	Cl	1	PWR	Dv (6)
†Codiaeum (croton)	Sh	foliage only		In Wm	1	N	Ct (5–6)
*Coleus	Pr	foliage only		Cl In	2	N	Sd (2–3), Ct (7–8)
Crossandra undulifolia	Pr	R	July–Aug	In Wm	1	N	Sd (3–4)
†Cryptanthus	Pr	foliage only		In Wm	1	PWR	Dv (3–4)
*Cyclamen	Bb	W P R C	Nov–Apr	Cl	1	PSR	Sd (4 or 8)
*Cyperus	Pr	foliage only		Cl In	1	N	Sd (3), Dv (3–4)
Didiscus	An	B	June–Sept	Cd Cl	1	N	Sd (3–5)
†Dieffenbachia	Pr	foliage only		In Wm	2	N	Ct (3–4), Sd (3–4)
Dipladenia	Cl	P	May–Sept	In Wm	2	N	Ct (3)
†Dizygotheca	Sh	foliage only		In Wm	2	N	Ct (6–8)
†Dracaena	Pr	foliage only		In Wm	1	N	Ct (3–4), Sd (3–4)
Eccremocarpus	Cl	O R	July–Oct	Cd Cl	2	WR	Sd (2–4)
Eucharis	Bb	W	Jan–Apr	In	1	PWR	Dv (5)
Euphorbia fulgens	Sh	R	Dec–Mar	In Wm	3	N	Ct (4–5)
,, pulcherrima (poinsettia)	Sh	R P	Dec–Mar	In Wm	3	N	Ct (4–5)
,, splendens	Sh	R	July–Sept	In Wm	1	PWR	Ct (6–7)
Eustoma	Bn	B	June–Aug	In Wm	1	N	Sd (3–6)
Exacum affine	An	B & Y	Aug–Dec	Cd Cl	2	N	Sd (3 or 9)
†Fatshedera	Sh	foliage only		Cd Cl	1	N	Ct (4–7)
†Fatsia	Sh	foliage only		Cd Cl	1	N	Ct (6–7)
†Ferns: *see* page 109							
†Ficus elastica (Rubber plant)	Sh	foliage only		Cl In	2	N	Ct (4–6)
†Fittonia	Pr	foliage only		In Wm	2	N	Ct (5–7)
*Francoa	Pr	R W	June–July	Cd Cl	2	N	Sd (3–4), Dv (3–4)
Fuchsia	Sh	P R Pl B W	May–Oct	Cl In	2	N	Ct (6–8)
Gardenia	Sh	W	all year	In Wm	2	N	Ct (3)
Genista	Sh	Y	Feb–May	Cd Cl	2	N	Ct (5–7), Sd (3–4)
Gerbera	Pr	Y O P R	May–Aug	Cl	1	PWR	Sd (3–4)
Gloxinia	Bb	B Pl R P & W	July–Sept	Cl In	1	WR	Sd (1–2)
†Grevillea robusta	Sh	foliage only		Cl In	1	N	Sd (3–4)
Hibiscus rosa-sinensis	Sh	Y R C P	May–Aug	In Wm	2	N	Ct (3–4)
Hippeastrum	Bb	W P R C	Nov–June	Cl In	1	WR	Dv (2–3)
Hoya bella	Tr	W & Pl	July–Sept	In	1	N	Ct (4–7)
* ,, carnosa	Cl	P & Pl	July–Sept	Cl In	1	N	Ct (4–7)
Humea elegans	Bn	brown	July–Sept	Cl	1	N	Sd (5–7)

Primula obconica Mixed

Name	Type	Colour	Season	House	Soil J.I.P.	Water	Increase
Hydrangea	Sh	W B P R C	May–July	Cd Cl	2	N	Ct (4–7)
*Impatiens	Pr	P C R W	all year	Cl In	1	N	Sd (3–4), Ct (6–8)
Jacaranda	Sh	foliage only		Cl	2	N	Sd (4)
*Kalanchoë	Pr	P C R W	all year	Cl	1	N	Sd (3), Ct (5)
Lachenalia	Bb	O Y	Mar–Apr	Cl	2	SR	Dv (8–9), Sd (3)
Lantana	Pr	Y P R	May–Oct	Cl In	1	N	Ct (3–8)
Lapageria	Cl	P W	June–Oct	Cl	1	PWR	layer
Lobelia tenuior	Tr	B	June–Sept	Cd Cl	1	N	Sd (2–3)
†Maranta	Pr	foliage only		In Wm	1	N	Dv (2–3)
Mesembryanthemum	Tr	Y O R C	May–Sept	Cl	1	N	Dv (2–3)
†Mimosa pudica (Sensitive plant)	Pr	foliage only		In Wm	1	N	Sd (3–4)
†Monstera	Cl	foliage only		In Wm	2	N	Ct (6–8)
†Neanthe bella	Palm	foliage only		Cl In	2	N	Sd (3–4)
†Neoregelia	Pr	foliage only		In Wm	see page 108		Dv (3)
Nerine	Bb	P R C M	Sept–Oct	Cl	1	SR	Dv (8)
Nerium (Oleander)	Sh	P W	May–Sept	Cl	2	N	Ct (6–8)
†Nidularium	Pr	foliage only		In Wm	see page 108		Dv (3)
*Oliveranthus	Pr	R & Y	Apr–May	Cl	1	PWR	Sd (3–4), Ct (6–7)

Orchids: *see* page 109

115

Name	Type	Colour	Season	House	Soil J.I.P.	Water	Increase
Pandanus	Pr	foliage only		Cl In	2	N	Dv (3–4)
Passiflora	Cl	W B R	June–Sept	Cl In	1	N	Sd (3), Ct (6)
*Pelargonium, ivy leaved	Tr	P R M	May–Oct	Cl In	1	PWR	Ct (7–8)
* ,, , regal	Pr	W P R C Pl M	May–July	Cl In	1	PSR	Ct (8)
* ,, , scented	Pr	foliage only		Cl In	1	PWR	Ct (7–8)
* ,, , zonal	Pr	W P R C	May–Nov	Cl In	1	PWR	Ct (7–8), Sd (2–3)
†Peperomia	Pr	foliage only		Cl In	2	N	Dv (3–4), Lc (6–7)
Petunia	An	all	June–Oct	Cd Cl	1	N	Sd (2–5)
†Philodendron	Cl	foliage only		In Wm	2	N	Ct (6–8)
†Phoenix roebelinii	Palm	foliage only		Cl In	1	N	Sd (4–5)
†Pilea	Pr	foliage only		Cl In	2	N	Sd (3–4), Ct (3–5)
Plumbago capensis	Cl	B	July–Oct	Cl	2	N	Sd (4–5), Ct (5–6)
Primula kewensis	Pr	Y	Nov–Mar	Cd Cl	2	N	Sd (3–4)
* ,, malacoides	An	P R M	Jan–Mar	Cl	2	N	Sd (4–7)
* ,, obconica	An	W P Pl C B M	Oct–Apr	Cl	2	N	Sd (3–7)
* ,, sinensis	An	P R C O B M	Dec–Mar	Cl	2	N	Sd (3–7)
†Rhoicissus	Cl	foliage only		Cl In	2	N	Ct (4–7)
Saintpaulia	Pr	B P M W	all year	In Wm	1	N	Lc (6–8)
†Sansevieria	Pr	foliage only		In Wm	2	N	Dv (3–4)
Schizanthus	An	W P R C	Apr–Oct	Cd Cl	1	N	Sd (1–9)
†Scindapsus	Cl	foliage only		In Wm	2	N	Ct (6–8)
†Setcreasia	Pr	foliage only		Cl In	2	N	Ct (4–7)
Smithiantha (Gesneria and Naegelia)	Bb	Y O P R	July–Sept	Cl In	1	WR	Sd (2–3), Dv (2–3)
Solanum capsicastrum	Pr	orange winter berries		Cl In	3	N	Sd (3)
*Sparmannia	Sh	W	Jan–Dec	Cl In	2	N	Ct (4–7)
†Spathiphyllum	Pr	W	Apr–May & Oct	In Wm	2	N	Sd (3–4), Dv (3–4)
Statice suworowii	An	P	July–Sept	Cd Cl	1	N	Sd (3–4), Dv (3–4)
Stephanotis	Cl	W	all year	In Wm	3	N	Ct (3–4)
Strelitzia	Pr	O & B	May–June	Cl In	1	PWR	Sd (3), Dv (3)
Streptocarpus	Pr	B P R W	Sept–June	Cl In	2	N	Sd (2 and 6)
Streptosolen	Cl	O	June–July	Cl	1	N	Ct (4–7)
†Syngonium	Cl	foliage only		In Wm	2	N	Ct (6–8)
Thunbergia alata	An	O W	June–Aug	Cd Cl	1	N	Sd (4)
Tibouchina	Sh	B	May–Oct	Cl In	2	N	Ct (4–7)
Torenia fournieri	An	B & Y	June–Sept	Cl	2	N	Sd (2–3)
Trachelium caeruleum	Pr	B	May–Sept	Cl	2	N	Sd (3 or 7)
†Tradescantia fluminensis	Pr	foliage only		Cl In	1	N	Ct (3–8)
Vallota	Bb	R P	Aug–Sept	Cl	1	PWR	Dv (4)
Veltheimia	Bb	Y & R	Nov–Apr	Cl	1	SR	Dv (8–9)
Vinca rosea	Pr	P W & R	all year	In Wm	2	N	Sd (2–4)
†Vreisia	Pr	R foliage	Apr–May	In Wm	see page 108		Dv (3)
Zantedeschia (Arum)	Bb	W Y	Jan–May	Cl Wm	1	N	Dv (8–9)
†Zebrina	Pr	foliage only		Cl In	2	N	Ct (3–8)

116

12 Vegetables

There is no need to consider vegetables as things apart, to be banished to the bottom of the garden or suitable only for allotments. There is no reason why they should not be considered as part of the overall design, and well grown vegetables in neat rows can be as satisfying to the eye as purely ornamental plants. Cottagers have always grown vegetables in this way where they can be seen and admired, and whether vegetables are in fact grown in beds in the ornamental garden or separately can be decided mainly on grounds of convenience.

What is important is that the ground allocated to vegetables can be prepared year after year without interfering with the roots of other more permanent plants, that routine cultivations can be carried out easily, with room to use a hoe freely to keep down weeds, and with access to the beds at all times without trampling through flower borders.

It is also desirable, though not absolutely essential, that there should be some rotation in the sequence of vegetables so that the same kinds are not grown in exactly the same place every year. In large vegetable gardens it is sometimes possible to work to a three year plan, which involves dividing the ground into approximately three equal parts. One of these is devoted to all the brassica crops (cabbages, cauliflowers, kales, turnips, etc.), a second to potatoes, and a third to peas, beans, salads, carrots, parsnips, and onions. Then in succeeding years the groups are moved on in a rota, the brassicas going to the potato plot, the potatoes to the pea, bean, and root plot, and the peas, beans, and roots to the brassica plot.

The merit of some such scheme is that each plot can be prepared to suit the crops to be grown on it, the brassicas and potatoes getting most of the animal manure, and the peas, beans, and roots being fed largely with chemicals but benefiting from what is left of the manure applied to their plot in the two preceding years. Moreover each plot gets a rest from any one type of crop for two years and that is beneficial as it checks the build up of soil borne diseases.

In little gardens no such rigid divisions are possible, but the general principle should be observed of moving things around and of knowing in advance where each crop is going so that the ground can be prepared appropriately.

Digging and forking are really just the same for vegetables as for ornamental plants, but it is done more often and this frequent cultivation will result in the soil deteriorating in structure and in fertility unless it is well fed. Animal manure, or manure substitutes such as rotted garden refuse, mushroom compost, town waste, sewage sludge, peat, and spent hops, are of great importance in the successful cultivation of vegetables because they help to preserve the structure of the soil as well as feed it. Yet even when available in quantity, they are rarely sufficient and need to be supplemented by chemical fertilizers, particularly by well blended compound fertilizers which will supply nitrogen, phosphorus, and potash, the elements most likely to be in short supply in a heavily cropped vegetable garden.

117

Lime is also of much greater importance for vegetables than for most ornamental plants since it helps to keep the soil fertile and prevent it from becoming too acid. Unless the soil is naturally rich in lime or chalk, it is usually wise to apply hydrated lime at about 100 grammes per square metre ($3\frac{1}{2}$ oz/sq yd) once in three years, and where a three year rotation is carried out, this is most conveniently done on the plot being prepared for peas, beans, etc. Where no such regular sequence is possible, the best advice that can be given is never to apply lime at the same time as manure, but a few months before or after, whichever is more convenient.

Many vegetables are grown from seed sown directly outdoors where the crop is to grow. To do this properly a good seed bed must be prepared, which means that the surface must be made level and crumbly. For this work the right soil conditions must be chosen, when it is moist but not wet and the clods easily break up when hit with a fork or rake.

It is also convenient to sow most of these crops in straight rows. To do this a garden line must be stretched tightly to mark the position of the row and then a little furrow or 'drill' must be made alongside the line. The corner of a hoe is convenient for this purpose, but really any pointed tool can be used. The important thing is that the drill must be of the same depth throughout so that, when the seeds have been sown and the displaced soil drawn back over them with a rake, they are all covered to approximately the same depth.

In small gardens it is wise to concentrate on salads that are so much better cut fresh as required, herbs, specially well flavoured vegetables, such as some peas and tomatoes, and on other specialities that are not readily available at the greengrocer's shop.

Many vegetable varieties are F_1 hybrids with the special qualities of vigour and uniformity which this method of breeding gives (*see* page 23).

Artichoke. There are two kinds of artichoke, globe and Jerusalem, and they are totally different plants.

The globe artichoke is a perennial with ornamental grey leaves and purple flowers rather like huge cornflowers. It is worth planting for ornament, but as a vegetable it is grown for its unopened flower heads, which are cooked so that the delicate flesh at the base of each scale can be eaten. Plants can be grown from seed sown in a frame or outdoors in April but better results are obtained by detaching rooted offshoots from old plants and planting them 1 m (3 ft) apart in rich soil and a sunny place. Cut off all the flower stems the first summer, crop the plants the second and third year, and then replace.

The Jerusalem artichoke is grown for its tubers, which look rather like knobbly potatoes. It is also a perennial but is grown from the tubers which are planted in February 40 cm (16 in.) apart in rows 0·75 m ($2\frac{1}{2}$ ft) apart in any reasonably good soil. Leave plants to grow all summer and dig them up as required in autumn and winter, reserving some tubers for replanting.

Asparagus. This is one vegetable which does not fit into any kind of rotation since it may be left undisturbed for many years. Asparagus can be grown from seed or from purchased roots, but seedlings will not give a crop for three years, whereas two year old roots will commence to crop the year after planting.

Sow seed outdoors in April or May in drills 4 cm ($1\frac{1}{2}$ in.) deep and 30 cm (1 ft) apart. It is an advantage to soak the seed for twenty-four hours before sowing to soften it. Thin the seedlings to 7–8 cm (3 in.) apart and in autumn transplant to the bed in which they are to grow. Space them 40 cm (16 in.) apart in rows 1 m (3 ft) apart, and during the next two summers gradually draw soil from between the rows towards the plants so that eventually each row becomes a low rounded ridge. Do not cut any asparagus until the third year.

Purchased plants are spaced and treated in a similar way except that planting is usually done in March or April.

Prepare ground for asparagus by thorough digging and generous manuring. Feed each March with a compound fertilizer and, if possible, manure. Cut young shoots 7–10 cm (3–4 in.) below soil level. Never cut after mid-June. Remove all top growth each November. Weed beds by hand.

Aubergine (Egg Plant). This is grown for its egg-shaped fruits. It can be grown throughout in pots in a sunny greenhouse or seed may be sown under glass in March in a temperature of 15–18 °C (60–65 °F), seedlings pricked off and later potted singly in 8 cm (3 in.) pots in J.I.P.2 compost, hardened off and planted outdoors in a sunny sheltered place in early June. Space plants 45 cm (18 in.) apart and cover with tall cloches if available to hasten growth and ripening. Whether grown in pots or outdoors pinch out the tip of each plant when about 15 cm (6 in.) high. Put a 1 m (3 ft) cane to each plant and tie to this. Restrict fruits to about six per plant.

Beans, Broad. In sheltered places, where the soil is well drained, broad beans can be sown in late October or early November to start cropping the following June. More reliable results can be obtained by sowing in boxes of J.I.S. compost in February in a greenhouse or frame, temperature 12–13 °C (55 °F), hardening off and planting out in mid-April. For a later crop sow outdoors in March–April, 5 cm (2 in.) deep and 15 cm (6 in.) apart in a double row 20 cm (8 in.) apart with 0·75 m (2½ ft) between each pair of rows. Whichever way the beans are grown, pinch out the tip of each plant when beans can be seen to be forming from the bottom truss of flowers. Pick pods as they become nicely filled but before beans start to get tough. It often pays to lime soil before growing broad beans.

(above) Egg Plant
(centre) Beetroot Boltardy
(below) Lettuce Trocadero Improved

Beans, French. There are both dwarf (or bush) and climbing types. The latter can be grown against fences or allowed to twine up poles like runner beans. Dwarf french beans need no support.

Sow outdoors from late April until early July 15–20 cm (6–8 in.) apart in drills 5 cm (2 in.) deep and 60 cm (2 ft) apart. Earlier crops can be obtained by sowing under cloches in March–April or in boxes of J.I.S. compost in a greenhouse or frame and planting out in May. Climbing french beans are grown in the same way as runner beans but may be sown about a fortnight earlier. Pick pods of all kinds regularly as they attain usable size.

Beans, Haricot. These are really varieties of french bean grown for their ripe seeds instead of for their young pods. Grow in the same way as french beans but leave plants until the leaves commence to wither, then pull them up, tie them in small bundles, and hang them in a greenhouse or shed to dry. Finally, shell out the beans and store in tins or bins for use at any time.

Beans, Runner. Normally these are vigorous twiners, but dwarf bushy varieties are also available. Streamline is a popular variety of the climbing type.

Sow from early May until late June 5 cm (2 in.) deep and 20 cm (8 in.) apart in a double row 30–40 cm (12–16 in.) apart and leave 2–2·5 m (6–8 ft) between each double row. Place long poles for each plant, cross them near the top and lash to horizontal poles laid in the forks. Alternatively sow in a single line against fences and strain string or wire up these for the beans to twine around; or sow in large circles and make a wigwam of poles or canes lashed together at the top. Water freely in dry weather. Gather beans regularly as they attain usable size. Sow dwarf varieties 20 cm (8 in.) apart in rows 45 cm (18 in.) apart. No support is required.

Beetroot. There are several distinct types, one with globe-shaped roots, another with long tapering roots, a third with cylindrical roots. Globe varieties are the most popular.

Make three or four small sowings between late April and early July. Sow in drills 2 cm (1 in.) deep and 30–40 cm (12–16 in.) apart. Thin seedlings of globe types to 10 or 12 cm (4 or 5 in.) and of long and cylindrical types to 18 or 20 m (7 or 8 in.). Pull a few roots at a time as required, starting as soon as they are large enough to use. Lift the remainder in late September, twist off the leaves and store in sand or soil in a shed or other reasonably sheltered place.

Borecole or Kale. Plants of the brassica family grown for their leaves which may be plain, curled, or much divided according to variety.

Sow in a seed bed in April–May and transplant seedlings when they are about 15 cm (6 in.) high. Space 60 cm (2 ft) apart. Do not gather leaves until there has been frost in autumn, then pick as required. Most kinds will stand right through the winter until April or even May when they run to flower. Dust seed bed and planting holes with calomel dust (*see* Cabbage).

Broccoli. The name is sometimes applied to the hardier winter and spring varieties of cauliflower, but more properly belongs to those varieties grown for the young flowering sprouts rather than for large curds. There are several types, including calabrese with medium size green heads followed by smaller sprouts in summer and early autumn, and the purple and white sprouting varieties with small sprouts in late winter and spring.

Sow all in a seed bed in April–May and plant out seedlings when about 15 cm (6 in.) high, 60 cm (2 ft) apart each way in fairly rich soil. Cut sprouts with about

15 cm (6 in.) of stem as they form and before they commence to get loose and show the individual flowers. Dust seed bed and planting holes with calomel dust as for cabbage.

Brussels Sprouts. Varieties are available to crop successively from September to February. Sow for an early crop in January–February in a frame or cool greenhouse, for later crops outdoors in March–April. Plant out seedlings when about 15 cm (6 in.) high on firm, well-manured soil, spacing them 60 cm (2 ft) apart in rows 1 m (3 ft) apart. When the buttons are well formed on the stem, cut the heads or tops and use these as greens. This will help the buttons to grow even larger. Gather buttons as required, starting with the most forward. Dust seed beds and planting holes with calomel dust as for cabbage.

Cabbage. There are several distinct types of cabbage: ballhead with almost globular hearts; pointed with conical hearts; and Savoy with wrinkled leaves. Savoy cabbage is particularly hardy and useful for winter cutting, but there are also varieties of the other types that can be used in winter. There are quick growing varieties, such as Velocity, specially suitable for summer use, and yet others, known as spring cabbage varieties, which if sown in summer, will stand the winter and be available for cutting in May–June.

Sow all in a seed bed: in March–April for summer and autumn cropping and in July–August for spring cropping. Sow 1·5 cm ($\frac{3}{4}$ in.) deep and transplant seedlings when about 15 cm (6 in.) high. Give cabbages good rich soil. Plant summer, autumn, and winter varieties 60 cm (2 ft) apart, spring varieties 30 cm (1 ft) apart in rows 45 cm (18 in.) apart. Dust seed beds and planting holes with 4 per cent calomel dust as a protection against club root disease and cabbage root fly maggots. Cut cabbages as required, starting as soon as they have made good firm hearts.

Carrot. There are several distinct types: very short, almost globular rooted, varieties particularly suitable for the earliest crops; stump rooted varieties with candle-shaped roots, such as Autumn King, the most generally useful kind; intermediate varieties with longer, tapering roots; and long carrots chiefly used for exhibition.

All do best on ground that has been well manured for a previous crop and fed with a compound fertilizer prior to sowing. Sow from early March to mid-June in drills 1 cm ($\frac{1}{2}$ in.) deep and 20–30 cm (8–12 in.) apart. The small round kinds need little or no thinning if thinly sown. Thin short horn carrots progressively to 5–8 cm (2–3 in.) apart, leaving the last thinning until the roots are just large enough to use. For large carrots thin to 15 cm (6 in.). Pull carrots for use as required, lift the remainder of the crop in mid-September and store in sand or dry soil in a shed. Dust rows of carrots every ten to fourteen days with flaked naphthalene from first thinning until late June to ward off attacks by carrot fly.

(left) Cabbage Velocity; (right) A basket of Cauliflower, Tomatoes, Cucumber, and Broad Beans

Cauliflower. These are grown for their close white heads or curds. Varieties are available to mature at different times so that cauliflowers can be available for the greater part of the year.

Sow in a seed bed from March to May according to variety, or for June–July cutting sow a quick maturing variety in a slightly heated greenhouse or frame in February–March. Plant out in firm, well manured, well drained soil when seedlings are about 15 cm (6 in.) high and keep well watered in dry weather. Space at least 60 cm (2 ft) apart each way. Dress seed beds and planting holes with calomel dust as for cabbages.

Celery. Two kinds are grown, self blanching, suitable for summer use, and the ordinary pink or white celery for autumn and winter use. Both like rather rich soil with plenty of water during the summer. Sow from early March to early April in pots or boxes of J.I.S. in a greenhouse or frame, temperature 15–18 °C (60–65 °F). Prick off seedlings 1 cm (2 in.) apart in boxes of J.I.P.1 compost and harden off for planting out from mid-May until late June.

Plant self blanching celery 20 cm (8 in.) apart each way in blocks so that the leaves shade the stems. Plant pink and white celery 30 cm (1 ft) apart in single rows in trenches and gradually draw soil towards the plants, mounding it up to cover the stems and so blanch them. Dig plants as required, starting at one end of the ridge so that the soil remains as a protection for the remaining plants. Use white celery first, since it is not as hardy as the pink.

Celeriac. This is also known as turnip rooted celery and is grown for its swollen, turnip-like roots which have the same flavour as celery. Sow in the same way as celery and plant out in May 20 cm (8 in.) apart in rows 30–40 cm (12–16 in.) apart. Use the roots as they become sufficiently large.

Chicory. This is grown outdoors in summer and then roots are lifted and forced in complete darkness in winter for their young blanched leaves, used as salad. Sow from mid-May to mid-June in drills 1 cm ($\frac{1}{2}$ in.) deep and 30 cm (12 in.) apart and thin plants to 20 cm (8 in.). Lift in November and store in sand or dry soil in a shed. Force a few roots at a time by packing them quite close together in large pots or deep boxes in sand and peat and putting them in any dark place in which a temperature of 10–15 °C (50–60 °F) can be maintained. Keep moist while forcing. Cut heads when about 15 cm (6 in.) high.

Cress. Sow in moist peat compost in shallow boxes or pans every seven to fourteen days, simply pressing the seed into the surface of the compost with a smooth block of wood. Cover with a sheet of glass and keep in a minimum night temperature of 10 °C (50 °F). Remove the glass as soon as the seeds germinate and cut seedlings for use as salad when 5–6 cm (2–2$\frac{1}{2}$ in.) high.

Cucumber. Two kinds are commonly grown, ridge cucumbers for planting outdoors in summer and frame cucumbers for cultivation in greenhouses or frames.

Sow seed of ridge varieties in pots in J.I.S. compost, temperature 15–18 °C (60–65 °F) from mid- to late April and harden off for planting outdoors in early June, 1 m (3 ft) apart in rich, well manured soil and a warm sunny place. Water freely in dry weather. Alternatively sow seeds in May in twos or threes 1 m (3 ft) apart outdoors where they are to grow, cover with cloches, and thin the seedlings to one per group. Cut cucumbers regularly as they become large enough for use.

Sow frame cucumbers in the same way under glass, but for an early crop sow in February. Pot seedlings singly in J.I.P.1 compost and, when about 15 cm (6 in.) high, plant in a cool or intermediate house 1 m (3 ft) apart on low mounds of

J.I.P.3 compost or a mixture of two parts loam and one part well rotted manure. Train stems to wires strained 15–20 cm (6–8 in.) below the glass. Remove all male flowers, recognizable by the fact that they have no embryo cucumber below them like the female flowers. This precaution is not necessary with the variety Femina, an F_1 hybrid with all female flowers. Pinch out the tip of each stem two leaves beyond the first fruit that appears on it. Water freely, maintain a damp atmosphere, and shade the glass with limewash or shading compound. Again it is important to cut fruits regularly and not allow any to ripen.

Endive. This is grown and used in a similar way to lettuce, but it is hardier and therefore particularly serviceable in autumn and winter. Sow from April to July in drills 1 cm ($\frac{1}{2}$ in.) deep and 30 cm (1 ft) apart. Thin seedlings to 20 cm (8 in.). When plants are large enough for use cover each with an inverted plate, or a flower pot with drainage hole blocked to exclude light, and blanch the leaves. Blanching will take from one to three weeks.

Garlic. This is grown from 'cloves', the separate sections of a garlic bulb, planted in March or April 20 cm (8 in.) apart in rows 30 cm (1 ft) apart in well-drained soil and a warm sunny place. Just cover the cloves with soil. Lift the plants in August, lay them in a sunny place to dry for a few weeks, and then store in a cool dry place.

Kale. *See* Borecole.

Kohl Rabi. This is grown for its swollen stems which are used in the same way as turnips. Sow from March to July in drills 1 cm ($\frac{1}{2}$ in.) deep and 45 cm (18 in.) apart. Thin seedlings to 20 cm (8 in.). Pull and use as the stems become of reasonable size.

Leek. These require rich, well worked soil. Sow seed in March–April in drills 1 cm ($\frac{1}{2}$ in.) deep and 30 cm (1 ft) apart and either thin the seedlings to 15–20 cm (6–8 in.) apart, or when they are 18–20 cm (7–8 in.) high lift them carefully and replant in 15 cm (6 in.) deep holes made with a stout stick or 'dibber'. Space the plants 20 cm (8 in.) apart in rows 45 cm (18 in.) apart. Do not fill in the holes but pour water into them after planting to wash some soil round the roots. Longer blanched stems can be obtained by planting in shallow trenches like celery and drawing the soil into the trenches and up the stems as the plants grow. Early leeks are obtained by sowing seed in boxes in February in a temperature of 12·5–15 °C (55–60 °F), hardening off the seedlings, and planting them out in May. Holborn Model is a good variety.

Lettuce. There are several different types of lettuce. Cabbage lettuces have more or less globular hearts and broad leaves: cos lettuces have long upstanding leaves forming ovoid hearts; and loose leaf lettuces make no hearts at all. The cabbage type is further split into butterhead varieties, with soft textured leaves, and crisp-head varieties, with much crisper, more brittle leaves. Cos lettuces are always crisp leaved.

Lettuces like rich soil and plenty of water in dry weather. Sow in small batches every two or three weeks from March to July, in drills 1 cm ($\frac{1}{2}$ in.) deep and 30 cm (1 ft) apart. Thin seedlings 20–30 cm (8–12 in.) apart. If the unwanted seedlings are lifted carefully with a handfork they can be replanted elsewhere. Early crops can be produced by sowing in a frame or unheated greenhouse during the first fortnight in October in drills 20 cm (8 in.) apart. Thin seedlings to 7–8 cm (3 in.) in November and in March transplant two out of three to cloches or another frame, leaving the remainder at 20–24 cm (9 in.) apart to mature.

For a winter crop use a special winter variety such as Cheshunt Early Giant, and sow every three or four weeks from September to December in boxes of J.I.S. compost in a cool greenhouse. Plant seedlings about 20 cm (8 in.) apart each way in a bed of fairly rich soil in the greenhouse and maintain a temperature of 10–12·5 °C (50–55 °F) throughout. A good light greenhouse is essential.

Melon. These can be grown in sunny greenhouses in which a minimum temperature of 10 °C (50 °F) can be maintained or in frames or under cloches. Culture is very similar to that for cucumbers, but the atmosphere should be drier (especially as the fruits ripen), no shading should be given, and each plant should be restricted to about four fruits. Moreover, unlike cucumbers, melons must be fertilized. Do this by picking off male flowers when fully open and shaking dry pollen on to the female flowers, each of which will have an embryo melon below it. Fertilize four flowers on a plant at the same time and then, when it is clear that pollination has been effective and that the fruits are swelling, remove all other flowers. Water freely except for the last fortnight as the fruits are ripening. Spread about 2 cm (1 in.) of well rotted manure or J.I.P.3 compost over the beds when white rootlets appear on the surface. Support ripening fruits in nets attached to the training wires. Under cloches or in frames support the fruits on inverted pots or bricks so that they are out of contact with the soil and fully exposed to the light.

Mushroom. These can be grown in the light or dark, the principal advantage of the latter being that it is easier to keep a shed or cellar at the necessary 10–15 °C (50–60 °F) than it is a greenhouse. Mushrooms dislike high temperatures and in summer it is difficult to keep greenhouses down to the required level.

Mushrooms can be grown in stable manure but nowadays are usually grown in straw, rotted with the aid of one of the proprietary mushroom compost makers. Manufacturer's instructions must be followed. When this compost is in the right condition, place it in boxes about 15 cm (6 in.) deep and of any convenient size. Check the temperature of the compost with a soil thermometer and when it has fallen to 21 °C (70 °F) obtain some mushroom spawn, break into pieces about 2 cm (1 in.) across, and push into the compost about 20 cm (8 in.) apart. Then cover the compost with a 15 cm (6 in.) layer of clean straw. After ten to fourteen days the white thread-like mycelium of the mushroom should be visible on the surface of the compost. When it is, remove the straw and cover the compost with a 2 cm (1 in.) thickness of a mixture of equal parts granulated peat and well broken chalk. Maintain a moist atmosphere and water lightly if the compost looks at all dry. Gather mushrooms as they appear by breaking them off complete with the stalk.

Mustard. This is grown in exactly the same way as cress, but grows a little more rapidly so should be sown three days later if both are required at the same time.

Onion. These can be grown from seed or from 'sets', i.e. from small onions specially grown for the purpose. Either way a fairly rich and crumbly soil is required and many expert growers prefer to keep onions out of the regular vegetable garden rotation and instead grow them on the same ground year after year, gradually improving it with manure, peat, wood ashes, lime, etc.

Sow in March–April in drills 1 cm ($\frac{1}{2}$ in.) deep and 20–30 cm (8–12 in.) apart. Thin seedlings to 15 cm (6 in.) apart for ordinary size onions, or to 20 cm (8 in.) for really large bulbs when the thinnings are large enough to be used as salad onions. Use bulbs as they attain suitable size and lift all bulbs when the foliage has partly died down in late August or September. Dry for a week or so in a dry, sunny place, then store in a cool, dry place.

Sets are easier to manage than seed, especially if it is difficult to prepare a fine, crumbly seed bed. Plant with a trowel or dibber in April, 15 to 20 cm (6 to 8 in.) apart in rows 30 cm (1 ft) apart at such a depth that the tips of the bulbs can just be seen. Lift, dry, and store in August–September as for onions grown from seed.

For an early crop varieties such as Autumn Queen can be sown in late August in well-drained soil and a fairly sheltered place and be transplanted in March–April 15 to 20 cm (6 to 8 in.) apart in rows 30 cm (1 ft) apart. Seed of all varieties can also be sown in a cool greenhouse in January in J.I.S. compost, seedlings pricked off 5 cm (2 in.) apart in boxes of J.I.P.1 compost, and hardened off for planting out in April.

Parsnip. These do best on soil manured for a previous crop and dusted with a compound fertilizer prior to sowing. Sow in March–April in drills 2 cm (1 in.) deep and 30–40 cm (12–16 in.) apart. Thin seedlings to 15–20 cm (6–8 in.). Dust rows with flaked naphthalene as advised for carrots. Dig roots as they obtain usable size. Parsnips can be left in the ground all winter as they are quite hardy, but it is often convenient to lift some roots in November and store in sand or ashes.

Pea. These are classified as first early, second early, maincrop, and late according to the time different varieties take to produce a crop under similar conditions. This varies from about ten weeks for the fastest maturing to sixteen weeks for the slowest. Peas also differ in height, from about 45 cm (18 in.) to 1·5 m (5 ft), and all but the shortest must have sticks, netting, or something of the kind for support. There are also round seeded and wrinkled seeded varieties, the former a little hardier but not so sweet and little grown in gardens today. Raynes Park is a reliable variety with wrinkled seeds taking fourteen weeks to mature and 1 m (3 ft) in height.

Peas like fairly rich soil containing plenty of lime or chalk. Sow from March until late June choosing an early variety for the later sowings. Sow in drills 5 cm (2 in.) deep, or scoop out flat

(above) A Selection of Radish, including Sparkler and Cherry Belle; (centre) Asparagus and Mixed Peppers; (below) Tomato Moneymaker

bottomed trenches 5 cm (2 in.) deep and 15–20 cm (6–8 in.) wide with a spade and space the seeds about 5 cm (2 in.) apart all over these. Space rows according to the height of the variety, 60 cm (2 ft) for a 60 cm high pea, 1 m (3 ft) for a 1 m pea, and so on. Do not thin seedlings. Put bushy sticks or well supported string or plastic netting for peas to climb on as soon as the seedlings appear. Water freely in dry weather. Pick peas as the pods become reasonably filled but while the peas are still tender.

Asparagus peas and sugar peas have edible pods which are picked as soon as they are well grown but before the peas in them mature. They are cooked whole and eaten like french beans.

Potato. These, too, are classified as early, second early, maincrop, and late according to the time varieties take to mature, from about twelve weeks from planting to lifting for the fastest to six months for the slowest. They are also classified according to shape and colour, as round or kidney (which is really ovoid) and as white skinned or coloured skinned. Varieties listed as 'immune' are immune to wart disease only, a disease that is troublesome in a few places and seasons.

'Seed' potatoes are small potatoes grown specially for planting. Scottish and Northern Irish seed is more likely to be free of virus disease than seed from other parts of Britain because of the late arrival of aphids (which carry the infection) in these two areas.

Potatoes like rather rich, well cultivated soil that has had some manure or manure substitute as well as a dressing of a compound fertilizer. They do not like lime, which encourages scabby skins.

Purchase seed potatoes in January–February and stand the tubers, eyed end uppermost, in shallow trays. Place them in a light but frost-proof place to sprout.

Plant in March–April in trenches 12–15 cm (5–6 in.) deep and 75 cm ($2\frac{1}{2}$ ft) apart. Space the tubers 30 cm (12 in.) apart for earlies, 40 cm (16 in.) for all other varieties, always with the sprouts uppermost. Cover by drawing back the displaced soil. When shoots appear draw a little soil from between the rows over them. Continue to draw soil towards the stems as they lengthen, until the soil is in low rounded ridges.

Spray potatoes in late June, mid-July, and early August with copper fungicide as a protection against potato blight disease.

Lift early and second early potatoes a few at a time as required, starting as soon as the tubers reach usable size. Lift all potatoes in late September or when leaves and stems wither (whichever is earlier) and store sound tubers only in a dark, dry, frost-proof place.

Radish. Grow in rich soil and sow every two or three weeks from March until August in drills 0·5 cm ($\frac{1}{4}$ in.) deep and 15–20 cm (6–8 in.) apart. Pull roots as required, starting as soon as they are of usable size.

Rhubarb. This is a semi-permanent crop to be grown in some places where the plants can be left undisturbed for years. It can be grown from seed sown in April in a drill 2 cm (1 in.) deep, seedlings thinned to 15 cm (6 in.) and transplanted to their permanent position in the autumn or spring, or from roots purchased in autumn or spring. Plant in fairly rich soil 1 m (3 ft) apart and do not pull any sticks the first year.

Early supplies are produced by covering strong roots with barrels, deep boxes or special earthenware forcing pots in early January and heaping straw, bracken or

126

dead leaves around them to keep out the cold. Even earlier supplies can be had by lifting roots in November–December and bringing them into a greenhouse or shed in which a minimum night temperature of 12·5 °C (55 °F) can be maintained, and from which light can be excluded. Pack soil around the roots and keep moist.

Salsify. This is grown for its parsnip-like roots and cultivation is the same as for parsnips.

Savoy. *See* Cabbage.

Seakale. This is grown for its young blanched shoots in winter and spring. It can be grown from seed sown 1 cm ($\frac{1}{2}$ in.) deep outdoors in April, the seedlings thinned to 30 cm (12 in.) apart, or alternatively pieces of root about 15 cm (6 in.) long can be planted in March in dibber holes 30 cm (12 in.) apart. Plant right way up and so that the top of each root is just covered with soil. Growth must be blanched for use and this can be done either by covering plants with boxes or pots, much as for early rhubarb, or by lifting roots in November, storing them in sand or soil and potting a few at a time, to be forced in darkness in any place in which a minimum night temperature of 12·5 °C (55 °F) can be maintained. Pot about four or five roots in each 18–20 cm (7–8 in.) pot. Cut shoots at soil level when 15–20 cm (6–8 in.) high.

Seakale Beet. A form of beetroot grown for its leaves, which have thick white mid-ribs with much the same flavour as seakale. Cultivation is the same as for spinach beet.

Shallot. Plant bulbs in February or March 15 cm (6 in.) apart in rows 30 cm (12 in.) apart, simply pressing the bulbs into the soil so that they are nearly, but not quite, covered. Lift the clusters of bulbs in July–August when the leaves turn yellow and treat in the same way as onions.

Spinach. Sow round seeded or summer spinach every three weeks from March to mid-July in drills 2 cm (1 in.) deep and 30 cm (12 in.) apart. When plants touch in the rows cut alternate ones for use and leave the rest to grow on. From these gather leaves as required. Sow prickly seeded or winter spinach about mid-August and treat in the same way.

Spinach Beet. A variety of beet grown for its leaves which are picked and used like spinach. Sow in March–April and again in mid-August in drills 2 cm (1 in.) deep and 40 cm (16 in.) apart. Thin seedlings to 20–30 cm (8–12 in.). Gather leaves as required.

Most vegetable seeds are sown in straight drills made with the corner of a hoe. The seed is scattered thinly and covered by drawing back the displaced soil with a rake. Leeks are planted in holes made with a dibber (right) and are watered in.

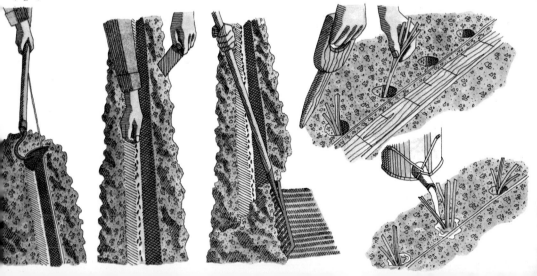

Swede. Grow in the same way as turnip, but give a little more room, rows 40 cm (16 in.) apart and seedlings thinned to 20 cm (8 in.)

Sweet Corn. Sow seeds singly in 6 cm (2½ in.) pots filled with J.I.S. compost in April in a temperature of 12·5–15 °C (55–60 °F). Plant out seedlings in late May 60 cm (2 ft) apart each way, in blocks rather than in long rows, for more effective pollination. Plant in fairly rich soil and a sunny sheltered position. Gather cobs as soon as the 'corn' is well formed on the cobs and before it commences to get hard.

Tomato. These can be grown in a greenhouse or in a warm, sunny place outdoors. For intermediate house culture sow seed in January, for cool house in February, and for cold house or outdoors in March–April, but in a propagator in which a temperature of 15 °C (60 °F) can be maintained. Sow in J.I.S. compost, prick off seedlings 5 cm (2 in.) apart in J.I.P.1 and later pot singly in 8 cm (3 in.) pots in J.I.P.2. For greenhouse culture either pot on into 20 cm (8 in.) pots in J.I.P.3; or plant in bottomless rings 25 cm (10 in.) in diameter filled with J.I.P.3 compost and placed on a 15 cm (6 in.) deep bed of gravel or cinders; or plant 45 cm (18 in.) apart in rows 0·75 m (2½ ft) apart in a bed of good soil on the floor of the greenhouse. Outdoors do not plant until early June, except in the mildest districts. Plant 45 cm (18 in.) apart in rows 1 m (3 ft) apart.

With the exception of bush varieties, which are allowed to branch naturally, restrict each plant to a single stem, removing all side shoots as they appear. Tie the main stem of each plant to a cane. Remove the tops of outdoor plants when they have formed four trusses of flowers and of greenhouse plants when they reach the roof. Place clean straw under bush tomatoes to keep fruits off the soil.

Water freely throughout, but only water the gravel or cinder base of ring culture plants after one good soaking of the soil in the ring at planting time. From the time the first fruits are set, feed every ten to fourteen days with a tomato fertilizer used according to label instructions. For ring culture apply this fertilizer, suitably diluted with water, only to the soil in the rings.

Spray outdoor plants in late June, mid-July, and mid-August with copper fungicide as a protection against potato blight disease. Change the soil in tomato beds every year.

Carters Fruit Tomato is recommended for its firm, well flavoured flesh.

Endive can be blanched by placing a plate over each mature plant. Potatoes are earthed up (centre) to prevent greening of tubers through exposure to light. Celery is planted in trenches (right) and is earthed up when fully grown to blanch the stems.

Pea Feltham First
Carrot Tip Top

Turnip. These like a fairly rich soil that has been manured for a previous crop and been dusted with a compound fertilizer prior to sowing. Sow every three or four weeks from March to mid-August in drills 1·5 cm ($\frac{3}{4}$ in.) deep and 30 cm (12 in.) apart. Thin summer crops to 10 to 15 cm (4–6 in.), but the July–August sowings to 15 to 20 cm (6–8 in.) to stand the winter. Turnips can also be sown in early September and left unthinned to provide turnip tops as greens in spring. Pull turnip roots as required, starting as soon as the roots reach usable size.

Vegetable Marrow. There are both bush and trailing kinds; also American varieties known as squashes; prolific varieties to be cut very young, known as courgettes; and pumpkins to be allowed to ripen before being cut.

All like very rich soil with plenty of manure or manure substitute and plenty of water in summer. Sow seeds two in each 8 cm (3 in.) pot of J.I.S. compost in April and germinate in a temperature of 15–18 °C (60–65 °F). Harden off for planting outdoors in late May or early June. Plant bush varieties 1 m (3 ft) apart; trailing varieties 1·5 m (5 ft) apart. Pinch out tips of the main growths of trailing varieties when 1 m (3 ft) long. Restrict pumpkins to two or three fruits per plant. Cut courgettes regularly as they attain usable size. Allow marrows to grow to medium size, but cut before they get really hard. Only pumpkins are permitted to ripen and turn orange.

129

13 Herb Beds

Fresh herbs gathered from one's own garden can make all the difference to a great many dishes. Herbs can also be very decorative and a bed reserved for them, or even a series of beds, perhaps enclosed in clipped box in the old fashioned manner, can be quite a feature in any garden. Add to this the fact that it is easy to dry herbs and so have an all the year round supply of many useful kinds that it would be difficult to buy and you will see that there are many excellent reasons for including herbs in the garden.

The most generally useful herbs are chives, mint, sage, and thyme, all perennials, and parsley grown as an annual. To these may be added lavender and rosemary for their fragrance. Other kinds will be grown according to what is required for kitchen use, for flavouring drinks or maybe just for old world associations. Nearly all are quite easily grown in any reasonably good soil and fairly open situation.

Shoots or leaves for drying should be cut in June–July, when well grown but before they get old and hard. Tie them in small bundles and suspend them in a dry airy place for a few weeks, after which they can be stored in tins, bowls or jars.

Angelica. A tall and handsome biennial grown for its leaves, stems, and also leaf stalks which are candied and used for decorating cakes. Sow it outdoors in April–May and thin the seedlings well. Once established, angelica will often renew itself for years by self-sown seedlings which appear in hundreds around the parent plants.

Balm. There are several kinds, but the most generally useful is the lemon balm, Melissa officinalis, a perennial grown for its lemon-scented leaves. It can be raised from seed sown outdoors in April–May or by division of the plants in spring.

Basil. There are two kinds, sweet basil, Ocimum basilicum and bush basil, O. minimum. Both are grown from seed, best sown in a temperature of 15 °C (60 °F) in March–April in J.I.S. compost and planted out in June.

Bay. An evergreen tree with aromatic leaves. It can be grown in tubs or other containers and clipped into cones, balls, formal standards, and other fancy shapes. Dwarfed pot specimens can also be grown on window-ledges. Bay trees may need winter protection in cold places.

Borage. An attractive annual plant with blue flowers. It is readily grown from seed sown outdoors in March–April.

Caraway. This is a biennial grown for its distinctively flavoured seeds. Sow outdoors in April, thin the seedlings well, and leave to flower and ripen their seeds the next year.

Chamomile. Several different plants share this name but the best for the herb

| Cotton Lavender | Rosemary | Bergamot | Lavender |

bed is Anthemis nobilis, a perennial with much divided leaves. It can be clipped like a lawn and emits a pleasant fragrance when bruised. Raise it from seed sown outdoors in March–April.

Chervil. A hardy annual with ferny leaves and an aniseed flavour. Grow if from seed sown outdoors in March–April.

Chives. This is a relative of the onion, a tufted perennial plant grown for its leaves, which have a mild onion flavour. It can be raised from seed sown outdoors in April–May or plants can be divided in the spring.

Coriander. A hardy annual grown for its aromatic seeds. Sow in April–May where it is to grow.

Dill. A hardy annual grown for its leaves which are used in a variety of ways. Sow in April–May.

Fennel. There are two different kinds, sweet fennel, Foeniculum officinale, grown for its aniseed scented leaves, and Florence fennel, F. dulce, grown for its swollen stems. Both have attractive ferny leaves and are grown from seed sown outdoors in April–May.

Hyssop. A small bushy plant which can be clipped like lavender to form a little hedge or make a formal edging to a bed. Grow it from seed sown outdoors in April–May or from cuttings taken in summer.

Lavender. *See* Chapter 8.

Marjoram. There are several different kinds of marjoram: one, known as the golden marjoram (Origanum vulgare aureum) with soft yellow leaves; another, the French marjoram (O. onites), with grey leaves; a third, the sweet or knotted marjoram (O. majorana), with a particularly spicy flavour. The first two are perennials but the sweet marjoram is a half-hardy annual. It is raised from seed sown in a greenhouse or frame in March and planted out in late May or early June.

Mint. There are several varieties of mint, differing in the scent and flavour of their leaves, but all are perennial and grown in exactly the same way. It is the spearmint, Mentha viridis, that is the most popular. All mints spread by underground shoots so should be planted where they will not interfere with other things. Plant in March, spreading the roots out thinly and covering with 3–4 cm (1½ in.) of soil. Pick leaves or young shoots as required.

Parsley. Two sowings outdoors, one in March–April, the second in June–July, will ensure a supply of fresh parsley for much of the year. Sow in drills 1 cm (½ in.) deep and 20 cm (8 in.) apart and thin seedlings to 15 cm (6 in.). Water freely in dry weather. Cover some plants with cloches in October.

Rosemary. *See* Chapter 8.

Rue. This 30–45 cm (12–18 in.) shrubby plant is grown for its finely divided blue-grey aromatic leaves. It is often clipped as an edging. Increase by division or seed.

Sage. A small evergreen bush with grey-green leaves, variegated with cream, yellow or purple in some varieties. It likes a sunny place and well-drained soil and can be grown from seed sown outdoors in April–May or from cuttings in summer. Plant in permanent positions about 40 cm (16 in.) apart.

| Chicory | Thyme | Marjoram | Fennel |

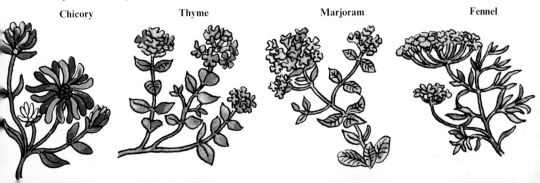

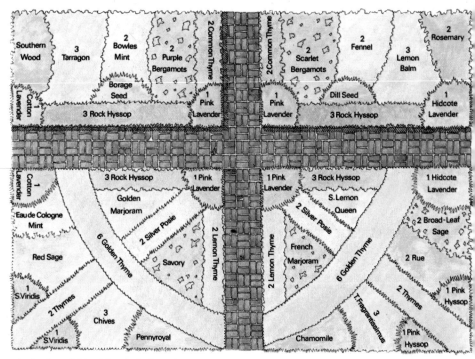

Labels in the plan (top row, left to right): Southern Wood; 3 Tarragon; 2 Bowles Mint; 2 Purple Bergamots; 2 Common Thyme; 2 Common Thyme; 2 Scarlet Bergamots; 2 Fennel; 3 Lemon Balm; 2 Rosemary

Borage Seed; Dill Seed

1 Cotton Lavender; 3 Rock Hyssop; 1 Pink Lavender; 1 Pink Lavender; 3 Rock Hyssop; 1 Hidcote Lavender

1 Cotton Lavender; 3 Rock Hyssop; 1 Pink Lavender; 1 Pink Lavender; 3 Rock Hyssop; 1 Hidcote Lavender

Eau de Cologne Mint; Golden Marjoram; S. Lemon Queen; 2 Broad-Leaf Sage

Red Sage; 6 Golden Thyme; 2 Silver Posie; 2 Lemon Thyme; 2 Silver Posie; 6 Golden Thyme; 2 Rue

Savory; 2 Lemon Thyme; French Marjoram

1 S. Viridis; 2 Thymes; 2 Thymes; 1 Pink Hyssop

1 S. Viridis; 3 Chives; Pennyroyal; Chamomile; T. Fragrantissimus; 1 Pink Hyssop

A plan for a fairly elaborate herb garden designed as an ornamental feature as well as a source of material both for use fresh and for drying.

Savory. There are two kinds, one the summer savory, a hardy annual to be grown from seed sown outdoors in March–April, the other, the winter savory, a small shrub which in well-drained soil will live for years. It, too, can be grown from seed, preferably sown in a greenhouse or frame in March–April, the seedlings transplanted outdoors in early June. Alternatively it can be increased by summer cuttings.

Thyme. There are several kinds of thyme: the common thyme, Thymus vulgaris, a small bush to 30 cm (12 in.) high; the lemon thyme, T. citriodorus, similar but lemon scented; and the prostrate thyme, T. serpyllum, making carpets of aromatic leaves and purple or white flowers. There are silver variegated varieties of the first two and also a golden leaved variety of lemon thyme. All like sunny places and well-drained soils containing lime or chalk. Grow from seed sown outdoors in April–May, or the common thyme and the lemon thyme from cuttings, and the prostrate thyme by division. Variegated varieties must be increased by cuttings.

14 Fruit

Fruit, like vegetables, can be combined in the general garden design or be given a place to itself, whichever is more convenient. Trained fruit trees make attractive divisions between one part of the garden and another or may be used to cover walls and fences. Standard fruit trees can be used in place of ornamental trees and can be quite as attractive. There are also special forms, such as pyramids and winged pyramids, which because of their formal outline can perform a similar function to topiary specimens, with the important difference that they will be bare of leaf in winter.

Fruits, like vegetables, need routine attention: spraying several times in spring and summer; pruning in winter and possibly also in summer; and picking. Because of this there must be easy access to the trees, bushes or canes at all seasons. Unlike vegetables, fruit crops, with the one exception of strawberries, are there to stay. After the first soil preparation, which should be thorough, the soil around fruit crops should never be disturbed more than a few centimetres (an inch or so) deep since the feeding roots are all quite near the surface. For this reason fruit trees and vegetables do not mix very well, since the frequent soil cultivation required by one is bad for the other. But there is no reason at all why hardy plants or small shrubs should not be grown with fruits, provided they do not crowd them too much.

Soil preparation and planting are similar to that for trees and shrubs. Manure or manure substitutes can be used freely, and since most fruit trees use a good deal of nitrogen and potash, hoof and horn meal at 100 grammes ($3\frac{1}{2}$ oz) and wood ashes at about 200 g (6–8 oz) per square metre (or square yard) are useful preparatory dressings.

Most fruit trees, bushes, and canes are sold 'bare root', i.e. lifted from the open ground from late October to late March, but some can also be purchased in containers at any time of the year. The major exception to this is the strawberry which is sold bare root from August to October and in containers mainly in March–April.

Apples, pears, plums, cherries, peaches, nectarines, and apricots are grafted by

Various forms in which fruit trees may be grown. From left to right they are bush, half standard, standard, single stem cordon, horizontal trained or espalier, and fan trained. Note that the last has no vertical main stem which would tend to monopolize growth.

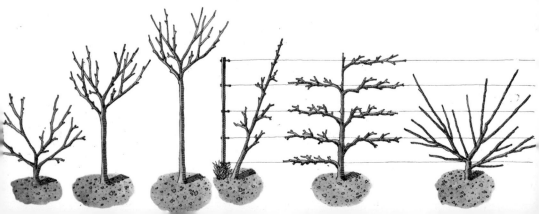

nurserymen on to stocks which provide them with their roots. A number of different stocks are in use and they influence the vigour and fruitfulness of the trees. In general the more strongly a tree grows the slower it will be in coming into bearing but the longer its life will be. However, since any well cared-for tree is likely to live for at least twenty years, longevity is not a first consideration in gardens and compact size, coupled with early and consistent bearing, are what really matter. Therefore what are known as moderately dwarfing stocks are more suitable than vigorous stocks and should be specified when ordering.

Fruit trees only produce crops when their blossom is fertilized. Pollen for fertilization is carried by wind and also by bees and other insects. If the weather is bad when the blossom is open it may be impossible for it to be fertilized properly and this accounts for many crop failures.

Though fruit trees are hardy, their flowers and the very small fruits can be killed by even a few degrees of frost, so fruit trees planted in hollows, and other places where cold air accumulates, often crop badly. The best site for most fruit trees is one that is reasonably open, with good circulation of air.

Some fruit trees cannot be fertilized by their own pollen or are only imperfectly fertilized by it. For good cropping they need pollen from another variety of the same kind of fruit, i.e. one variety of apple needs pollen from another variety of apple, one variety of cherry needs another cherry as a mate. The lone fruit tree is often barren or nearly so for this reason. Nurserymen who specialize in fruit trees are able to give advice on suitable varieties to plant together. Some graft several different varieties on the same tree so that each fertilizes the others. Another method is to restrict fruit trees to one stem, the single cordon system, and so get quite a lot of varieties in a small space.

Cordon trees are usually planted at an angle of 45–60° against a wall, fence or wires strained horizontally between stout posts. Fan-trained trees have radiating branches like the ribs of a fan and are also suitable for walls or fences. Horizontal-trained trees have a vertical central stem with horizontal branches on each side but in one plane only. They, too, can be grown against walls, fences, or strained wire.

Standard trees have a tall main trunk with a head of branches and bushes have a similar head but on quite a short main 'leg' or trunk.

Pyramids are conical like a Christmas tree, with a central stem and branches radiating from it. Winged pyramids have the branches turned up and grafted at the ends to the next lot above to produce an even more regular shape, like a cage. There are other shapes, some very 'fancy' indeed, but the more complicated they are the more difficult it is to look after them.

Standard, half-standard, bush, and pyramid trees are often planted in grass, but it is wise to keep a circle of bare soil at least 1 metre (3 ft) in diameter around each tree. Grass too close to the tree will check its growth unduly, especially during the first few years.

Spacing of trees must vary according to variety and the kind of stock on which the tree is grafted, but it is seldom wise to plant standard or half-standard trees closer than 6 m (20 ft); bush, normal pyramid, fan-trained, and horizontal-trained trees closer than 3·5 m (11–12 ft); dwarf pyramids closer than 2 m (6 ft); or cordons closer than 60 cm (2 ft).

Shoots coming direct from the roots are known as suckers. If the tree is grafted these suckers will be from the stock and will not produce good fruit. They must be removed as soon as they are seen. Do this by baring the sucker right to the

root from which it grows and cutting it off close against this. Shoots growing from the main trunk of grafted trees below the point of grafting are also from the stock and must be removed. The point of grafting can be seen as a swelling on the main stem, usually about 25 cm (10 in.) above soil level.

Currants, gooseberries, raspberries, and other soft fruits are not grafted, so suckers from these are of the same character as the rest of the plant. Whether they are kept or removed depends mainly on the shape of the plant one is trying to form, but raspberry suckers are always retained.

Apples. These grow well in all reasonably well-drained soils. There are many varieties, some intended primarily for cooking, some for dessert, a few that are dual purpose. Some varieties also ripen much earlier than others, the first being ready in late July or early August, the latest keeping until April. All make a fine display when in flower in May and those with brightly coloured fruits are also decorative in autumn.

Apples bear their flowers and fruit on stems that are two years or more old. When trees are grown as standards, half-standards, or bushes it will be sufficient to prune each winter, any time between November and March, when badly placed branches are removed and overcrowded ones thinned out. Aim at maintaining a goblet-shaped head of branches, fairly open in the centre with main branches evenly and well spaced. If branches grow too tall cut them back to a point at which there is a fork or new stem. Do not leave stumps unprovided with growth.

Cordon and horizontal-trained trees are pruned in summer and winter. In July–August shorten all side shoots growing from the main stems to four or five fully developed leaves (do not count the rosette of small leaves at the base of each shoot). In winter shorten the shoots that have grown at the extremities of the main stems to about 30–40 cm (12–16 in.). When the tree reaches the limits of the space allotted to it, cut out these extension growths each winter. At the same time look for fruit buds, which are fatter, rounder, and more prominent than growth buds, and cut back small shoots to these buds.

Pick early apples (July to October ripening) as soon as they part readily from the tree and use as quickly as possible. Pick late apples in the second half of October, store in boxes in layers three or four deep, and keep in a cool place, such as a shed with an earthen floor. Use at the correct season as stated in the fruit catalogue.

Feed apples in February–March with a top dressing of manure or manure substitute, plus hoof and horn meal at 100 grammes ($3\frac{1}{2}$ oz) and sulphate of potash at 25 g (1 oz) per square metre (or square yard).

Summer pruning a trained apple tree. Side growths, known as laterals, are shortened to five leaves when the stems commence to get woody at the base, usually some time in July. Pears, gooseberries, and red and white currants can be pruned in the same way.

Spray apples occasionally from March to July with captan, and if greenflies or caterpillars are seen spray at once with a reliable insecticide.

Apricots. Only suitable for warm sunny walls or fences and rather rich well-drained soil. Plant fan-trained trees and prune in June–July by removing badly placed shoots, particularly those growing forwards or backwards, and shortening other side shoots to six leaves each. Tie in all growths neatly to strained wire, spreading them to fill the available space evenly. Feed as for apples. Spray after flowering and again in May and June with a good greenfly killer.

Blackberries, Loganberries, etc. These vigorous bramble fruits make good cover for fences, screens, sheds, etc. They grow readily in any reasonably good soil and in sun or partial shade. Plant canes at least 2·5 m (8 ft) apart. Cut all stems to within 30 cm (12 in.) of the ground after planting. Train new growth fanwise. No crop will be produced the first year. The following summer, fruit should be produced on the previous year's stems. Meanwhile train the new growths more or less vertically. When the crop has been gathered cut out the old shoots (or canes) completely, untie the new shoots, and spread them out fanwise to replace the old ones. Continue in the same way in succeeding years.

Feed as for apples, but if possible give a second top dressing of manure or manure substitute in May.

Blackcurrants. These succeed well on rather rich and moist soil. They are nearly always grown as bushes planted about 1·5 m (5 ft) apart. Cut all stems to within 15–20 cm (6–8 in.) of ground level after planting. No crop will be produced until the second summer. When the crop has been gathered cut out as much as possible of the growth that has just fruited, without losing any of the good new shoots that will fruit the following year. Retain all shoots

(from top) Dessert Apple Worcester Pearmain; Cooking Apple Arthur Turner; Dessert Apple Sunset; (below left) Cooking Apple Bramley's Seedling; (below right) Dessert Apple Charles Ross

growing direct from the roots as they help to strengthen the bush and keep it well provided with new growth.

Feed as for apples but if possible give a second top dressing of manure or manure substitute in May. Keep bushes well watered in dry weather. In winter pick off and burn any swollen, globular buds, which are infested with almost microscopic mites. If such buds are seen spray bushes in March with lime sulphur at twice the normal winter strength as stated on the label.

Cherries. Sweet cherries make handsome standard trees but are too large for small gardens. The Morello cherry does well fan trained against a wall or fence and will succeed in sun or shade. Sweet cherries require very little pruning beyond the removal of misplaced or overgrown branches, best done in March or August. Morello cherries are pruned as soon as the crop has been gathered, when the best young stems are retained and older or weaker ones cut out. Every few years it may be necessary to cut one or two branches well back to prevent trees becoming leggy.

Morello cherries are self fertile, i.e. they will set good crops when fertilized with their own pollen. Sweet cherries are self sterile, i.e. they must have 'mates' for pollination and, as the compatibility of varieties is rather complicated, nursery advice should be sought on this matter when purchasing trees.

Feed as for apples but give a second application of hoof and horn meal in June. Use a good greenfly killer if greenflies or blackflies are seen.

Figs. The trees are hardy but crops of ripe figs are only produced in warm, sunny, sheltered places. Figs may be trained fanwise against sunny walls or fences and they like well-drained but not very rich soil containing lime or chalk. In July–August, shorten side shoots to five or six leaves each and in winter cut out weak or badly placed stems. Feed with hoof and horn meal and sulphate of potash as for apples, but without manure. Every third year apply ground chalk at 20 g/sq m (8 oz/sq yd) in autumn.

Gooseberries. These like fairly rich well-drained soil. They are usually grown as small bushes on a short main stem or leg but can also be trained as cordons, usually with two or three stems each, like the prongs of a fork. Plant bushes about 1·25 m (4 ft) apart, double stem cordons 60 cm (2 ft) apart, triple stem cordons 1 m (3 ft) apart. Prune cordons in summer, shortening all new side shoots to four or five leaves. Prune bushes at any time between October and March by removing some of the older branches and thinning out overcrowded stems, particularly in the centre of the bush where they make picking difficult. Also remove suckers (growths direct from the roots) not because they will not produce good fruit but because they, too, crowd the centre of the bush.

Start to pick gooseberries as soon as the berries are large enough for cooking, but only thin the fruits at this stage and leave some to grow larger and ripen.

Feed as for apples. Spray with BHC or trichlorphon if caterpillars are seen. If mildew is troublesome (it produces a felt-like growth on leaves and fruits) spray with washing soda and soft soap in April, May, and June. This spray is prepared by dissolving 5 g (2 oz) each of washing soda and soft soap in 5 litres (1 gal) of water.

Grape Vines. These can be grown outdoors, as the vines themselves are quite hardy, but they do not crop very reliably and so are usually grown under glass. A fairly large greenhouse is required since even one vine makes a good deal of growth. Vines can be grown in large pots or tubs filled with J.I.P.3 compost, but these take a good deal of watering and feeding and so vines are usually grown in borders of good soil, either inside or outside the greenhouse. Inside borders give earlier crops but outside borders require less attention since they get much of their water from rain. If vines are planted outside, the main growth of each is brought into the house through a hole in the wall.

Prepare borders for vines by excavating all soil to a depth of 1 m (3 ft), putting a good layer of stones or broken bricks in the bottom for drainage and filling up with good soil mixed with about a quarter of its volume of peat, plus a sprinkling of ground chalk, hoof and horn meal, bone meal, and wood ashes.

Plant vines in February–March 2 m (6 ft) apart. Train the main stem of each towards the ridge of the house, tying to wires strained horizontally 20–25 cm (8–10 in.) below the glass. These wires should be about 40 cm (16 in.) apart. Pinch out the tip of the main stem when it reaches the ridge. Train side shoots every 40 cm (16 in.) or so on each side of the main stem, tying them to the wires provided. Each winter shorten each side growth to two dormant growth buds (about 2 cm or 1 in.). In spring retain the best growth from each pruned stem, or 'spur', and rub out the weaker. Train to the wires and pinch out the tip one leaf beyond the first flower truss. Pinch out the tips of secondary shoots at the first leaf.

Ventilate vines freely from November to February and use no heat. Then water well, close ventilators, and raise temperature to 10–15 °C (50–60 °F) to start growth. No heat is likely to be necessary after April, except possibly while grapes are ripening in September. Syringe vines daily with water from March until grapes begin to ripen, except for the period when the flowers are open when a drier atmosphere will help fertilization. Thin the bunches

(top) Red Currant Laxton's No. 1; (centre) Peach Peregrine; (below) Gooseberry Careless

of grapes with pointed vine scissors, starting about a fortnight after they begin to swell. Thin the bottom of each bunch more than the top and take great care not to damage the berries.

Feed vines each February–March with a top dressing of well rotted manure, or manure substitute, plus hoof and horn meal and bone meal, each at 100 g ($3\frac{1}{2}$ oz), plus sulphate of potash at 25 g (1 oz), all per square metre (or square yard). Give ground chalk at 225 g/sq m (8 oz/sq yd) every third autumn.

Dust vines with flowers of sulphur in summer if mildew appears as a white powdery outgrowth on the leaves. Rub off loose bark from the main stem (rod) in winter and paint rods with Gishurst Compound or spray with tar oil wash.

Medlar. This can be grown as an ornamental and useful standard tree. One is usually sufficient and the medlar will fruit without a mate. Little pruning is required, simply removal of badly placed or overcrowded branches in autumn or winter. Fruits are gathered in late October and stored in single layers, eyed ends downwards, in a cool, dry place until fully ripe.

Mulberry. Another very ornamental tree but mulberries take years to produce fruit and make a great mess when they do. One standard tree is usually sufficient. Little pruning is required but young trees should be well staked as they are easily blown over.

Peaches and Nectarines. The nectarine is simply a type of peach with a smooth skin and so cultivation of the two is identical. They like warm, sunny places and rather rich, well-drained soils. They are usually planted either as bushes or as fan-trained trees, the latter planted against a wall or fence. Bush trees require little pruning, simply the removal of some of the older stems to prevent over-crowding, and to preserve a good balance. Fan-trained trees are pruned gradually as they grow in spring and early summer. Surplus young shoots are rubbed out while still quite small, approximately three being retained on each existing side shoot, one at the tip and another near the middle to draw sap through it and the third as near the base as possible to replace it after the crop has been gathered. Then in autumn old shoots are cut out and new ones trained in. For best results fruits are thinned to about 20 cm (8 in.) apart when as large as walnuts.

Peaches and nectarines are also grown in greenhouses, often trained against the back wall of a lean-to house. Exactly the same system of pruning is adopted. The greenhouse must be ventilated in spring and summer and trees syringed daily with water to discourage red spider mites, which cause a grey mottling of the foliage.

Outdoor peaches and nectarines often suffer from leaf curl disease, which causes a thickening, curling, and reddening of the leaves. To prevent this spray with copper fungicide in late February or early March.

Some varieties ripen earlier than others. Only July–August ripening varieties should be planted out of doors.

Pears. The cultivation of these is very similar to that of apples but they require a warmer place and even better drained soil. Pears usually do well as single stem cordons or horizontal-trained trees planted against sunny fences or walls. Feeding, pruning, and picking are the same as for apples, but pears ripen more rapidly than apples and quickly spoil if left too long, so should be examined frequently and used directly they are ready. They are best stored in single layers in a dry place and in a temperature of 10–12 °C (50–54 °F).

Plums and Damsons. These can be very attractive in flower and fruit but grow rapidly and make quite large trees. Good quality dessert plums, including the several varieties of gage, are often trained as fans against walls, but again there is the problem of size and a fairly large wall is required to accommodate even one fan-trained plum tree.

Planting and feeding are very much as for apples, but plums need rather more nitrogen and if surrounded by grass should be given an extra dressing of a fertilizer, such as Nitro-chalk, at 25 g/sq m (1 oz/ sq yd) in April–May.

Prune standard and bush trees lightly in late summer as soon as the crop has been gathered, simply thinning out overcrowded branches and removing badly placed ones. With fan-trained trees pinch out the tips of well placed shoots as they attain 12–15 cm (5–6 in.) length from June to August and rub out badly placed shoots at an early stage. In autumn look for fruit buds on the older stems and cut back to these to keep the trees neat.

Spray plums with a greenfly killer if aphids (usually present as grey-lice on plums) are seen in spring or summer. Watch for silver-leaf disease, indicated by a metallic silvering of the leaves. Cut out any branches showing this symptom and paint wounds with a good wound dressing. Burn the affected wood immediately.

Raspberries. These like rather cool, rich soil. Use manure or manure substitutes freely in preparation and top dress liberally with one of these substances each March, repeating if possible in May. Plant canes 1 m (3 ft) apart in rows 2 m (6 ft) apart. Cut all canes down to 5 cm (2 in.) after planting. No crop will be produced the first summer. Tie young canes to wires strained horizontally between strong posts, the topmost wire 2 m (6 ft) above ground level. Shorten long canes to 15 cm (6 in.) above this top wire in February. Fruit should be produced annually from the second summer. As soon as the crop has been gathered, cut out all canes that have fruited but retain five to seven of the best new canes per root and tie in their place. Cut out all other canes.

A different method of pruning is required for autumn fruiting raspberries. Cut all canes almost to ground level each February. Thin out young canes to the five to seven best per root.

In addition to top dressing with manure or manure substitute in March and May, apply a compound fertilizer in April as advised by the manufacturer. Spray raspberries with derris when the blossom begins to fall and again when the first fruits turn pink to kill maggots of the raspberry beetle.

141

Dessert Pear Conference

Dessert Pear Beurre Superfin

Dessert Pear Louise Bonne of Jersey

(left) Removing surplus young growth on a peach: a young growth retained at the base for replacement. (right) Removing a branch that is rubbing against another. The cut is made immediately above a side branch.

Red and White Currants. These are simply colour variations of the same fruit and require identical treatment. They can be grown as bushes, usually on a short main stem or 'leg', or they can be trained as double or triple stem cordons. Planting distances and feeding are as for gooseberries. Prune in July–August, when young side shoots can be shortened to about five leaves each, and again in autumn, when older stems can be cut back to fruit bud clusters where these have formed. The clusters stand out quite prominently on the stems. Pests and diseases are not, as a rule, very troublesome and routine spraying is unnecessary.

Strawberries. These should always be grown as a short term crop, to be renewed at least every three years and preferably every two years. New stock of summer fruiting strawberries can be produced by pegging down a few of the natural runners around the best plants in June–July, but it is better to purchase new plants because of the readiness with which strawberries become infected with virus disease. If home propagation is tried do not retain more than six runners per plant, peg the first plantlet on each runner to the soil with a piece of wire bent like a hairpin, and cut off the runner beyond this plantlet. In August–September, when the plantlet has formed roots, sever the runner between it and the parent plant, lift carefully with a trowel a week later, and replant where it is to fruit.

Plant the purchased runners in August–September or in March and plant in rather rich, well-manured ground. Space plants 40 cm (16 in.) apart in rows 1 m (3 ft) apart. Top dress with manure or manure substitute in March and give a

A blackcurrant bush before and after pruning. As much as possible of the the old growth that has carried a crop has been cut out to make room for the current year's stems which will bear fruit the following summer. Good feeding helps to produce this new growth.

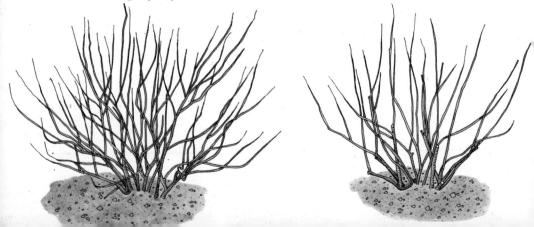

sprinkling of compound fertilizer in April. Spread clean straw under the plants in May or use special strawberry mats to keep fruits off the soil. Cut off all runners as they appear, unless required for propagation. Spray every ten days with captan or thiram from the time the plants start to flower until the fruits are nearly ripe.

Remontant or perpetual fruiting strawberries continue to crop until September or October. Some varieties do not produce runners and are increased by divisions at planting time.

Alpine strawberries also produce no runners and are grown from seed. Sow this in a cool greenhouse or frame from January to May in J.I.S. compost. Prick off seedlings into boxes of J.I.P.1 compost and plant out when they have made sturdy little plants. Space 30 cm (1 ft) apart each way in fairly rich soil and a partially shaded place. Replace plants with new seedlings every two or three years. The fruits of the alpine strawberry are small but well flavoured and freely produced.

The fruits of the alpine strawberry are small but well flavoured and freely produced.

Walnuts. These are planted in gardens more for ornament than for cropping, since they make handsome trees of large size. No special feeding or pruning is necessary. The common walnut is usually raised from seed, may be very slow in coming into bearing, and of uncertain quality when it does. Improved varieties are available, but these are more expensive since they have to be increased by grafting.

**(right, from top) Plum Warwickshire Drooper; Plum Belle de Louvain; Plum Denniston's Superb; Plum Coe's Golden Drop
(below) Strawberry Royal Sovereign**

15 Feeding Plants

Plants with leaves obtain the bulk of their food from air and water. Through the agency of the green colouring matter in their leaves and the energy derived from sunlight they are able to combine simple chemicals derived from these into the far more complex sugars, starches, proteins, etc., that they require. In this they are totally unlike animals (including human beings) which are dependent on plants for these organic compounds and could not exist without them.

So the first essentials for healthy plant growth are air, water, and light, plus the required amount of warmth to make use of them. But in addition plants need small quantities of numerous minerals, obtained mainly from the soil. Most of these are normally present in sufficient quantity, but when land is intensively cropped some may be used up more rapidly than they are replaced and some are also removed by leaching. As a rule it is simple to replace these minerals by applying fertilizers and it is quite possible, though not always desirable, to confine feeding to the application of a few chemicals in relatively small quantities. Nitrogen, phosphorus, and potash are the three most likely to need renewal and most compound fertilizers are blended to supply these three in varying proportions.

However, there is a little more to feeding plants than that. The soil contains living organisms as well as minerals. There are vast numbers of bacteria and fungi, as well as earthworms and many other creatures, some harmful to plants, some beneficial. Some help to bring about decay of dead matter and to release the minerals it contains so that they are available to plants again. Many help to preserve the texture of the soil, so that water can pass through it freely, air can reach the roots, and plant foods be retained in it.

So in addition to feeding the soil with chemical fertilizers the gardener must also supply it with bulky organic substances such as manure, garden refuse, and peat. Some of these also contain chemicals which plants require, though usually they are not immediately available to plants but must be liberated by decay.

This is one reason why decayed manure is usually to be preferred to fresh manure, and it is better to let vegetable refuse rot in a compost heap than to dig it in fresh. For best decay compost heaps should be not more than 1 m (3 ft) wide and high though they may be of any length. They are built up in layers each 15–20 cm (6–8 in.) thick with a little sulphate of ammonia, Nitro chalk or compost accelerator sprinkled between each layer. After six to eight weeks the heap is turned inside out and any dry places wetted. It is ready for use when everything has decayed to a uniform brown mass fairly crumbly in texture.

This then is the basic pattern of feeding; bulky 'manures' to improve or maintain texture and to supply a slowly available reservoir of minerals, plus chemical fertilizers to supply minerals more rapidly or to supply particular minerals that are known to be required.

Fertilizers are themselves of two basically different types. Organic fertilizers, such as bone meal, hoof and horn meal, fish meal, and dried blood, contain minerals, such as phosphorus, and nitrogen that must be liberated by decay like those in manure or compost. This takes time and so such fertilizers are sometimes said to be slow acting, though the term is a relative one. But they are also long lasting and steady in their action and they supply other chemicals besides the main ones for which they are principally applied and all these things can be an advantage.

By contrast inorganic fertilizers, such as sulphate of ammonia, superphosphate of lime, and sulphate of potash, are much more readily available to plants and act quickly, but it is necessary to be careful not to apply too much at a time or the plant may find its roots in too strong a solution of chemicals and suffer severe damage, or even be killed outright. Chemical fertilizers are safe and beneficial if used strictly according to label instructions, but can be dangerous if they are used carelessly.

Each chemical reacts on the others and so it can be misleading to assign a particular function to each. Nevertheless it is easy to see that nitrogen rapidly deepens the green colouring and increases the size of leaves, that phosphorus stimulates root growth, and that potash improves the colour of fruit and helps to ripen the growth of plants. An adequate supply of phosphates is particularly necessary for seedlings and young plants, nitrogen is needed to keep plants growing, and potash becomes of special importance towards the end of the summer.

Skilled gardeners can use individual chemicals for particular crops, or at selected periods, but usually it is better to make use of compounds containing nitrogen, phosphorus, and potash – in about equal parts for general feeding, with high nitrogen to stimulate growth and with high potash to encourage ripening. Such mixtures can be purchased from any garden shop and the percentage of each mineral will be stated on the package in the order in which they are given above, i.e. nitrogen first, phosphorus (stated as phosphoric acid) second, and potash third. National Growmore fertilizer has 6 per cent of each, and is a well balanced fertilizer suitable for a great many purposes in the garden. Most manufacturers prepare fertilizers of similar type and some offer mixtures which, in addition to supplying nitrogen, phosphorus, and potash, also contain other chemicals used by plants, such as magnesium, iron, manganese, and others known as trace elements (because they are required in such minute quantities). Phostrogen is a compound fertilizer of this all-embracing type.

Fertilizers can be applied dry or in solution. Since plants can only take minerals from the soil in solution, liquid fertilizers act even more rapidly than dry fertilizers, unless the latter are watered in or rain follows their application. Whichever method is used the fertilizer must always be distributed as evenly as possible over the whole area covered by the roots of the plant, which may well be a metre or so (several feet) around it.

Dry fertilizers should always be kept off leaves as much as possible, but dilute liquid fertilizers can sometimes be applied to leaves as well as to the soil, a process known as foliar feeding. This can be particularly useful when there is something in the soil which is liable to counteract the fertilizer. In soils containing a great deal of lime or chalk, iron and manganese – two chemicals essential to plants – may become completely insoluble and so be unavailable. Foliar feeding with sulphate of iron or sulphate of manganese can bring an almost immediate improvement, but an even better method is to apply iron and manganese sequestrols to the soil, i.e. iron and manganese in special chemical combinations which secure

145

them, at least for some weeks or months, from chemical interaction with the lime or chalk in the soil.

Lime and chalk perform two functions in the garden. They supply the soil with calcium, one of the elements that all plants require, and they make the soil less acid or more alkaline, whichever it happens to be already. Some plants, such as lavender, scabious, clematis, peas, beans, and all the cabbage tribe, like a lot of lime or chalk in the soil. To some others, notably rhododendrons, camellias, and many heathers and magnolias, too much lime or chalk is poison. So in the ornamental garden it is necessary to be careful where one uses them and if in doubt the best advice is not to use them without expert opinion that they are required. In the vegetable garden, with its frequent cultivation of the soil and free use of manures and fertilizers, which usually tend to make soils more acid (or less alkaline) than they were, it is usually wise to give lime or chalk at least once in three years. Both substances perform exactly the same function but hydrated lime does it rather more quickly than finely ground chalk and also gets used up more quickly. So if hydrated lime is used it may be best to give 100 g/sq m ($3\frac{1}{2}$–4 oz/sq yd) and repeat every two years, whereas ground chalk may be used at twice that rate and be repeated every three years. If in doubt get the soil tested or test it with a simple home kit, and if the result shows a reading below pH 6·5, give lime or chalk.

When particular chemicals are lacking, or are in very short supply, plants may react with symptoms that are easily mistaken for diseases – indeed they really are diseases, but of a physiological nature and not caused by insects, fungi, or other outside agents attacking the plants. Thus plants that are very short of iron or manganese, perhaps because there is too much lime or chalk in the soil locking up the iron or manganese in a form which is not available to the plants, produce bright yellow leaves, a condition known as chlorosis. The leaves of plants that are very short of potash may appear scorched around the edges or if magnesium is deficient they may show brown smudges between the veins. When symptoms of this kind occur it is usually wise to seek the advice of an expert before taking action unless it is quite clear what is lacking.

Some physiological disorders are due to irregularity in the water supply. If tomato plants are allowed to become very dry it is probable that a few weeks later all the fruits will show black patches at the bottom, a condition known as blossom end rot. Apple trees that are alternately too wet and too dry may produce fruits with little patches of corky flesh just below the skin, a condition known as bitter pit. There are many more such conditions in other plants. An example is spraying of potatoes, in which the flesh may crack internally and be marked with brown, which is prevalent in varieties which produce very large tubers under alternating very wet and very dry conditions. Improvement of drainage and the digging in of bulky manure and other absorbent materials, together with watering in very dry spells will prevent all these troubles.

16 Keeping Plants Healthy

It is broadly true that sturdy, well grown plants are less likely to succumb to the attack of pests or diseases than weak, starved, poorly grown plants, but good cultivation is not a guarantee of immunity. Both pests and diseases come and go with the seasons, encouraged by weather conditions or suddenly becoming epidemic. The gardener must therefore be constantly watchful for trouble, ready to take remedial action at once or prepared to carry out routine preventive treatment if this seems necessary.

Many of the pests of plants are insects and these broadly fall into two classes according to their mode of attack. One class is composed of insects that puncture the leaves, stems, petals or fruits and suck sap from them; the other of insects that chew pieces out of the plant.

The sucking insects include aphids, a name that covers a number of plant lice, including the all too familiar greenflies and blackflies, also capsid bugs, thrips, leaf hoppers, frog hoppers or 'cuckoo-spit' insects, and scale insects. To these may be added various mites, including red spider mites, which are not insects but do similar damage by sucking the sap.

These pests leave no obvious wounds, but they weaken plants, cause leaves to cockle or curl or to change colour. Thrips produce distinctive silvery or dark streaks, particularly on stems and petals, and give leaves a greyish colour. Red spider mites impart a mottled grey or bronze colour to the leaves. These are all warnings to the gardener to look closer and see what is causing the trouble. Greenflies, blackflies, and other aphids are usually easily detected clustering around the young shoots and leaves. Capsid bugs are often a little more difficult to find since they are more active and fewer in number. Leaf hoppers leave their discarded white skins sticking to the undersides of leaves and frog hoppers protect themselves with a frothy mass which indicates their presence. Scales adhere like minute limpets or mussels to the leaves or stems. Red spider mites usually cluster close to the veins on the undersides of leaves but are so small that a lens is required to see them clearly.

Biting insects are mainly caterpillars, weevils, and the grubs of various flies. Earwigs have a particular fondness for the petals of chrysanthemums and dahlias. To these may be added slugs and snails which are not insects but eat leaves in so similar a manner that it is often difficult to decide what is doing it until the marauders are found. Caterpillars are easy to see, but not so weevils, slugs, and snails. The time to look for them is after dark, with an electric torch, and slugs in particular are likely to be most active in warm, damp weather.

There are chemicals to deal with all these pests but no single chemical will kill

Aphid (Green Fly)	Black Spot (Rose)	Big Bud Mite	Carrot Fly Grub

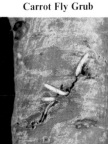

all pests. Manufacturers prepare mixtures of chemicals, such as menazon or dimethoate (Rogor), both first-rate aphid killers, with BHC carbaryl or trichlorphon, which are effective against caterpillars and weevils. Such combined insecticides are very useful to the gardener, enabling him to carry out blanket treatment against a variety of foes. However, there are also single chemicals with quite a broad band of effectiveness, including malathion and derris, which will both kill red spider mites as well as many true insects. They are justly popular with gardeners.

All these are applied as sprays or dusts, either direct to the plants or to the soil in which they are growing, if that is where the pests are. Some caterpillars are soil dwellers and so are leather-jackets, wireworms, and millepedes, which do a great deal of damage to the roots of plants. Sometimes flaked naphthalene is forked into the soil to kill or drive out these pests and BHC dust is also widely used as a soil insecticide, though it can impart an unpleasant musty flavour to potatoes and carrots. Trichlorphon does not have this drawback and is effective in solution watered on to the soil.

None of these chemicals is of any use against slugs and snails which are usually killed with metaldehyde, either applied combined with bran as a bait or in liquid form to be watered wherever it is likely that slugs and snails are hiding. It is most effective in dry weather, but methiocarb is also effective in wet weather.

Diseases are mainly caused by fungi, bacteria, and viruses. For the last no effective remedies have yet been discovered, though since they are spread from plant to plant by sucking insects, particularly greenflies, anything done to eliminate these will help to check virus diseases. In addition all infected plants should be removed and burned. Common virus symptoms are yellow mottling of the leaves, leaf distortion, dry brown spotting, and dwarfing, but as all these can also be caused by bad cultivation, bad weather, and mineral deficiencies in the soil, it is wise to seek expert advice if virus infection is suspected.

Bacterial diseases are also difficult to treat and often difficult to diagnose, and since there are no effective remedies and seriously infected plants must be destroyed, it is wise to seek advice before doing so.

Fortunately most of the common diseases of garden plants are caused by fungi, are fairly easily recognized, and can be prevented, if not actually cured, by timely spraying or dusting. A number of distinct types may be distinguished. Spot diseases produce more or less circular black or purple spots on the leaves, the spots increasing in size and causing premature leaf drop. Rusts produce small rust coloured or orange spots, often on the underside of leaves. Powdery mildews cover plants with a white or grey flour-like outgrowth. Downy mildews cover plants with a felt-like white or grey out-

1 Club Root; 2 Cutworm; 3 Earwig;
4 Leaf Hopper; 5 Leaf Miner; 6 Mealy Bug (enlarged)

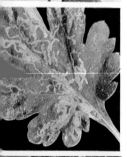

growth. Moulds, of which grey mould or botrytis is by far the most widespread, blacken stems or leaves and later a fluffy white mould appears on the diseased parts. Cankers attack stems, causing them to split and produce gaping wounds, usually with gnarled edges. Scab diseases produce rough, scabby outgrowths, usually on fruits or tubers (apples and potatoes both suffer from their own scab disease) though there may be other damage as well.

The sprays and dusts used against pests are totally ineffective against these diseases, for which a different group of chemicals, known as fungicides, are used. Another difference is that diseases can seldom be cured, only prevented. This means that the fungicides must be applied before the infection occurs, the object being to coat the leaves and stems with a thin chemical film which will make it impossible for fungus spores to germinate. Since plants are growing for months, it is usually necessary to spray several times, both to protect the new growth and to replace fungicide that has been washed off by rain.

As with insecticides, there is no one chemical that will prevent all fungal diseases, though several, such as Bordeaux mixture and other copper preparations, thiram, and various sulphur preparations have a fairly wide band of effectiveness. But again combinations of chemicals are available or chemicals can be chosen for particular groups of diseases. Captan is very good against rose black spot and apple and pear scab, and dinocap is one of the most effective chemicals against powdery mildews.

Some diseases are carried in the soil and cause root and stem rots. Damping-off disease is of this kind and it attacks seedlings, particularly if they are overcrowded. As a result they rot at soil level and topple over. Sometimes a whole potful may go in a day or so. These soil diseases can be controlled by partial soil sterilization and the loam in the various John Innes seed and potting composts should always be steam sterilized before use. They can also be checked by watering soil with Cheshunt Compound, which can be applied safely even to small seedlings. Other stronger chemicals, such as formalin and metham-sodium, are also used but can only be applied to vacant ground, are rather dangerous to handle, and should only be used with expert knowledge or advice.

In greenhouses both pests and diseases can be controlled by fumigation. Various insecticides and at least one good fungicide, tecnazene (TCNB), are available in convenient pellets which give off dense clouds of smoke when ignited. This smoke carries the insecticide or fungicide to all parts of the house and deposits it on the leaves. There are also devices for vaporizing chemicals by electrically generated heat, and impregnated strips can be suspended in the house to give a continuous fumigation.

Some chemicals are described as systemic. This means that,

1 Mildew (Rose); 2 Peach Leaf Curl; 3 Scab (Apple);
4 White Fly; 5 Wireworm; 6 Woolly Aphid

149

instead of remaining on the outside of the plant, they enter it and are carried around in the sap. This has both advantages and drawbacks. Systemic chemicals cannot be washed off by rain and often remain effective for several weeks. Equally they cannot be removed by wiping or washing, so if applied to food crops a safety period must be allowed to elapse before the crop is used. This differs according to the chemical, so that the label instructions must be followed. In general, systemic insecticides are less harmful to useful insects than surface chemicals since these do not eat the plants and so are unlikely to acquire a fatal dose.

Finally, all chemicals should be handled with care. Some are highly poisonous and most are harmful if consumed in any quantity. Some can irritate the skin, especially in their concentrated form. All should be stored in a safe place, away from food, and out of reach of children. It is wise to wear rubber gloves when mixing chemicals and to wash out all utensils thoroughly after use. Above all never neglect to read label instructions and always follow them to the letter.

WEED CONTROL

In small gardens weedkillers are of greatest use to keep paths and terraces clean and to remove weeds from lawns. In large gardens they may be used to kill weeds around many plants, including roses, shrubs, herbaceous plants, vegetables, and fruit trees, and to prevent any re-emergence of weed seedlings for several months. This is specially useful if there is a shortage of labour for hoeing and handweeding, the traditional methods of keeping cultivated ground clear and ones which still have a great deal to commend them.

The experts do not talk of weedkillers at all but of herbicides, which means plant killers, and that is exactly what they are. No chemical can distinguish between a weed and a garden plant, but some do distinguish between different types of plant and the gardener can make use of this. Chemicals of this kind are called 'selective herbicides' and the most important for the gardener are those that kill a great many plants but not grasses. These are the selective lawn weed-killers that can be purchased in every garden shop and which have so greatly lightened the work of lawn maintenance. There are several of them, and since some are more effective than others against particular types of lawn weeds, manufacturers often prepare mixtures. All will kill or damage most ornamental plants if splashed or sprayed on them and so must be carefully applied to the lawn only, or if there are only isolated patches of weeds, directly to these.

Herbicides that kill or damage all, or almost all, plants are called total herbicides. They are the most useful ones for keeping paths, drives, and terraces clean, but if garden plants are growing in the crevices between the paving slabs they will be killed, too, if the total herbicide reaches them. Sodium chlorate is such a chemical and it has the twin merits of being cheap and effective, but it can be carried considerable distances by water passing through the soil and so it is unwise to use it near flower beds. It is also highly inflammable, but many garden brands are mixed with a fire depressant to reduce this risk. Sodium chlorate can be used in solution or dry, sprinkled on the weeds.

Two other total herbicides, paraquat and simazine, are of great use to the gardener. The first is absorbed through the leaves of plants but is inactivated by the soil. If it is applied direct to the weed leaves, but kept off the leaves of garden plants, it can be made selective. The best way to do this is to apply it from a

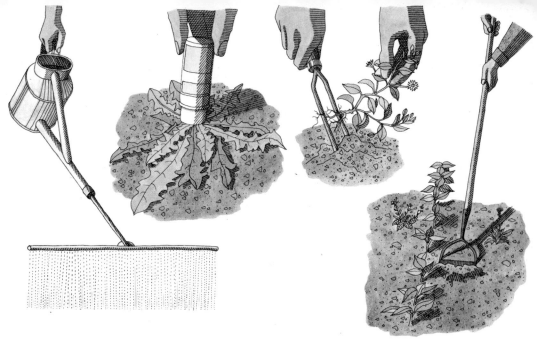

To apply weedkillers over large areas a wide sprinkle bar is convenient. Spot treatment can be done with various chemical packs or individual weeds can be dug out with a two-pronged fork. Frequent hoeing will kill seedling weeds and is good for most crops.

watering can or special applicator fitted with a narrow sprinkle bar which can be held quite close to the ground below the leaves of garden plants but over the leaves of young weeds.

Simazine is what is termed a residual herbicide. It remains for a long time in the soil but does not penetrate very far. Applied in moderation as a spray or with a sprinkle bar, it will stay in the top 2 cm (1 in.) of soil and prevent the emergence of most weed seedlings for two or three months. But to be effective the surface must not be broken by hoeing or other cultivation and the odd weed that does come through should be removed by hand.

As with all other garden chemicals, correct dosage and correct method of application are vital to success. Label instructions must always be carefully read and followed to the letter. Watering cans or applicators used for herbicides are best reserved for that purpose alone. If this is impossible they must be washed out thoroughly after each use. Special plastic applicators are available complete with interchangeable sprinkle bars of several different widths. These have several advantages. They are unlikely to be used for anything but weedkilling; they are closed by a screw cap so there is little risk of accidental splashing; and the choice of sprinkle bars enables a narrow one to be used for close work between plants and a wide one for rapidly covering lawns or vacant ground.

Index to Plants

Illustrations indicated by *italic numerals*

153